COMING THROUGH

COMING THROUGH

Expeditions to Chogolisa and Menlungtse

ANDY FANSHAWE

Hodder & Stoughton
LONDON SYDNEY AUCKLAND TORONTO

British Library Cataloguing in Publication Data

Fanshawe, Andy
  Coming through.
  1. Mountaineering – Biographies
  I. Title
  796.522092

  ISBN 0-340-52079-5

First published in Great Britain 1990

Published by Hodder and Stoughton,
a division of Hodder and Stoughton Ltd,
Mill Road, Dunton Green, Sevenoaks, Kent TN13 2YA
Editorial Office: 47 Bedford Square, London WC1B 3DP

Photoset by Rowland Phototypesetting Ltd,
Bury St Edmunds, Suffolk

Printed in Great Britain by St Edmundsbury Press Ltd,
Bury St Edmunds, Suffolk

To my parents
Ralph and Joyce

CONTENTS

MAPS AND DRAWING

COLOUR ILLUSTRATIONS

ACKNOWLEDGEMENTS

I wish to record my thanks to the following friends for their guidance and encouragement in the writing of this book. Acknowledgement of supporters of the expeditions themselves appears in Appendix IV.

I am indebted to Maggie Body, my editor, for her professional advice and sharp wit, for amusing and prodding me toward the finishing line and for trusting me to produce the goods in the first place; Ed Douglas, for his meticulous scrutiny of the original manuscript and his mix of bluntness and poignancy in comment; Xavier Eguskitza for checking the historical details; Helen Jamieson for allowing me to reproduce two of Liam Elliot's photographs; Chris Bonington, Jim Curran, Ulric Jessop, Alan Hinkes and Jess Stock for the use of their excellent photographs; Iain Peter for the very generous loan of his Amstrad word processor; and Caroline for her unending encouragement and support.

AF

1

Creating the space

It was the middle of July. The rain pelted on the polythene strung out between our tents. Raising my eyes above the waterlogged field on which we, and hundreds of other British climbers camped, revealed only thick clouds rolling down from the Alps. There was nothing else for it. We would get drunk. John Taylor arrived back from Chamonix. His tangled hair was wet like seaweed. As he carefully placed his rucsac down on the grass, I heard the chinking of bottles. Cheap French wine. From his pocket he produced tobacco and papers dressed in a torn plastic bag.

'How many could you get?' I enquired. He had traded our collection of empties, some which we had owned and some we had scavenged from the rubbish bins or in the scruffy forest around camp.

'Some.'

I dived into my tent and pulled out a long stick of bread, broke off a bit and gave the rest to John. Then I reached for one of the bottles, tinted red and simply labelled 12%.

'Last supper,' I offered.

John peered up at the sky. 'I doubt it,' he said.

Six months passed. It was Christmas Eve. We sat with our backs against the wall of a sérac on the North Face of the Aiguille du Plan. Between John's knees balanced our stove, melting snow for a brew. A light breeze rode up the face and cut gently into the stillness. The flame shook itself and then steadied. Below us lay the rocky ridge, blanketed with powder snow, that we had only barely been able to climb. In summer we might not have even employed a rope. Beyond that the lights of Chamonix sprawled on the valley floor, stretching to left and right. Above, 600 metres of icefall led to the summit, and from there the Midi-Plan Traverse, a snowy ridge to the Aiguille du Midi and the *téléphérique* that would take us down to Chamonix. In summer the traverse

11

might take only three hours. It was not an ambitious project and, looking back now four years later, I wonder whether with more experience we could have avoided the epic struggle of the next few days.

John turned to look curiously at me. I was manufacturing a cigarette. Half the tobacco fell in the snow as I squeezed and rolled it between white fingers, wetting the paper and choking the tobacco of air. After only a couple of draws I had no option but to throw it at the slope.

'Bloody thing,' I spat in anger. In fact, the cigarette had been a success, as its assembly had killed some time. 'Do you want one, a cigarette?' No, he did not.

John was a powerful and gentle man; on the hill ragged-arsed and demanding, yet on the ground he was open and sensitive with a dry wit. I watched as he poked his finger into his ear and scratched an itch, cocking his head gently and raising his eyebrows to the experience, blanking his expression. He looked unperturbed by the cold, as usual.

'The average age of my clothing is seven years,' I remembered him saying, as we had packed our rucsacs, in the quiet, confident tone that meant he was feeling pleased with himself. 'This,' he had said, pinching the fabric of his fleece jacket, 'this belongs to the old man, Pettit, God knows how old this is.'

The older and cheaper the better. I admired how he managed to keep out of debt on a student grant. It was something that I could never do. To afford the present trip he, with his friend Si Yates, had dug graves in Leicester. Simon had gone on to be an alpine binman, a term given to the lads who worked the Chamonix streets in winter, in their spare time climbing some of the hardest routes in the range. The characters were formidable – Millar, Curtis, Tinker, and their climbs impressive. John admired their devotion and he was friends of them all. They were all probably in town at this moment, 1200 metres below and, as I couldn't help reminding myself, 1200 metres warmer, whilst we sat like fibre-pile Buddhas on our tiny bivouac. I had known John less than a year, though in the summer we had climbed together often in the Alps. We were alike in many respects and good enough friends not to be embarrassed by pregnant pauses in conversation. And there was little to talk about now.

Of the summer I had remembered those days in Chamonix best, discussing what we would do when the rain stopped. When it was really heavy we joined the other impoverished alpinists gathered under the tunnel where the Chamonix–Argentière road crosses the Snell's Field service road. Not that the field was serviced much. Invaded more like; first by the climbers and then, as it had seemed to us, by the gendarmes

12

clearing us off. Of course, we were not impoverished, few were, but we chose to think so. This was the way it was. In the tunnel, someone would have a ghetto-blaster and someone else their stove producing endless brews for those who didn't want wine. Here we could pontificate for hours at a time about the Grandes Courses, the hundreds of routes we would like to do, content in the knowledge that most were safely out of reach above the clouds. John loved the visual appeal of the Alps, particularly their rock architecture. To him the actual summits meant less than the routes – bold pillars of granite thrown into relief by the oblique sun were best. These were logical and direct lines. And reaching the summit meant much less than the style of ascent.

'The Droites North Pillar,' he had once suddenly said, 'that's a real line. It cuts straight to the summit. It's black because it's steep. The Walker, that's another.'

John was not intimidated by the remoteness of a climb, nor its technical difficulty, but he hated unnecessary risks and poured derision on the idiots who flirted with them. More than once, while I related a story of my own to him, he had raised his eyebrows and I had cringed, fearing his anger, but only because it never once came – I think he must have liked me too much. Of course, we recognised and accepted dangers that could never be avoided. We had to, simply to get the job done. John was a safe partner, as well as something of an achiever in the hills.

After a few days in Chamonix that summer, we would go back up into the mountains and try one of the lines that we had talked about. Three times we walked up into the Argentière basin before we had finally been able to trust the weather, in a summer broken by storms, enough to climb the Droites, which we did late in August just a few days before hitching back to Britain. It had been a wonderful climb, like so many others. We had arrived on the summit a few minutes before dusk and, rather than descend to the start of the abseils in fading light, we bivouacked on the very top. I had sat contently under the settled sky, leaning against the hard, warm stone, to let my gaze meander through the dark valleys and over the alpenglow tops laid out before me. We had talked all night, opening our minds to each other and absorbing the sights and sounds of the mountains. Such moments were some of the happiest of my life. At dawn we had enjoyed far-reaching views of the range before descending by abseil to the Mer de Glace railway, where we had queued with tourists for a ticket to Chamonix. We might have thought we were poor but we knew when we were tired.

I remember a rather sheepish man with his children appearing a few metres ahead and edging nervously into the queue. He was obviously pushing in. I would have said nothing.

'Monsieur,' John said calmly above the general level of background noise.

The man turned his head, followed by everyone else's. John and I must, I think, have looked pretty intimidating standing there in huge plastic boots and a pair of thermal tights and little else, John, unkempt, unshaven, very untidy and very lean. The pot belly was long gone, his physique honed by ten long alpine routes. He was pointing to the back of the queue. A moment passed before the embarrassed man led his children away and John's warm smile had returned. Everyone else had eased a sigh of relief.

Smiling from this summer memory, still sitting on our winter North Face bivouac, I attempted another cigarette. This time, by crushing the burnt end between my fingers, each time it went out, I was able to smoke most of it over the tea that John passed to me silently. I held the tea close to my lips and breathed into the liquid so that the hot steam swept my face. John removed the cylinder of gas and thrust it down his sleeping bag and replaced the stove in his rucsac. We sat quietly for a few minutes more. Then, pulling my bivouac bag over my face, I lolled back against the ice and struggled for sleep.

Our dawn was indefinite. Clouds had extinguished the lights of Chamonix in the night. Now we could see barely thirty metres. The small icy cliffs among which we were nestled assumed grand proportions and a gothic style. We waited just a few minutes in the still, cold air, watching the cauldron of churning mist, welling up in the abyss beneath. I felt strangely committed.

At first I moved stiffly, slowly loosening up on the icy slopes. A hundred metres above our bivouac site we were stopped by a vertical cliff of corrugated ice rising about twenty-five metres above a deep crevasse which extended to left and right across the width of the face. The ice hung in columns like huge organ pipes, some of them completely detached. Unable to free climb the chandelier face we reverted to an aid technique that was clumsy and laborious. This single pitch of climbing took us most of the morning! During the afternoon, as we picked our way slowly towards the top of the face, the wind strengthened dramatically, so that when we did eventually reach the summit, at dusk, we were barely able to stand up against the force of rushing air. An alpine storm had arrived. I tried to be defensive, sealing all my clothes and staggering like a drunk, turning my back to the stinging wind and covering my frozen eyelids with ice-encrusted woollen mitts, fumbling

14

clumsily. But the storm raped. It was a frightening experience.

By the following morning we had not moved. We had spent the night huddled against each other and the summit tower, conscious of the sinister humming and occasional cracking of electricity around us. In the night snow had drifted against our bodies, and forced its way through the tiniest flaws in our rucsacs and bivouac bags. At best my clothes were lightly dusted with snow, at worst, where the warmth from my body had melted it, they were wet and I was cold. There had been no respite in the storm. Without a proper shelter it had been futile to try to keep the stove alight and just by having the stove out at all we had clogged its jets with snow.

We were virtually pinned to the ridge. We slowly worked our way towards the Aiguille du Midi. The seriousness of our situation was initially more shocking than frightening but as time went by and I started to lose my mental grip, depression, that most negative and destructive of emotions, set in. For liquid at night I sucked on the inside of my sleeping bag or packed powder snow into my mouth. My fingers felt wooden, my heels stung and I couldn't feel my toes at all. During the third night on the ridge I stopped shivering, feeling almost comfortable for the first time, a sure sign of hypothermia. I sat up, awake, fighting an urge to sleep. Extricating the ropes the next morning from under yet another metre of fresh snow, still witness to the ripping wind screaming over the crest of the ridge, I no longer believed that we could survive another night and I doubted that we could make the *téléphérique* that day. John kicked me to move but he too looked lost in his fear.

We struggled on pitifully, bulldozing through the snow, or skating recklessly on the hard black ice. On the ridge John screamed angrily at me 'Keep left!', fearing that I would walk through one of the cornices hanging over the Chamonix side. Too tired to comprehend his advice I trod slowly on until at last we recognised the steepening ridge that led to the *téléphérique* station perched just below the summit of the Aiguille du Midi. At that moment, it seemed to me, the storm subsided. The station stood tall and imposing in the silent mist above us, like a malevolent castle from medieval times. Normally the icy tunnel between the underground of the station and the ridge leading up to its entrance is three metres high but on this day it was completely covered; instead there was just a smooth snow slope. As we approached, wondering what to do, a fist appeared through the snow near our feet and then an arm and finally the face of a smiling Frenchman. John enlarged the hole that the man had made and fell into it. Only when he saw me at the entrance did he both laugh and cry his relief.

15

'*Les Anglais!*' the man called behind him as he walked back, through his deserted tunnels.

I spent the next week in Chamonix hospital with frostbite in three toes. John said to me, 'Me and Si. We've been thinking. If the Doc even *hints* he's going to have your toes, we'll get you out. Here, from this balcony. It can be a midnight raid.' He was so excited! His wild eyes longed for the doctor to announce the worst. It was just the sort of thing he would do. I could only laugh.

But after two days, with no improvement forecast in the weather, John left to go back to Britain and I began to feel fear. Another anxious few days passed before Francine wheeled me into the operating theatre and gave me a shot of morphine which immediately made me feel very happy. This, she said, was quite normal. I looked around the room for bone saws. Dr Forey strolled in and gave me one of those benevolent smiles that I immediately took as sadistic. I sat up in bed, all of a sudden taking a keen interest and watched him preparing to operate. Then he plunged his scalpel into my blistering toes. I looked away. He scraped away at the flesh beneath and at last declared it '*vivant*'. Everyone wanted to cheer. And I hadn't felt a thing. Nice bloke, Dr Forey.

Soon after, I resumed my life in London. In Chamonix, one of the alpine binmen, John Tinker, had told me that my frostbite would kill my plans for the summer. I convinced myself he was a fatalist. I had to, for I had committed a lot to the summer and an expedition to a mountain in Pakistan called Chogolisa.

Before the alpine summer of 1985 I had worked for an oil company as a geologist. In June I had asked them for leave, not just for the expedition, planned for the following year, but also for a couple of months in 1985 so I could spend the summer in Chamonix; 'necessary training' I told them. I was only twenty-two, no age to be stuck in a career, I thought. Predictably they had declined, and I had quit. After the summer in Chamonix with John, I took shop work in London. This way, I thought, I could do more climbing and devote more time to the expedition. The logic had been false. I had less money and less time, and because I was not using my brain at work, less motivation as well.

Now in January 1986, London was cold and wet. My frostbite kept me off the British hills and there were few other things that I could divert my energies towards. As a Philistine student, when I first came to London in 1981 I had rarely explored the city and I didn't feel the urge to do so now. I was working for a climbing equipment retailer, temporary and unabsorbing work and living in Finchley, a long tube ride out of

16

Central London. I rented a room in a house with some similarly engaged Antipodeans. I loathed the tubes, each day shuffling along from one place to another, pressed against hundreds of other passengers, victims of their self-affliction. My left foot was swathed in bandage and I carried a crutch to support me but this would not usually guarantee me a seat. London, I had already discovered, was so desperately uncivilised.

Through tedium and by a process of exclusion of other things in my mind I found myself thinking more and more about the summer and the mountain that I wanted to climb. I drew a picture of Chogolisa in my mind, with long elegant fluted lines, draped silk on a cobbled floor, a stunning young Bride.

In her most photographed pose the twin-summited Chogolisa appears as a trapezium peak guarding the junctions of the Vigne, Baltoro and Godwin Austen Glaciers in the heart of the Karakoram, just a few kilometres from K2, the world's second summit. The ridge between the two summits (7665 and 7654 metres) is over a kilometre in length and never falls below 7600 metres. The North-East summit which Martin Conway, the American explorer at the turn of the last century had christened Bride Peak was attempted in 1957 by Austrians Hermann Buhl and Kurt Diemberger after they had climbed Broad Peak. In a gathering mist Buhl had strayed onto a cornice which collapsed, throwing him down the North Face to his death. Diemberger, alone, had retreated. A year later, in 1958, the Japanese Hirai and Furijara reached the top one August morning. But it was not until 1975 that the higher, South-West summit was climbed by another team of Austrians led by Eduard Koblmuller. They approached from the south via the Kaberi Glacier and fixed over a kilometre of rope. Such indulgence, I can still not imagine! Our expedition planned to climb both peaks, ascending to the higher top and then traversing north-east along the connecting ridge to Bride Peak, and descending to the Upper Baltoro, the way that the Japanese and Diemberger had. We would take no ropes to fix and climb purely in an alpine style.

The idea of a traverse of Chogolisa belonged to Mark Dixon, a friend from university with whom I had climbed in Ecuador and Peru and on a couple of alpine excursions. We had made a habit in our first alpine visits of being over-zealous and we had suffered for it, such as when we had been bombarded by rocks descending the Gspaltenhorn North Face in an electric storm. Once or twice a month each winter we hired a car and thrashed it mercilessly up to Scotland on a Friday evening, returning on Monday morning in time for a shower on the way to work. Mark and I met Hamish Irvine in 1983 on one such weekend. We had arrived on a January day, after driving through the night and slogging up the Allt a'Mhuillin from the golf course carpark to the bottom of the Orion Face of Ben Nevis. Hamish and his friend Pete Smith had planned on doing Pointfive Gully. So had we. Hamish, leading, was half way up the second pitch when I set out on the first, overflowing with confidence. I had actually never climbed ice before but I reckoned it wouldn't be too hard. Alas my inability was quickly apparent and my technique inefficient and costly on my arms. I hadn't placed a single piece of protection and was about to fall back down the twenty metres that I had climbed when Pete dropped me a loop of rope. I lunged for it and hauled myself up, all the while preventing Hamish, attached to another part of the rope, from moving. I was very grateful. Hamish was not.

'Get that utter *wanker* off my rope!' he called down, ranging the pitch of his voice over an octave in a single sentence.

We gave up on Pointfive and did a rather easier climb around the corner instead, meeting Hamish and Pete on the summit where we, perhaps unexpectedly after the earlier incident, made an acquaintance that would lead us to be close friends.

Hamish, Mark and I became the founder members of the Chogolisa project. Mark and I invited Simon Lamb, a university friend with whom we had both climbed in Ecuador, and Hamish invited Liam Elliot from Edinburgh. I did not know John Taylor well then, and he was committed to Ama Dablam for the following year anyway. We decided on five, only because this was the maximum number of members of an expedition to a large Karakoram peak that the Pakistan authorities would allow without a qualified doctor. As we didn't have any doctor friends, or even vets, which Dai Lampard proved was an acceptable alternative on his trip to the Nameless Tower in 1984, we decided to stick to five, and when Mark had to drop out in the summer of 1985, we filled his place with Ulric Jessop, a friend of Hamish and Liam.

In the autumn of 1985, in that dead period when it is rather too cold for rock-climbing and still too mild in Scotland for ice to form, John and I travelled to the National Centre for Mountain Activities at Plas y Brenin in North Wales to commemorate the death of Don Whillans, one of Britain's best loved mountaineers. We had recognised Whillans leaving a bar in Chamonix the previous summer and riding off on a very large motorcycle that he was taking back to Britain. Before he reached his home in North Wales he had died of a heart attack. The Brenin was bursting with people, though the mood of the gathering was far from solemn. Most attending came more as an excuse for a good social than to pay their respects to the big man, great though these may have been.

Through the masses of bodies lurking at the Brenin that weekend I recognised Dennis Gray, the long-suffering General Secretary of the British Mountaineering Council. I approached him with the idea that a letter of support from the BMC would make a suitable foreword for our expedition prospectus.

'I'll send you a copy of the prospectus,' I said to him hopefully.

Before the BMC could endorse us we had to be screened by the Mount Everest Foundation, but eventually both committees greeted our proposals with vigour, each granting us £800 towards our costs, while the Nick Estcourt Award gave us their annual grant of £1000 and a letter of good luck. Such support did wonders for our morale. Traverses of mountains it seemed, were very much in vogue.

As our departure date approached, so my excitement grew and working in London became more tedious. In June I noticed an advertisement placed by the BMC seeking a National Officer to replace Mark Hutchinson whose contract had expired. Like most climbers, I presumed that to make a living from one's interest was attractive. But I had deliberately avoided instructing. Above all, mountaineering was for me about escapism and I disliked strenuous physical effort other than that which is required solely to climb rock or ice. I rarely enjoyed walking in the mountains and I viewed long approaches to mountains or crags as necessary evils to ensure the remoteness and quality of nature I sought. So instructing or guiding in the mountains did not appeal. However, the job of the National Officer was office-based and one which would still allow me to visit the mountains in my spare time. I applied, despite putting my chances of being shortlisted as extremely limited. Even if I was considered a suitable candidate, I could not disguise the fact that I was leaving on a ten-week expedition the following month. Judging by two previous National Officers, Peter Boardman and Alex MacIntyre – two of Britain's finest climbers – my biggest doubts about getting the job stemmed from my lack of expedition experience. But when I received a letter inviting me to an interview, I concluded that such qualities were only desirable, not essential, and I quickly started to swat up on the political affairs of the climbing world.

At the interview, the chair of the appointments panel, George Band, stressed to my surprise the Council's express wish that the new National Officer should *not* go on any expeditions but instead stay in Britain with his or her work. I said that I quite understood. John Neill, the President of the Council expressed his view, which was quite correct, that the first time I ever seriously considered what the BMC did was when I was researching for the interview. Paul Nunn, of the International Committee asked an unpalpable question; what would I do on Chogolisa if I got oedema?

'Go down,' was the answer I gave but it was not the answer he wanted.

'What if you were in the middle of the traverse?'

Although I could see him willing me on like a driving-test examiner asking the routine Highway Code questions at the end of the test, I could not read his mind. Paul wanted precisely the answer that was in his head, but he first wanted my detailed reasoning before I delivered the punchline. I did not offer one so George intervened and the interview drew to a rather stilted close. Dennis Gray looked at me through one eye for the whole of the hour-long dialogue, muttering what I now know was encouragement but was unfathomable and terrifying at the time. When I left the interview I collected my bag and headed immediately for the door, rushing for an imminent train back south, except the door I swung through coolly was the other door that led straight back into the interview room. Someone must have seen the funny side because they gave me the job.

The first person I told was Mr Kelleher, the loans officer at my bank.

'I'm delighted,' he said. 'A civil servant!'

'Thank you,' I replied, rather taken aback by his terminology. 'A civil servant, yes, I hadn't thought of it that way.'

In fact I was seeing him for another reason. The Pakistan Government insisted that our expedition deposited a helicopter bond of $4000 (US) on arrival in their country which would be returned as we left ten weeks later, so long as the expedition didn't call a rescue. By stressing to the bank the unlikelihood of us needing a rescue and hinting that helicopters cannot fly anyway at the altitudes that we were going, I tried to convince him that we were a financially safe risk for a short term loan. I succeeded. Mr Kelleher led all the members of our team into a windowless room with a single table, no chairs and a shadeless light hanging from the ceiling to sign an indemnity and guarantee. He need not have gone to the trouble. He handed over four crisp, $1000 International Money Orders. Then I explained to him that I was the only member of the team who hadn't paid all of his personal contribution into the expedition. I was in need of £500.

'Your account is already overdrawn,' he reminded me.

So what's new? I felt like saying. 'I wonder . . . would you consider . . .' I felt sure he wouldn't.

Hamish saw that I was struggling and put his arm around Mr Kelleher and squeezed his shoulders gently. 'Go on,' he said, 'give him the money.'

Thus concluded our business with the bank. The following day I had to sign my contract with the BMC at George Band's office in Knightsbridge, have a tetanus and hepatitis jab in Regent Street, and make forty-five kilos of airline luggage weigh only twenty-five kilos. The next day we took a tube to Heathrow to board our flight to Pakistan. It was 27th June.

A great burden was lifting. The hectic months of planning were behind us. We were five friends on an expedition to a high mountain peak in the Karakoram. For a first time visit to the Himalaya this was an ambitious project, though wobbling through the airport terminal under a considerable load, dressed in plastic mountain boots and fleece salopettes and dragging twenty kilos of hand luggage behind us, it did not feel like it. We felt humbly insignificant.

2
Getting in the swing

Karachi, on 28th June in the early morning. A stench was already rising under the oppressive heat of dawn. Hundreds of people were gathering at the station some of whom had slept there, some perhaps lived there. Most of the smells were of rotting meat and vegetables, though the fragrance of excrement and urine was particularly pungent and appeared most intense in the sheltered cubbyholes of the building. I wondered what it would be like at midday under the overhead sun, or in a monsoon storm. Inside the ticket office a ceiling fan revolved at a painfully slow pace stirring the thick air to mix and equalise the smells in the room. There were three classes on the train; one that had no Urdu translation, a middle one, and one that had no English translation. Not knowing any of this, we joined the only queue that appeared to be leading to a ticket booth, finally exchanging 120 Rupees (about £5) for a ticket to Islamabad, the capital, where we had our first appointment with the Ministry of Tourism.

Simon was not with us. He would fly direct, with his employers British Airways, to Islamabad. Our longer route via Karachi with Royal Jordanian Airlines, had cost us only £300, thus saving us each about £250 on the direct fare. Our other privilege was the twenty-six-hour train journey.

We found seats on a hard wooden bench next to the window. The temperature in the Thar Desert that day was considerably more than body temperature and we discovered that sitting by the window had the reverse effect of what we had hoped for. Occasionally a Coca Cola vendor came by, but despite several bottles, we dehydrated quickly. At the beginning of the journey I would not have dreamed of drinking the untreated water that passed about the train in shiny metal jugs, but now, only six hours into the journey, I sat with one in front of me, and the mixture of fear and excitement that one feels on the top board at a diving pool for the first time. I could not see the bottom of the jug; the water

22

was warm and murky, like used dishwater. As I psyched up for a tentative sip, Ulric snatched the jug from me and poured its contents straight down his throat. Hamish and Liam were horrified, Ulric expressionless, whilst I was just plain thirsty. Another jug came and I drained it. We were getting into the swing of things.

Mysterious and endless halts in the desert allowed us to walk beside the track to stretch our cramped muscles. At one time hundreds of people were squatting or standing along the line, blurred figures against the shimmering heat. By dusk and the town of Lahore, our seats had been occupied by a family who claimed to have reserved them. They lay out on the benches, each filling a space where three or four women had sat. The women took to the floor whilst we stood or bridged out across the seats for the remainder of the night, which was thankfully cool.

In Islamabad, and Rawalpindi, connected to Islamabad by a twenty-kilometre stretch of dual carriageway, we rode for a couple of hours from hotel to hotel in an overloaded Morris Minor taxi until the Al Farooq in Rawalpindi eventually took us in. I had never seen so many tenderly nursed cars of the same type. All were painted black with yellow roofs and immaculately shiny chromework. For decoration, and a kind of mysterious class symbolism, most had metal AA shields attached to their grilles. Their drivers were also their mechanics, and they were remarkably inventive. Some Rawalpindi Morris Minors had been rebuilt several times, from components of other cars. Less crucial parts, such as the screenwash fluid container might, when worn out, be replaced by a tin can. But the climate of Islamabad and the absence of salt on their roads had protected the bodywork of these cars and some were over thirty years old. The only other vehicles that we saw in Rawalpindi were Ford Transits and huge bare coaches. These travelled to and fro between Rawalpindi and Islamabad and one simply gave a rupee to the driver's mate when boarding. If buses could have elastic walls, then Pakistan would be full of them.

It was in one such bus that we first arrived at the Ministry of Tourism in Islamabad, where we hoped to meet our Liaison Officer. Two months previously Mr Qaiser had sent us an outline drawing of his foot and a chart of his considerable frame – over six foot tall and forty-two-inch chest. We had brought him some modern plastic boots and some clothing from Britain and we had no doubt that he would like them. There was no sign of him at the Ministry but we were assured that he would come directly to the hotel. When he did we could hardly believe our luck, or rather lack of it.

'Mr Fanshav?'

'Er, hello. You are Wasim Qaiser?' I knew this was unlikely, looking at the size of him.

'No. I am Captain Gulzar Jamal, I am a doctor with the Pakistan Army, I am your appointed Liaison Officer. May I see my equipments, please.'

He had wasted little time raising the subject of 'his equipments', but his anxiety caused him some embarrassment. Of course nothing fitted. His boots were size eleven, yet his feet would have rattled in a seven. His duvet was size 'XL', yet Captain Jamal was five foot six at the most.

'It's the latest style,' Hamish lied, passing the Captain his duvet jacket, 'and of course we can adjust the length of the sleeves.'

'But it will not look smart,' he said. This was obvious, though we had mistakenly not thought this important. Simon tried to model the duvet, whilst Liam turned up the arms and tightened the draw cords. 'No, it is no good,' he at last said. 'I do not like this colour.'

Captain Gulzar Jamal had not made a favourable impression. He left soon after our introduction, declaring he would be back the following evening. He wanted a completely new set of clothes, or a dress allowance. In fact the Captain did not return the next day, or the next. Meanwhile we had much to do, buying all of our food for the next two months, insuring and buying shoes and sunglasses for our estimated thirty-five porters, importing our air cargo that arrived with Simon and arranging to have it transported by road to Skardu, a thousand miles to the north.

On 6th July, in the early morning, we were at last treated to our debriefing at the Ministry. The Captain showed up and suffered the indignity of having his complaints squashed by the rather aggressive civil servant, and his chief of operations, the legendary Muneeruddin with whom every expedition coming to Pakistan in the past twenty years had liaised. Gulzar, for we had now drawn a delicate truce and agreed to call each other by our first names, was happy to accept the clothes we had provided and even agreed to eat with us, provided we bought him a giant tub of lime pickle. To be called Gulzar by us must have sounded as strange to him as being 'Mr Andy' was to me. The next day, with business in Islamabad complete, we flew to Skardu.

To reach Chogolisa we would follow the route that all expeditions visiting Concordia used. From Skardu we would take the fifty-kilometre jeep and tractor road in the Shigar valley to Dasso, from where a six-day walk up the hugely impressive Braldu Gorge, via the isolated village of Askole, would lead to the snout of the Baltoro Glacier. Another five days' march on this would take us to the meeting place of three enormous glacier systems, the Baltoro, Upper Baltoro and Godwin Austen Glaciers. Concordia is reputedly one of the most impressive places on earth. It was near here that we would make Base Camp.

My first view of the Karakoram came at 8500 metres from the flightdeck of a Boeing 727. The jet service to Skardu had only been in operation a week, so we were the first expedition to use it. Previously the altitude ceiling on this flight had been 5500 metres, the highest the Fokker Friendship propeller aircraft could safely fly. To the east, hundreds of dark foothills lay below a cloudless sky and a piercing low sun. In some valleys the silvery threads of rivers, the range's deepest lines, splintered through the enveloping haze. West, the range was cleansed in light, and to the north, projected precisely across the glass of the flightdeck's window, lay hundreds of huge mountains. The summit pyramid of K2 rose above the smoky blanket of haze – it was the only peak that did; it was, after all, the only summit higher than ourselves. Our journey also took us above Nanga Parbat. I imagined what it would be like seeing the same view from its summit. Gulzar was becoming inspired too.

'Mr Andy, I am very happy to be coming with you to the mountain.'

'I'm very glad.'

'When I was dropped from the Army expedition to Gasherbrum,' he explained, 'I was very disappointed.'

I knew that the Pakistan Army were that year trying to climb Gasherbrum II, which is said to be the easiest 8000-metre peak, but I did not know that Gulzar was at one time to be their doctor.

'I didn't know that, Gulzar.'

'Yes, I was very sad. I had not enough experience for an 8000-metre peak. But now I am thinking philosophically; if I climb Chogolisa, well, it will . . .'

'Hold on a minute, Gulzar. Who said anything about climbing!' Gulzar had admitted to us that he had done no climbing in his life, but even if he was a brilliant climber we would not have agreed to him climbing with us. 'Gulzar, we are a team of five, this is how we have planned it.'

'But this is why I am on your expedition,' he insisted, 'to get experience. Chogolisa will be good training for me.'

'No, Gulzar, this is not the case.'

'I will carry loads for you to the higher camps, and maybe if I am fit . . .'

'No, Gulzar!' I had raised my voice, unnecessarily. I had to apologise. 'Sorry, Gulzar, what I meant was, we won't have any camps.'

'No camps?'

'We won't have ropes either. Only small lengths that we carry, none that we leave on the mountain.'

'No ropes?' Gulzar looked surprised. 'This is dangerous.'

'Yes, but it is very modern.' I had lied twice in a single sentence. Alpine-style climbing was commonplace in the Himalaya, even before the wars, and there is nothing especially dangerous about it. Gulzar had nothing to add on the subject, but I hoped that he had understood that we didn't want him on the mountain.

The flight lasted just forty-five minutes. Within another thirty we had collected our baggage and been driven quickly through the scrub-littered landscape and along the sandbanks of the Indus to Skardu itself; a hot and dusty little town beneath high unstable cliffs and a ring of high mountain peaks. The Skardu summer is so hot that none of the surrounding mountains are snow-covered, despite being higher than the Mont Blanc massif. We were taken to the K2 Motel, which is as much an institution for climbers as Camp 4 in Yosemite or Snell's Field in Chamonix. We camped on the front lawn, paying half the price of a room, but still enjoying the facilities of the motel, an arrangement the management make with most expeditions. Gulzar was given a room.

With the help of the local Government tourism official and Gulzar, who was suddenly extremely helpful, we engaged a Sirdar or head porter, Hamsa Ali, who would be responsible for buying further supplies and hiring porters for the walk-in to Concordia. Hamsa's energy and enthusiasm easily matched the task, and his warm infectious personality won the respect of us all. Hamsa was a Balti, one of the indigenous people of the northern area of Pakistan. His village, Satpara, was renowned for producing very strong porters and sirdars. Certainly Hamsa's small stature belied his strength and the respect he commanded in the villages enabled him to round up the thirty-five porters that we had agreed with him were necessary. However, no sooner had Hamsa brought the porters to our tents to be enlisted, than they were wooed away at double the Government rate to carry water for a Swiss extreme skier, Sylvan Saudain, who had in 1982 skied from the summit of Gasherbrum I, and was now organising a five-day mountain marathon, sponsored by Swatch Watches. He hardly allowed himself to notice our small expedition and I was beginning to dislike him, when John Porter and Jim Hargreaves of the British Fullers K2 Expedition returning prematurely from their mountain, mentioned that they had seen brightly red painted Ms on boulders during the last two days of their walk-out from Concordia. More seriously, the villages of Askole and Chongo had the paintmarks on the sides of their houses. I wondered at the arrogance of someone

26

who could wantonly inflict such graffiti on the countryside and villages of others.

With John and Jim came other expeditions and parts of expeditions, which reminded us that we were unusually late to be travelling up the Baltoro Glacier. An Australian-American expedition had successfully climbed the North-West Ridge of Gasherbrum IV, the nearest major peak to Concordia, and was now happy to be back in Skardu. Andy Tathill, one of the Americans, whilst within near certain grasp of the top, had decided against going for the summit which would have committed him to a bivouac without equipment. He had waited at their camp at 7900 metres until the other three returned from the summit a day later. I had no way of imagining what a night out at that altitude could be like, inside or outside a tent.

'I didn't want it bad enough,' he said, when I probed.

'What about the others, the bivouac?'

'Ah well, pretty okay, I guess.' And then, 'Greg got cold feet.'

'Did *he* bottle as well?' I offered, trying to keep up with the colloquialism.

'No?' he said looking confused. 'He stuck 'em in Tim's stomach.' In fact Andy himself had not bottled – he had decided not to go on. There was a distinction.

I admired his resolve, though wondered whether he felt any regret, with one of the summiteers, Tim McCartney-Snape, sitting beside him. It was probably as hard to stay as it was to continue, and with less promise of rewards. Tim, more to encourage than to warn, told us that he thought that the traverse of Chogolisa was 'very ambitious'. Thankfully I wrote in my diary that evening, 'we're under no obligation'. We, of course, had a duty to our supporters, not least the Nick Estcourt Award. But we were a young expedition with nothing to prove and lots to gain. I personally felt no overbearing pressure to succeed; only to try.

Gulzar helped us to enlist fresh porters by writing their names in my little black book: Mohammed Ali son of Hussain, Hussain s/o Ali, Mohammed s/o Mohammed Ali, Mohammed Hussain s/o Hussain, etc. I shuddered at the thought that one team that year, the Korean K2 Expedition, had reputedly had to find 600 porters, only about half of whom would be carrying essential gear and food for Base Camp and the mountain. The rest would be carrying food for 600.

With a tentative hold on most of the porters we needed, we left for Dasso in the hope of picking up the remainder out of the reach of Saudain. Simon, Liam, Ulric and Gulzar had already left during the night in a small jeep to ford a river we were obliged to cross before its meltwater feeds swelled under the day's heat. Hamish and I, accompanying the loads, left at dawn on 11th July. Our tractor would have no trouble with the river and the driver insisted on having light for the journey. Dawn arrived and departed quickly, the soft gentle light and cool breeze fanning up from the Indus giving in to the harshness of the Karakoram day – arid and hot. Small dust storms were dancing in the thermals across the valley. John and Jim came to see us off.

'Look in on our K2 team,' they instructed, calling after us, 'they could use the company.' According to John and Jim, they would have food and even, though I couldn't believe it, beer left over at the end of their stay. We shouted, 'We will.'

After about an hour we were overtaken by the leading marathon runners setting a ludicrously fast pace. The Shigar valley was wide and sandy, with the occasional scrub as the only form of life. Our tractor tyres either spun in the soft deep sand or leaped over hard baked ruts giving Hamish and me our first lesson in riding rodeo. Apricot plantations lined the road, though we would have to wait until our return in late August before enjoying them. Interestingly, the Baltis prize the bitter tasting kernels more than the fruit. The marathon runners began to overtake us again where we stopped at Shigar for what a sign misleadingly called 'refreshments'. Many of the houses were Sherpa in style, a throwback to the times when Buddhism had an influence in this area, before Islam. The only two women in the race were British – Lesley Watson and Kate Fitzgibbon – and as they ran past, both in deliberately baggy shorts and as concealing shirts as they could bare, every head in the village turned towards them. Some of the men simply could not believe their eyes. For the older inhabitants with failing sight they were the strangest looking men they had ever seen. For surely these people striding through their village, sweating, panting and spitting could not be women. Some of the younger men in the village took off after them, catching them up and running with them for as far as they could, which wasn't far. Of course, very few local women were outside to witness the spectacle.

At Dasso we met a team of Americans returning from K2, where two of their climbers had been killed in an avalanche. Here Hamsa gathered the porters together and gave them their loads. A day's work, carrying twenty-five kilos, earned them each sixty rupees, about two pounds, and 'fringe benefits'. These consisted of a pair of loopstitch stockings, a vinyl poncho, meant for weather protection, though they made good tablecloths, a length of rope for tying on their loads, though most of these got used on their animals, and a pair of shoes. Because the porters all mysteriously 'lost' their rope on the first day and asked for another

28

length, we decided to wait until we reached the glacier before giving them their sunglasses to protect them from snow blindness. These, at least, were essential.

Catching the eye of the older porters, we would trade smiles, the furrowed lines on their faces creasing. Their skin was dark, dry and unwashed, and their hair was black. Most had a beard of sorts – what some would call 'designer stubble'. Their expressions revealed hard, uncomplaining men, yet the manner in which they handled themselves and each other was gentle. No two Baltis, even to my unaccustomed eyes, looked remotely alike. These were our very own porters and seeing them all together filled me with delight and excitement for the days and weeks ahead.

3

Looking towards Concordia

As soon as I started walking from Dasso I felt horribly unfit. Lifting my eyes from the baked mud path revealed a huge gorge almost two kilometres deep – the Braldu river valley, up which we were walking. The brown colour in the landscape was grass, the greys and blacks were scree and crags. The base of the gorge was strewn with huge boulders, under which it was common to find the porters resting, shaded from the intense desert heat. Although the river was huge in itself, it looked lost and insignificant against the backdrop of the gorge that a relict form of itself had cut. Apart from beneath the boulders, or within the lonely clusters of trees, there was no shade, and no water either – just the silt-suspended contents of the Braldu river. The snout of the Baltoro Glacier lay five wearisome days ahead. This became my first goal. I looked up the long steep slope on the side of the gorge and tried to imagine being at its top. That would be, I guessed, about the altitude of the snout.

A few hundred metres from Dasso we crossed the river to reach its true left bank by means of a *jolla*, a wooden box suspended from a pulley-wheel on a wire a few metres above the river, hauled across by the previous passenger. Soon after we had crossed the river, I noticed several porters upstream on the right bank and, looking at the torrent between us, wondered when I would next see them and their loads. We had walked only fifteen kilometres when we stopped for the night. Hamsa assured us that having only half the porters with us at the night halt was quite normal. Although the sound of the turbulent river was not loud, it was inescapable, and I lay awake, mesmerised by its constant pitch.

The next morning we regained the true right bank by two wet planks of weathered wood, twenty-five metres beneath which white water roared between marble smooth walls. Once across, I off-loaded my sack and

30

took out my camera. Gulzar, who had not been with us when we crossed the previous *jolla*, came marching over.

'What are you doing?' he said. The question was rhetorical.

'I'm taking a picture. What does it look like?'

'You have read the regulations.' This time a statement.

I had, but I didn't remember anything about taking pictures of log bridges, so I let Gulzar go on.

'This is a bridge.'

'Yes, Gulzar.'

'The regulations are clear.'

I remembered more efficient conversations, though by now I had sussed what he meant. The reason he was not immediately forthcoming was that he was a little embarrassed by the regulations, but nevertheless felt it his duty to see them observed.

'No pictures of military bases, equipment, personnel or installations – is that it, Gulzar?' I said.

'Mr Andy, the rules are the rules. I must confiscate your film.'

When I refused, he got in a huff. It was the first of several embarrassing incidents.

On the right bank the path deteriorated and climbed steeply. I could not have been more exhausted. In places it was no more than a line of subsiding footholds across a scree slope and the angle was steep, uninterrupted into the river a hundred metres below. This was serious stuff. Some of the runners in the marathon passed us, and I wondered whether they were finding the terrain as terrifying as I was. Our group, like the runners, was strung out along the path. Walking alone, I arrived on top of another interminable slope clasping my knees with tired hands and was surprised but pleased to see a couple of Baltis guarding a small barrel of water. Water! They treated me to a single mugful. Then to my amazement Kate appeared, her long lithe legs springing effortlessly across the sand. She seemed to me a mirage. Coming from Dasso that day, she didn't stop for more than a minute. I stood up to greet her, but as quickly lowered myself back onto the desert. I felt inadequate, and suddenly too weak to climb a mountain. After sipping carefully at the water she bounced back onto the path and bounded off. A little later I caught her up again, relaxing at the third marathon night halt by the river. Hamish was at the camp, too, and he and I set off as late as we dared, to reach Chongo, a small village about 150 metres above the river, by nightfall. In this section we faced the crux of the whole approach to Concordia. At the end of an already tiring day, we found ourselves rock-climbing in short steep sections above a certain death fall. I hobbled

31

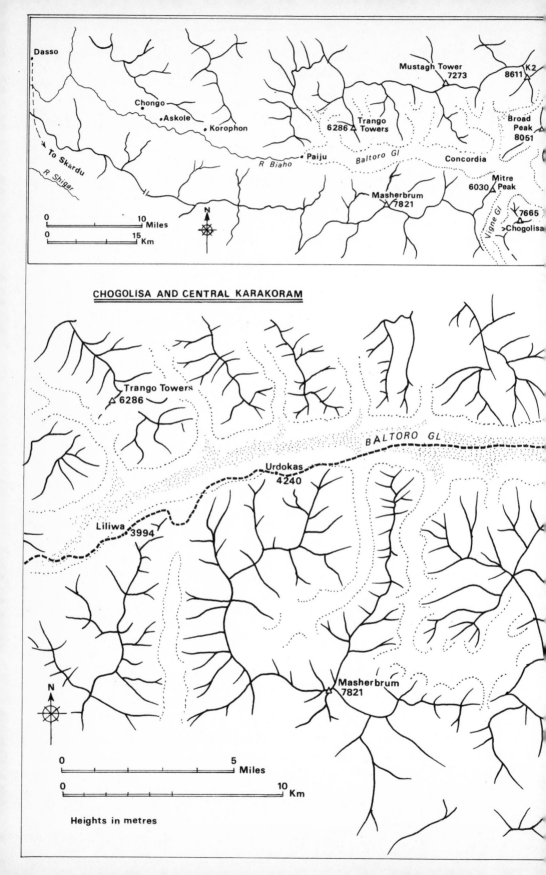

CHOGOLISA AND CENTRAL KARAKORAM

Dasso

Chongo
• Askole • Korophon

To Skardu
R Shigar

Mustagh Tower
7273

K2
8611

Broad
Peak
8051

Trango
Towers
6286

R Biaho • Paiju Baltoro Gl Concordia

Mitre
Peak
6030

Masherbrum
7821

7665
Chogolisa

Vigne Gl

0   10 Miles
0   15 Km

N

Trango Towers
6286

BALTORO GL

Urdokas
4240

Liliwa 3994

Masherbrum
7821

N

0   5 Miles
0   10 Km

Heights in metres

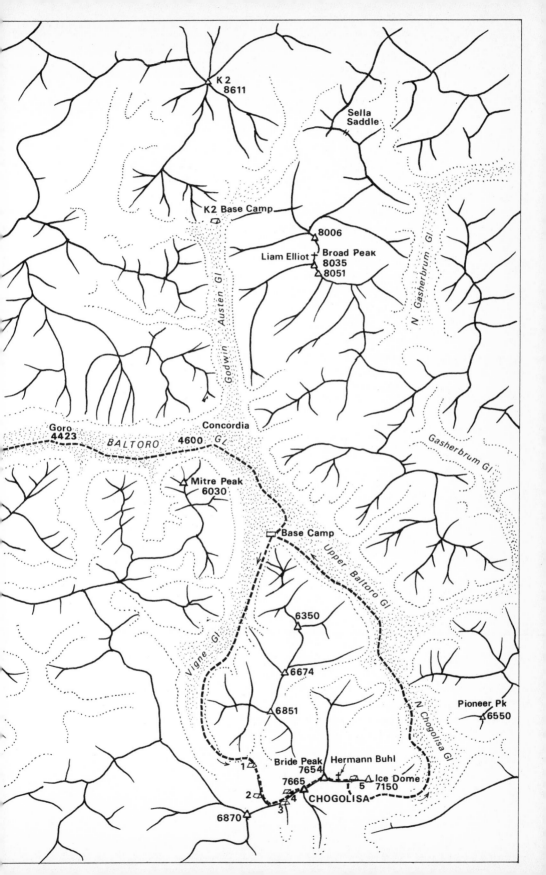

and balanced my thirty-kilo pack across crumbling slabs of sun-shattered rock and bottomless nullahs, terrifyingly steep grooves eroded in the mud in which boulders were suspended against every law of physics. My legs, jellylike from fear and fatigue, did their best to guide me up each mortal pitch. My throat dried out – a tell-tale sign of fear – which left me more or less speechless when I eventually subsided onto the horizontal above the difficulties.

The sky had darkened when Hamish and I neared Chongo. Rosi and Mohammed, two of our porters, ran out to greet us a few hundred metres from the village, and offered to take our sacks. Hamish did not hesitate to hand his over, but a stupidly stubborn side of me would not part with mine. It seemed very important to me that I completed the day's walk under my own steam. We approached Chongo together. Just before the village, Rosi, who had puzzled over why I had not let Mohammed take my sack, offered his burden back to Hamish with a grin. Hamish took his sack and we walked into the village with the porters lining the dusty alleys and Rosi and Mohammed marching behind.

Ulric handed me a mug of water. It had come neat out of the stream that ran through the village. 'I've drunk some,' he said when he saw the expression of horror on my face.

I had already learnt that there was no reasonable correlation between water that was fit for human consumption and water that Ulric had remained on his feet after drinking. What he had handed me might have been Bovril, judging by its colour. He grinned and watched me quench my considerable thirst. A little later I wandered around the village, and discovered that the black liquid I had drunk earlier ran beneath half the baked mud homes in the village and through several filthy chicken ranches before it reached our camping spot, where Mohammed Ali, our cook, had a scrawny chicken boiling in a smoky pot. The lanky chickens, tightly wrapped in tourniquet skin, ran madly around the village. All I saw them eat was their own shit. Mohammed gave me a meagre portion of the decaying meal. I picked at the emaciated leg, choking on its bones and spilling gravy down my gritty chin, which I reluctantly licked back into my mouth.

The Chongo chickens reminded me of the horses that we had seen in Rawalpindi, pulling carts, scraggy sunken bodies on stick-like legs. As Simon had put it, like a scene out of hell. He particularly loathed cruelty to animals, and just the thought of it would sometimes bring tears of hatred to his eyes. I knew Simon better than I knew the others, and had enjoyed climbing with him in the Alps and at home. I saw him as a very intelligent person; but socially shy. He rarely started a conversation, but

34

then his doggedness would never let one finish, until all of his points had been made. As a technical climber he was probably the least experienced of the team, and a little clumsy, unusual for his slight frame. Though he was remarkably determined and, like me, what he sought most on our expedition was a sense of personal achievement.

After an early start from Chongo, we were passed for the last time by Kate. Soon after, at Askole, the last civilisation on the route to Concordia, she would cross the Braldu river and climb steeply, in one more day, to a col at 5000 metres, the Skori La, which marked the end of her run. By the finish she would have run over 150 kilometres in five consecutive days.

This would be the shortest stage of our journey, and pleasantly unstrenuous. Before Askole we had a chance to bathe in hot-spring pools. Hamsa, no less modest than the other Baltis, found our naked splashing slightly perturbing but felt obliged to guide us to and from the pools, though he sat discreetly divorced from our group until we emerged from the murky and soapy waters. The pools provide the first and last thorough wash for expeditioners travelling to and from the Baltoro, and I hesitated to think how many dirty bodies had shared my experience.

Askole was so remote that many of its inhabitants, particularly the women, would never have been further than Chongo in their entire lives. Too close intermarriage had resulted in some inevitable retardation. When we were there, the Government engineers were surveying the area to decide upon the route of a road that would link Askole to the national network. At Dasso construction of the first bridge over the Braldu had already begun. This might relieve one problem, we thought, but ultimately create others.

Askole matched my idea of what a medieval English town might have looked like. An occasional western artifact, and the ludicrous red paintmarks that Saudain had daubed onto the sides of some of the houses, brought us back to the vulgarity of modern times. Many of the homes were built into the ground, below the level of the paths, to protect their occupants from the heat of the summer and intense cold of the winter. The village was a huge warren, with seemingly hundreds of passages and ladders leading up and down. Many of the houses were framed in wood, painted in seedy, once glossy paint. Their roofs were flat mud, upon which a woman sorting through her blanket of rice was a common sight. The headman, Haji Mehdi, lived in the grandest house which, unlike the others, was raised on stilts. After offering us tea and explaining that it was 'traditional' for an expedition to leave him a present, he displayed examples of gifts from other expeditions. Messner, he informed us, had given him a pair of skis.

'How useful,' came Hamish's wisecrack, as he produced and handed Haji a lighter that we had earlier agreed was superfluous to our needs.

Haji allowed us to camp in the village square for a small fee and provided us with a chicken and a goat. Mohammed Ali took the chicken away for slaughter but the goat, which we had promised our porters, would accompany us as far as the Baltoro snout. Haji showed us the goat when we had showed him a fistful of rupees, and it was then allowed to roam freely in the village. Hamish, practical as ever, wrote 'British' on one horn and 'Chogolisa' on the other. This he hoped would help us find it in the morning.

Once under the poplar tree in the middle of the square, fending off the dust and flies, Ulric, Liam and Hamish, who had organised our food for the expedition, allowed a number of 'luxuries' to be revealed. Simon and I had deliberately not enquired what these consisted of to maintain the suspense for as long as we could. One of the 'luxuries' was a kind of sherbet drink called Cremola Foam. The powder, bright yellow or orange, was contained in a neat little cardboard packet. Gulzar thought they were great and wanted to know what other goodies there were. We explained we had a few chocolate bars, but they were reserved for when we went on the mountain. 'I'll have mine now,' was his predictable response, and he was not best pleased when Liam explained they were climbers' perks only.

Liam had a quiet, content manner and I noticed his ability to detach himself quite naturally from the group, whenever the whim came. When I met him for the first time in the summer of 1985, I had been struck then by his single-mindedness. In his first alpine season he climbed many impressive lines including the North Faces of the Matterhorn and Grand Charmoz. The following winter, Liam took a young climber from Edinburgh on *his* first alpine route up the North Face of Les Droites. Such audacity reminded me of John Taylor, except where John was gentle in the company of friends, Liam appeared a little more rugged, nervous even and short fused. When pushed beyond the limits of his natural reserve, Liam could become quite argumentative, even if he was in a minority of one. When I, quite autocratically, appointed an agent for the hiring of porters in Skardu, nobody voiced an objection except Liam who was deeply critical. Admirably, he chose not to remind me now that this man had been an absolute waste of money, and indeed had been responsible for side-tracking many of our porters to Saudain, for whom he was also agent.

The next morning we climbed gently above Askole, through cultivated fields, bordered by skilfully engineered irrigation channels, passing women hunched under bales of fodder, twice their size and almost half their weight, that they had collected for their animals. Small trees, protected by a byelaw introduced by the villagers, lined the paths and offered gratifying shade before we were once again plunged into the natural, water-parched, colours of the Upper Braldu Gorge. Three porter-stages lay between us and the snout of the Baltoro, but we paid the porters for three days as well as a bonus as an encouragement for them to cover the distance in just two days. It was the masochistic in me that welcomed the saving of a day, for I found it harder each morning to rise from sleep and my legs and back were becoming progressively stiffer.

As Askole receded behind us, a lunar landscape of huge boulders and red mud channels rose ahead – the snout of the Biafo Glacier (which combined with the Hispar is reputedly the largest single volume of ice outside the polar regions) projected across our own valley and thus forced an obligatory day of scrabbling on moraine. Here was a taster of the thirty-five kilometres of Baltoro Glacier still to come. On my feet were a pair of threadbare trainers; I had decided to save weight by not bringing walking boots, but instead I carried a potentially redundant pair of rock boots, thinking that the bouldering around every corner would be Utopian and that I would have excess energy to burn. It was all I could do just to keep moving. I was beginning to feel pretty stupid. The only other footwear I had were my plastic high-altitude double-boots, which were unbearable even to put on, let alone walk in, and I risked looking like a wimp next to the porters in their open-top sandals. I wobbled nervously behind them following a line of small cairns, on the tenuous route across the glacier.

To my amusement more than surprise I found myself at the bottom of an ice pitch, maybe ten metres high. At first I assumed this was a joke, or at best an optional extra to relieve what the porters might have thought was a boring voyage. The first few porters took to the ice. It clearly wasn't a joke. On the left a steep impending groove – a real chop route – cut a direct line. The obvious line was a chimney which started about two metres up the ice on the right, and up which the porters wriggled, occasionally stemming wildly across the void, hacking a step out of the ice with their sticks. I was astonished. I looked at the goat. Surely not. Then to my utter bewilderment one of the Baltis, Ibraham, went for the groove. He thrust his arse out from the ice and padded delicately leftwards from the base of the chimney to the base of the groove. Already about three metres above us, he faced a painful landing, particularly as the base of the slab down which I imagined him accelerating was undercut. He brought his feet up high underneath his body, and inverted his hands, down-pressuring on the ice, whilst his eyes scanned the surface for a slight relaxation in the angle. It was masterful. The ice was pitted with tiny pieces of grit, and was actually quite rough, despite looking flawless, as it gleamed under the sun. Ibraham thus climbed the pitch as a rock-climber would climb a slab. He cruised to the top, which made me think I could do it, though when one of the porters had to pull me up the first move over the undercut, I saw sense and took the chimney. So did the goat, on the end of a very taut rope. Simon was beginning to think that the Askole Goat was getting as rough a deal out of life as the Pindi Horse or Chongo Chicken.

The porters pulled ahead again after this bottleneck, so that even before I arrived at Korofan on the other side of the snout I could see the familiar smoke columns rising out of the stone circles built on the dusty scrub. The porters were settling down for, although this was not our night halt, they were certainly not moving for a few hours at least, whilst they waited for the heat of the day to subside. For some of the Baltis this was their third journey to Concordia that year, and between them they had the route well rehearsed. We could do no better than follow their lead. It was, after all, a lovely place. Brightly coloured flowers were growing here and already snowy peaks were coming into view on the edge of the valley. Their laundered white contrasted sharply with the dirty greys and brushwood greens and browns that we had become accustomed to.

The valley was wider now and the river, no longer fed by the Biafo meltwater, was less energetic, braided and winding noiselessly beside us. The river, now the Biaho, had banks here too, adding a sandy red or in places creamy white colour to our landscape, and beaches along which it was effortless to walk. Tucked under some of the boulders, that had rolled from the long slopes on either side of the river, were pools of perfect clear spring water with a refreshing effervescence. Curiously the porters, even at the height of the day's heat, did not drink water and ignored these pools. What they did drink, when they took the trouble, was nauseously salty tea in tiny cups.

The end of our day involved another *jolla* across the Panmah River which brought the meltwater from glaciers in the Choktoi group in from the north. Earlier in the season expeditions had been able to ford this river at its widest point, where it fans gently into the Biaho, but now expeditions were forced to make a long detour to the *jolla* thrown up between two boulders buried to unknown depths in the sand.

'It's not what I would call dodgy,' commented Ulric, casting a critical scientific eye on the construction, 'just homespun.'

From a cave on the near side of the *jolla*, emerged a scruffy Balti with long greasy hair and a bushy beard who reminded me of Brian from the Monty Python's *Life of*. He announced that the bridge was on toll, and he was the toll collector. This was the first Balti troglodyte-cum-capitalist we had met and I hope I am excused for thinking he might not have been what he said he was, though, as he looked as ridiculous as the notion, I didn't question it publicly. He demanded five rupees for each porter and, as if upset that we only had thirty porters, five rupees for each load as well. And another five rupees for the goat.

On the other side of the river, we stopped for the night. Another British team was already there, having come from Paiju that day. Hamish knew the Scots among them, Rhona Lampard and Al Scott, already. Dai Lampard, Al Phizacklea and Bob Wightman made up the piratical-looking party. Rhona was distinguishable by her lack of beard. They had been on Gasherbrum IV and had, sensibly I thought, decided against their first objective of repeating Voytek Kurtyka's and Robert Schauer's West Face line. Instead they had ferried all their gear around the other side of the mountain to try the South Ridge, without success, but reaching 7300 metres. One of their porters had been killed above their first Base Camp, lured onto the mountain by a chance of swag. I wondered how they felt.

'He was a thieving bastard anyway!' Al Phizacklea said. I shouldn't have expected to get a serious answer.

Despite Hamsa's instruction that we should leave early in the morning in order to cover the distance to Paiju via the normal night halt of Bardumal in a single day, it was well after dawn before we thought about climbing out of our sleeping bags. Most of the porters had already gone. Sultan Ali brought us tea whilst we sprawled out on the sand under yet another cloudless sky. Sultan was wearing Hamish's red tartan scarf over his head. He had 'borrowed' it in Askole, and ever since had been convincing himself that it had been a 'present' in preparation for the moment when Hamish would ask for it back. Sultan did have a remarkably persuasive manner. Firstly he had convinced us that we should hire an extra porter in Askole in view of the fact that we now had a goat to herd and secondly he convinced us that the new porter should take his load whilst he took the rope of the unwilling animal. Sultan was therefore carrying only a small western rucsac, no doubt a 'present' from a previous expedition. Thus he was in no hurry to leave early that morning and sat around with us until the moment came when we had to hoist our thirty-kilo loads onto our backs and put our heads down and the sun behind us.

By lunchtime we had passed most of the porters on the path or resting at Bardumal around their smoky fires. Hamsa made a head count – common sense on a small expedition but totally impractical on a larger one – and disclosed we were one porter short. Apart from being bright, Sultan was also very kind and willing, and he volunteered to go back to look for the straggler. He left the goat with Hamish, Simon and me to take to Paiju.

Herding an ill-disposed goat through a desert was not as we thought it would be. I had the evil thought that the goat was an unusually difficult one and Sultan had taken the first opportunity he could to relieve himself of his duties with it. Simon's previous fondness for the goat and his reservations about Sultan's tight rope on the ice pitch quickly dissolved when his turn came. Every ten paces would be broken by the goat's sudden attraction to one of the shrubs by the path. It would resist encouragement from the front by locking its front legs solid and squatting low to the ground like an alert sheepdog. When finally it could resist the pull no more it would suddenly come running, sending its herder stumbling forward onto the hard earth and entangling itself in the slack rope. Simon was being reduced to anger.

'Ignorant sod!' he shouted at it. But probably the goat knew how the day was to end. In Paiju it was beheaded, chopped up and thrown into a huge stew for the voracious porters. With no other implement for the job the porter with the short straw chopped the meat into digestible pieces with an ice axe Hamish had found at the bottom of Number 2 Gully on Ben Nevis on one of his bounty hunting days in spring when he and Liam had visited the bottom of every popular gully in Scotland.

Paiju provided the last wood on the walk-in to Concordia. Porters use wood for cooking if they can get it, sometimes hacking down living trees and unearthing large bushes when they are unable to use dead wood. Because of this the Ministry in Islamabad has required that expeditions carry kerosene and stoves. Many of our porters were using the stoves. However, in the morning, we saw wood strapped to their loads for the following nights on the glacier. The wood at Paiju was almost spent, a fragile weakling on the side of a stark dry landscape. It was also a toilet, for most Baltis, shy of exposing their bodies, went upstream above the camp where they could not be overlooked, to relieve themselves. The toxic waters of the stream also contend with western garbage – sharp-edged cans and shredded packaging discarded by ungrateful visitors.

Everyone should take some blame. Certainly we played a part in the area's deterioration. Our expedition had seemed so negligible against the other larger parties, and the scale of the terrain. But forces, I realise now, are cumulative. We added our mite, no matter how small.

I sat in the morning on the far side of the starving oasis and looked ahead to the Baltoro and understood in an instant why so many people had come before us. It was very beautiful. A new magnitude of scale was introduced and it took a while for my mind to calibrate itself. On the north side of the glacier, itself three kilometres across, rose tall elegant steeples of granite. They were not the scattered hostile shards that I had visualised, but clean inviting features. Only until later in the day, when established on the glacier ourselves, did we see the base of these spires and appreciate that as flawless teeth they rose from decidedly unhealthy gums. Negotiating a route onto the snout of the Baltoro had taken us up a rubble slope close to the edge of a steep sweep of ice above the riotous jet of meltwater that gushed from the icy tunnels. This face itself was 300 metres high. We were passing magnificent scenery. Paiju Peak was already behind us. Opposite lay the Trango group, with the distinctive profile of the Nameless Tower, and ahead rose snowy mountains.

Our camping spot that night, at Liliwa, was on a small terrace above the glacier. We could hear the ice groaning restlessly beneath us. A tall unstable cliff of boulder clay overhung our site. Even at the edge of the terrace, at the farthest point from the threatening wall, we ran a risk of rockfall. Thus I was a little alarmed when Mohammed Ali put his cooking shelter up at the very base of the cliff, draping his tarpaulin over the boulders that had recently fallen.

The path to Urdokas kept to the steep scree and grass slopes on the south of the glacier, except in those places where the gradient was too steep, or where a spur had been truncated by the glacier to produce a vertical cliff. At one point, a few hours above Liliwa, we were obliged to cross a river of meltwater braided into several channels, some deep and narrow, others wide and shallow, all of which had to be waded forcefully. The water was cold enough to have you gasping and the torrent strong enough to carry any faller a few metres downstream, into deeper waters. Our porters never faltered. I remember Mahedi most of all. In places the water came over his thighs. Upon reaching the far bank he hurled his load onto the sand, ran on the spot, stomping his feet until the circulation returned before leaping energetically back into the river to help carry our loads and guide us on the best route across. Many

41

expeditions have had problems with the Baltis, reporting that they were unhelpful and liable to strike for wage increases. I found these stories difficult to believe and characters like Mahedi were typical rather than unusual. I sadly concluded, perhaps unfairly, that in the past, expeditions must have treated them badly.

The afternoon was spent at Urdokas, bouldering on perfect granite. Urdokas has several flat tent sites which were manufactured by the Duke of Abruzzi's party in its travels to these parts in the early years of this century and have weathered over the years so as to look like natural quirks of nature. From our site, the glacier below looked like a giant mining conveyor belt overloaded with rocks. In each direction I saw only boulders, some the size of houses toppled on one another in struggling heaps. The Cathedral group of granite spires stood opposite, with one of their faces, a vertical wall almost a kilometre high, falling into the far side of the river of rocks. Up the glacier was Broad Peak. This mountain like many others in that direction was much whiter than the rocky peaks opposite. The mountains around Concordia are comprised of layered rocks and their small ledges hold snow.

The Nameless Tower, now in view on the right of the main Trango peak, was the finest piece of rock I had ever seen. Even next to the 1500-metre East Spur of the main Trango peak, whose reddish colour gave it a strange autumnal glow, it dominated. In Skardu, the Aussie/ American team from Gasherbrum IV had said that three of their members had stayed on the Baltoro to try a new route on the Nameless Tower. Thus it was with only some surprise that I recognised Greg Child and Randy Leavitt appear that afternoon at Urdokas in search of porters to clear their camp beneath the Spire and to take them home. They had thrown hard free climbing and A4 artificial at the wall and got nowhere near climbing it. Randy, in particular, had a reputation as a brilliant Yosemite big-wall climber. He knew all there was to know about granite. He wandered about the boulders inspecting our problems and looking for new ones.

Just as I was showing my excitement at a crack we had seen from ten metres, cutting a pure split-line through a large boulder, he dampened my enthusiasm.

'Forget it. That's a one and a quarter.'

Had I measured the crack with a pair of calipers, I feel sure it would have measured exactly one and a quarter inches. But then I didn't need to; he had told me. And if he couldn't climb it . . .

Though we had got on well with our porters, at Urdokas we fell foul of the prickly dignity of Gulzar who took exception to a hasty remark and had the porters ready to pack up for home. A formal letter of apology, worded as tersely as I could make it, got the show back on the road, but reminded us of the fragility of our Liaison Officer's ego.

After our rest day during which it rained continuously, we walked to Goro in the middle of the Baltoro. We had split up as usual, only this time Gulzar said we shouldn't, quoting verbatim from the Ministry's rules: 'A team shall stay together at all times.'

I said, 'Gulzar, that's *ridiculous*! We're only walking with the porters!'

This was not the response that he wanted, so he resumed his sulk, the biggest of the trip so far, and disappeared into his tent. It occurred to me, for the first time, that as a team of climbers we were happy, but as an expedition we were not. Being a pain-in-the-neck was only part of the reason why Gulzar was being isolated from the group – he was the expedition's scapegoat.

The view that evening from Goro was enough to soothe anyone's temper; except Gulzar, buried in his tent, could not see it. The cloud veiling Masherbrum and Mustagh Tower cleared to reveal their dark shapes. This was our first view of them, yet we had already passed them by. They seemed to have risen up behind us. We were being slowly consumed by the mountains as we progressed, moving deeper and deeper into their gate. Paiju Peak, beyond the snout in the very jaws of the range twenty-five kilometres away, was a hazy silhouette beneath the setting sun. Behind us Gasherbrum IV's west side glowed gently, burning in the intense cold of its face. Mitre Peak, though small in itself, was difficult not to notice. It stood above Concordia like a crooked church spire that I remembered seeing in Chesterfield.

Al Burgess and Phil Burke, returning from K2, shared our site that night, and told us that the British team had given up on the unclimbed North-West Ridge, and were attempting a last ditch effort on the Abruzzi Spur, the original south-east route up K2. There were many climbers of many nationalities camped on the 'Strip' – the name given to the ridge of moraine on the glacier where most expeditions had made their Base Camp. In 1986, there were eleven expeditions to K2, and more tents, said Al and Phil, than you could expect to see on Snell's Field in Chamonix. Like John and Jim before them, they instructed us to call in on the British team. There was food in excess; Al even said we could probably claim some skis.

They also said that there had been many deaths already on the mountain, most notably (if one death can be more notable than another) of Renato Casarotto, the brilliant Italian who was trying to make a solo ascent of the mountain's 'magic line' – the South Pillar. He had died leaping a crevasse, the last before Base Camp, on his return from what he had vowed to his wife at Base Camp would be his last attempt. The story shocked me deeply.

Al gave us a piece of advice that stuck very firmly in my consciousness. We were talking about the changeability of weather and the commitment that our traverse required. He said, 'Go for it when the wind blows from China. Look for the plume on K2.' Each clear day after that, my eyes were drawn to the summit of the world's second peak.

At Concordia, we could not see Chogolisa, as we had expected. Our view was obstructed by smaller and nearer peaks in its own massif. Yet our eyes did not spend time searching. They had been drawn to the simple pyramidal outline of K2. It stood at the end of the Godwin Austen Glacier, seven kilometres to the north, the summit three and a half kilometres above. From Concordia its sheer bulk, more than its height, impressed me most. Concordia represented the heart of the range. Broad Peak formed a colossal wall at the far side of the Godwin Austen, and with Gasherbrum IV towering immediately above, the area felt almost claustrophobic, despite its implausible scale. The visitor here is thrown into a monochrome world. The rocks vary from black to grey, the snow, white to grey. There are no flowers, no grass and the only animal life comes in the form of jet black squawking crows that scavenge for garbage on the edge of the base camps. In the evening, some of the mountain faces assume a red hue, but such colours are short lived. The only exception is the sky.

4

The Baltoro Bin Boys

On 22nd July, our eleventh day from Dasso, Base Camp was established at the junction of the Vigne and Upper Baltoro Glaciers. The porters helped us build the shelter and put up the tents, as they had insisted on doing every day of the walk-in. Then they formed a long line to one of the tents where we supervised Hamsa, giving them each a modest wad of rupees. After the cheesy grins and solid handshakes of valediction, the Baltis huddled close together and started a lively chant that lasted, sadly, only ten seconds, but consisted, according to Hamsa, of a good-luck message. Grateful, we watched them disappear over the standing waves of moraine on the glacier. Hamsa lingered a little while longer before he too skipped effortlessly away with the promise that he would return on 10th September with ten porters to take us back home. I breathed deeply the thin air. We were alone.

Base Camp consisted of three Ultimate Phazor Dome tents; one for Gulzar, one for Hamish and Ulric and one for Simon and me; a small ridge tent for Mohammed Ali, a tiny Gemini mountain tent in which Liam slept, and a polythene cooking shelter draped over dry-stone walls that we had built on the ice. Two ski sticks acted as upright poles. In the course of the expedition the walls of the shelter shifted on the melting ice and had to be rebuilt three or four times. For bivouacking on the mountain we had only brought two Gemini tents, so Liam had to dismantle his Base Camp tent each time we went on the hill. Water came from a small stream that trickled past camp. It was a tiny and cosy Base Camp, huddled in a shallow depression in the moraine, and each of us was proud of what it represented.

I reflected on the journey, and in particular the Baltis who had each carried twenty-five kilos for over a hundred kilometres of difficult terrain, slept in temperatures below freezing for three successive nights huddled together under a blanket, one between two, and not once complained.

Ten months of organisation, fund-raising and travel, and now eleven days of walking had landed us, at last, at Base Camp in one of the remotest points in the Karakoram. None of us had yet seen Chogolisa. The only task left for us was to acclimatise and wait for the China wind.

We ate at regular times; a breakfast of tea and chapatis brought to our tents, and two main meals. Carbohydrates came from rice and chapatis, protein from lentils (dahl) and dehydrated meat, brought from Britain, and liquid came as tea or powdered fruit drinks. Ours was a basic diet, which made our tiny personal rations of boiled sweets and Cremola Foam all the more tempting, and ultimately all the more delicious.

From the top of the slope in front of us, that leaned gently up to the crest of the moraine ridge, we could see that we were camped in the middle of an ocean of rock and ice, and nothing else. It creaked constantly, shifting beneath us. Occasionally we heard louder sounds; avalanches, distant but very real, and rockfall. All around us the glacier and mountains were moving, yet equally they were inert rock and ice. I could sit and watch the glacier for hours. At nights the temperature at camp dipped below freezing but the daytime sun was warm and our site sheltered from winds. During the day we were able to relax totally, reading or tidying our possessions, packing and repacking our rucsacs. Ulric soloed a twenty-metre high vertical sérac ice wall near camp, dressed in a pair of shorts and plastic boots. Gulzar was gobsmacked; I was pretty impressed myself.

Our first exploration was to the K2 Base Camps. Al Rouse called us the Baltoro Bin Boys because we arrived on the Strip with empty rucsacs, and left with them full. We were given some food by the various expeditions, but mostly we picked it up off huge sprawling rubbish tips. We collected, or were given, German salami, Polish jam, Korean seaweed, and Fullers beer. Some of the tins were blackened by charcoal and smoke. Clearly someone had lobbed the cans in a bonfire, not expecting them to burn, but thinking that this was the extent of their responsibility towards waste disposal. Each collection of tents represented an expedition; some were arranged like inwardly facing castles with national flags blowing from their turrets, others in a more open welcoming pattern. Some blended indefinitely into others. This huge village of cloth, extending for a hundred metres or more towards the foot of the Abruzzi Spur had a bizarre medieval feel to it. Distance was measured in numbers of hours, young men in immaculate dress mixed with wizened veterans, Diemberger, not least, in tattered though functional robes. A light, bright mist swirled between the tents like a scene from *Ivanhoe*. The British Base Camp was some two hundred metres separate from the main group, isolated by what the Europeans called La Manche. There were fewer visitors here.

By the time we arrived they had already abandoned the North-West Ridge, their original objective, and had one attempt on the Abruzzi Spur. But my diary of our visit to the British Base Camp tells of a 'very happy expedition, lots of fun between them – all excellent people' and this, being the most accurate and first-hand record that I have, is the one which I will remember them by. Certainly we were entertained. Bev Holt, the team doctor, had found the skeletal hand of a porter who had died here in 1979. He kept it in a tin with some Kit-Kats.

'The four-finger snack,' he reminded us.

Rouse was playing a hot-seat act, as if everywhere he settled was a bed of burning coals. When he did sit down next to me, he pointed to Mrufka Wolf, the experienced Polish woman climber, and said he was going back on the Abruzzi with her. He seemed to be trying to persuade me that it was a good idea. Then he jumped up again and ran over to the barometer, talking to it like some people talk to plants. John Barry, recumbent the whole time, watched Al run about with what I took as an Oh-Al-sit-down-for-God's-sake look of despair in his eyes.

They were camped under the Gilkey memorial cairn, which would have reminded them each time they saw it of the deaths that had already come to K2. To come to terms with this blackness (for they had to – they could hardly ignore what was happening around them) they employed a kind of macabre humour, commenting that they were getting a little pissed off with the number of bodies that were piling up behind their camp, and that Renato Casarotto had failed to qualify in the K2 long jumping championships. I can't say that I find this at all funny now, out of context, but it would be very wrong for onlookers who were not there to pronounce these comments as grotesque. This was how it was; climbers, like them, were dying, and everyone had to come to terms with this horrible truth – or go home.

Apart from the North-East summit, that Simon and I had glimpsed after a brief wander from our own camp the day we had arrived, the view from K2 was the first I had of Chogolisa. In the evening a pale orange glow swept across her front face, beneath the perfectly flat summit ridge. No wonder that Conway called her the Great White Roof, I thought. The mountain was almost entirely snow-covered, and for the most part stylishly fluted. A plume was tossed from her left side; in truth an ice-raged wind but in appearance a delicate veil of soft silk. I sat for a long time watching the sunlight that warmed her gently glowing skin, slowly fade and die. As the evening moved to night, my eyes were drawn to her figure, stark and flawless. Without doubt, this was the most beautiful peak I had ever seen.

In the morning we traversed around to the Savoia Glacier, to the British expedition's ski park where we collected a pair of skis each to carry back to their Base Camp. Dave Wilkinson was there. He had slept the night in a tent without a sleeping bag because the previous day he had chosen not to make the traverse back in the dark.

'Wilkie? Oh, he'll be fine. He likes it,' John had told us the night before.

I was looking forward to meeting him – this was the man who Al Burgess had said at Goro was the least tent-trained person he knew. After leaving his tent one night in a storm to relieve himself, he had come back inside to wipe his arse.

'Like Rouse,' Al had said. 'He would puke in his tent if you let him.'

It was still early when we reached the ski park and Dave had barely woken up. He was wiping his eyes and yawning in his yellow fibre-pile romper suit – his pyjamas for the freezing cold night. He had been fast asleep since dusk.

The rest of the day I spent walking back over the five hours of glacier to our Base Camp. We had eaten an impressive amount of food at K2. Such gluttony came as a surprise to my stomach and it found its own way of making me regret being such a pig. I staggered into camp, dizzy, feverish and about two kilos lighter than when I had set off. The Jimmies, as I was calling Hamish, Ulric and Liam collectively in my diary, had rushed back. By the time I arrived they had already filled our 'Happy' barrel with the promise of real ale in three weeks' time. 'Happy' was so code-named in a childish attempt to disguise its contents from Gulzar and Mohammed who, we surmised, would as Muslims be offended by the contents. We removed the rubber seal from the lid and locked it firmly in place. At night we prepared a Sigg bottle full of boiling water as an immersion heater, and in the daytime we let the barrel bathe in the sunshine.

Hamish, Simon and I wandered up the Vigne Glacier the next day for a view of the North-West (Vigne) Face which leads to the col on the South-West Ridge. We knew nothing about the face, except that somewhere a 1983 German expedition had forced a line up it. It bristled with séracs and held the very last throes of Karakoram light each day. We returned a little happier in our knowledge. Liam and Ulric had climbed a small rocky peak behind Base Camp to about 6000 metres. Base Camp itself stood at about 4900 metres, higher, I reminded myself when panting from the slightest exercise, than Mont Blanc.

Our next plan was to climb up onto the North-East slopes of Chogolisa; partly to acclimatise and partly to recce our descent from Bride Peak, should we succeed in our traverse. The morning of our departure I fell ill and opted out. We had planned to negotiate a route up to the very end of the Upper Baltoro and, by way of a long ice slope, climb onto a rognon at the foot of the North Chogolisa Icefall. From this it was possible, we thought, to move up to slopes on the Ice Dome, a peak on the North-East Ridge near to where Hermann Buhl had been killed, from where we would be able to view our proposed descent. By the evening I was feeling a lot better and decided to go alone after the others. Gulzar would have found these activities 'unacceptable', but thankfully Gulzar had decided that he too could break the rules and leave us to go and spend a couple of days with the Pakistan Army Gasherbrum II Expedition, a few hours up the glacier. I was glad that he had found some company. He took Mohammed Ali with him, who had, it must be said, much better mountain sense than the Captain. Thus when I left, just an hour before sundown, the site was completely empty.

At eight o'clock I bivied beneath the rognon, and in the morning started out to reach the ice slope. The route to it was not obvious, so I decided reluctantly to try to cut directly across the icefall. Because at the edge of the icefall there was a huge gaping slot, I found myself climbing higher and higher, looking for a route across. By eleven o'clock, under a burning sun, I sat down despairingly in the middle of the choppy terrain. It was a hideously dangerous place to be. The séracs on which I sat groaned endlessly, giving the true impression that they were slowly collapsing. Trusting my weight on the snow bridges that spanned the crevasses might have been an acceptable risk in the cold-shaded morning, but certainly not now. I sat impatiently for nine hours until after dark and the air had chilled a little, but no sooner had I stood up and made a few steps in the pool of my torchlight than I had to sit down again. The snow was still much too soft. Furious, I produced my sleeping bag and Gore-tex liner and settled down for the night. I had covered only 200 metres that day. In the morning, my crampons biting on perfect névé snow, I climbed a little higher through the séracs until at last I found a way across to the ice slope on the side of the rognon. Below, skirting the icefall, I could see steep scree leading from the main glacier to the base of the ice slope. I was mildly enraged at the time I had wasted. By 7.30 I had met the tracks of the others and followed them to their tents at about 6400 metres, near the col between Baltoro Kangri and the Ice Dome.

The tents were empty, but by letting my eyes follow a line of steps

49

(the holes were black under the oblique sun) I spotted four tiny figures moving up onto the Ice Dome. I set off immediately after them, sinking a little further with each step into the softening snow. After only an hour I saw that the figures had started to come back, so I returned to the tent to put on a brew for their arrival. I lay outside, slightly dizzy from my exertion, listening to the gentle burr of the stove, just as I had done with John above Chamonix in the winter. Except I was wholly comfortable today. I extracted a Karrimat from one of the tents and laid myself out on it. The sunshine warmed my face.

Baltoro Kangri was a much bigger mountain than I had at first noticed. From Base Camp, looking at the mountain end on, I had not appreciated that it had several distinct summits connected by a ridge about three kilometres long. Pioneer Peak, a small rise on the ridge in front of me that led to the most westerly summit, was reached in 1892 by Martin Conway. He had stood on its summit, presumably on a leisurely day such as this, with his crayons and easel, carried up by 'coolies', and made a drawing of Bride Peak. His impression was accurate; from the north-east Bride Peak is steep and pyramidal, but Conway, giving the mountain an afternoon hue, had backlit the facing slopes – far from the soft welcoming light that I witnessed on that clear morning.

The snow had deteriorated so badly that we decided to stay another night at the camp and return in the morning at first light. Impressively, the Jimmies and Simon had been to almost 7000 metres and commented that the Japanese Ridge on Bride Peak looked straightforward. They proposed that the best descent from the summit would be down this ridge to the col at about 7000 metres, between Bride Peak and the Ice Dome. They further recommended that, instead of climbing over the Dome, we descend the south side of the ridge onto the basin between the Ice Dome and Kaberi Peak and follow this around to the slopes that they had earlier visited. We spent the rest of the day brewing tea, relaxing and talking, though I was too embarrassed to tell them how I had spent a whole day in the icefall. The sunset was memorable. Across the col to the east we could see the glowing tops of peaks in India above the Siachen Glacier. To the north and west, a sharp jumbled skyline outlined the Mustagh Tower, K2, Broad Peak and the Gasherbrums. Most distant, and most elegant was the unclimbed Crown Peak. This steeple of rock, shimmering against the burning red sky, lay wholly in the Xinjiang Province of China.

That night I slept in the open under a star-studded sky and in the morning balanced down the ice slope on the front points of my crampons, concentrating on the features of the landscape, in case we came this way

50

again in less settled weather after the traverse. We reached camp at about midday. The weather was still remarkably settled.

It was the second day of August. Optimism hovered over the camp, with talk of going for the traverse as soon as we had rested. On 3rd and 4th August, we stayed at Base Camp and I packed and repacked my sack several times, trying to slim the contents down. It was agreed that Simon and I would climb as one rope, and the Jimmies as another. We had brought a hundred metres of 7mm static rope, in case we needed to fix a difficult section of glacier, and we had also brought 8.5mm ropes for climbing. However, the weight saving that the thinner ropes offered was too great a temptation, and Simon and I cut a thirty-metre length for climbing, and the Jimmies, a forty-five-metre length. We made other weight savings by removing the internal aluminium frames from our rucsacs, taking no clothing spares whatsoever, and even reducing our food and gas supplies to five, instead of six days. Incredible, as it seems in retrospect, I decided against carrying a spare headtorch battery. My rucsac, including an ice axe and a pair of crampons, weighed just sixteen kilos for a week-long traverse above 7500 metres. I felt supremely confident about our chances. We decided that on the next day, 5th August, we would go for it.

At dawn on the 5th, bad weather poured in to the area, rolling up the Baltoro Glacier. Thus began a week-long period of snow and sleet, isolating us at our camp. We were not to know that on K2 a great disaster was beginning. The pace of life slowed and I was later each day in rising to the familiar sight of fresh snow on the ground. Even in the cloud, when the mist seemed to pervade the tents, the effect of the sun was deceptive and by midday the snow of the night would have melted and wetted the rocks around camp. In the evenings we sat under the polythene with our books or a pack of cards, before the cold would sting our toes and force a retreat to our tents. Simon and I shared *War and Peace* keeping about 200 pages between us, slowly ripping the book to pieces as we progressed. By the 9th, our fifth day of bad weather, the Jimmies' resolve weakened and they distributed the very last ration of boiled sweets – the last of the goodies.

'That's twenty you've given me since Skardu,' Gulzar said, 'I've been counting!'

5

The traverse of Chogolisa

The dawn sky of 10th August was clear and bright. There were tiny, icy tears suspended from the fabric of our tent. Outside the dark shapes appeared more pointed than before, cutting into a deep blue. I rose with optimism and climbed the verglassed rocks of the moraine slope behind our cooking shelter. The summit of K2 was washed in eastern promise and a tiny plume blew leftwards from its summit. A China wind! We all rose early that day. It would give us the chance to dry out our clothes under the promised sun. We could reorganise our lives, wash, lie out and relax.

'Let's go for it today,' Hamish said.

'Tomorrow,' came the consensus reply. I nodded with the majority, though had failed to think. A moment later I voiced my own view.

'No, come on, let's do it today.' I looked at Ulric.

Of course after a period of snow the risks of avalanche are far greater, but by the time we reached the face at the head of the Vigne, I thought to myself, it would have had a chance to slide and stabilise itself. I reckoned that we could watch the face for a day and judge its risk far better from under it, but at a safe distance away, than at Base Camp where we could not even see it.

'Okay, today,' he agreed.

Moments later Liam, the most reluctant, and Simon shrugged and nodded too. I felt relieved that the waiting had finished. Most of all I had a positive gut feeling. These feelings, I know now, are important and I want never to forget them. Climbing is much more than physical effort. It is about judgement and mental drive.

Mohammed disappeared into the kitchen to produce a final hot meal before we left. The sun crept over the Conway Saddle and I felt its warmth against my face. The crusty snow beneath my feet slushed and melted. I emptied out the contents of my sack, again, and lay them on the dry stone, determined to find another few grammes of superfluous kit. Weight had become a dangerous obsession.

'I won't need that,' I said to myself, discarding a grain bar of the kind that I couldn't even eat at home. For the moment at least, I was satisfied.

At eleven o'clock, packed and fed, we walked briskly up the Vigne Glacier. Clouds were building up. We could no longer see the plume on K2 and I began to question whether our optimism hadn't been a little hasty. After six hours we approached large crevasses. These marked the place where the glacier, unable to deform as it flowed over the break in slope at the lip of its enormous feeding cirque, had fractured. On my earlier reconnaissance I had not seen the full extent of the terrain; only Liam and Ulric had been this far and knew where to lead us. We skirted the glacier on its true right side and traversed a small terrace above the ice until we were able to cross the smooth flat snow above the slots to a point about ten minutes short of the face. We were in an impressive amphitheatre. The icy wall that we had come to climb loomed 1500 metres high. It captured the last of the day's sun whose oblique rays overstated the features of the face. Bristling séracs sent wavy shadows across the snow. The avalanche cones that fanned out from the bottom of the slope were small and few. It was certainly a cold face – and appeared safe too. An obvious line beckoned. It ran the full height of the wall from left to right and appeared only threatened by séracs on its lower part.

Our tents were cramped for two. Simon and I shared one tent, and the three Scots squeezed into the other. Both Hamish and Ulric are over six feet tall. There was no room for them to cook, once all inside, so they took it in turns each mealtime – once in the morning and once in the evening – to stand outside in the snow. Simon and I offered to rotate, so that five climbers shared two tents. But the logistics, even at that altitude, seemed awesome and would doubtless prove even more confusing higher up, so they decided to suffer bravely.

At one o'clock our small alarm blittered. I stuck my head out of the tent and saw one of the Jimmies standing in the snow. The night had been mostly clear, though clouds now spinning lightly in the cirque did threaten to hamper our route-finding. After drinking our statutory pint of water, melted from the snow, Simon and I finally emerged, packed our tent and filed into line behind Liam who started the day's trail-breaking. He led us over the bergschrund at the base of the face via an avalanche cone and continued as we had sketched in our memory the previous day. There were two torches on at any one time – two pools of light that bobbed to and fro. Normally the pools were circular, sometimes elliptical. Occasionally Liam stopped and we killed all the lights, and peered silently up the slope trying to recognise the outline of shapes that we had observed from the foot of the face. It was cold and quiet; I could hear only my own breathing. Then without words, and perhaps a quick glance behind, the front of the centipede would start again. I stepped rhythmically in the snow buckets in front of me, leaning on my gauntlet gloves. I breathed deeply, exhaling warm air into the fabric of my balaclava which I pulled over my face with just my nose and eyes exposed. This way, I hoped, I could keep my lips wet, and inhale warm moist air, rather than the dry air of the face, which was so cold it stung. It was effortless. We each climbed at our own comfortable pace, so that when the cold light came at five o'clock I noticed that our line had stretched, both up and across. We were five lonely figures on a fantastically exposed sweep of snow. The scale was absurd. Already I could look over smaller peaks on the south side of the Baltoro Glacier and up at Mustagh Tower on the other side. But it was the extent of the slope that shocked me most. I could look left and right across the snow for a kilometre in each direction. The ridge above looked unattainable, and the base of the face, thankfully remote.

We climbed for a few hours in the shade of the mountain until sunlight that had crept down from the ridge above reached us. It was not at all welcome. Its effect on the snow was gradual but on us quite sudden. We overheated and slowed down and immediately looked for places to sleep. At Base Camp the day was just beginning for Gulzar and Mohammed Ali, but for us it was now practically finished. Of course we had intended to reach the top of the face, but we had not. The snow would soon be soft and wet, and we were already very tired. We found a levelling. Above us a smooth unthreatening slope ran to the ridge. The weather was settled, cloudless and windless. Lying outside the tent in the bright sunshine, I could feel at last my legs recharging. We were on the back wall of a huge amphitheatre. Whilst climbing our noses had been pressed up against the snow. Now resting, we could look out towards Mustagh Tower. The view to the highest summits, to K2, Broad Peak and the Gasherbrums, was obstructed by peaks on the northern flanks of the Chogolisa massif. And Masherbrum, almost twenty kilometres distant, was hidden below the western arm of the amphitheatre. The following morning, at the top of the face and beneath the South-West Ridge of Chogolisa, I supposed that I would see the whole of the Eastern Karakoram.

At midnight we set off again, much as we had done the day before, except we were higher now and the climbing was more strenuous. At dawn we reached the col above the face, at about 6600 metres. Life was given to the dark outlines in the north – K2, the enormity of its pyramid, flanked on its right by Broad Peak, and the long line of Gasherbrums – unearthly monster shapes. I had never seen such an impressive sight.

Reaching the very crest of the ridge, momentarily razor thin and flawless, I could look south for the first time, to the Hushe valley and peaks that I had never seen. K7 and K6 were obvious, the only peaks that rose above the southern horizon. A little further on, the ridge broadened slightly to the col, a place that I presumed the Austrians had made their Camp IV in 1975 on the mountain's first ascent. We all sat down together on the snow. After two days of wading through the cold powder on the face, I should not have been surprised when I lost the feeling in my toes. Initially they had been sharply painful, later numb, but now I simply could not feel them. Ulric, voicing a similar complaint, removed his boots and tried to rub some life back into his feet, finally gaining the sympathy of Liam who offered to warm them against his stomach. To my amazement and gratitude Simon also volunteered himself for the same purpose. Simon and Liam suffered for fifteen minutes, at the end of which Ulric and I could still not feel a thing. I put the memory of last Christmas with John and the subsequent frostbite I had incurred to the back of my mind, and continued undeterred. We seemed anyway to have left the powder snow behind.

For the rest of the morning we meandered purposefully along the crest, finally turning a small sérac on its right edge to a sheltered levelling of snow, where we decided to stop for the day. The ridge reared up more steeply here, and beyond a collection of séracs immediately ahead, we could see, far above, the summit of Chogolisa at the top of a long continuous steep slope. This slope formed the left side of the ridge. On its right side it was abruptly cut by the Kaberi (South) Face of Chogolisa. The séracs were large but not complex. We guessed we were at about 6800 metres, still a long way from the summit, but half-confident that we might make it there the next day. Had we not been traversing the mountain, I feel sure that we would have decided in the morning to leave our tents, and try for the summit and back in a single push. A light gusty wind now blew across our faces as a mist rose, seemingly from nowhere, to envelop us. Simon and I sat sober in our tent. By dusk clouds and a more formidable wind had arrived, and with them fear that our good fortune had given out.

The midnight alarm did not wake me. I had remained fitfully conscious for most of the night, anticipating its unwelcome arrival. When it came I quickly killed it and reluctantly extracted my arm from the depths of my sleeping bag and, with it, my headtorch. Frost rained from the ceiling. I switched on the light which had already been reduced to a feeble beam. Carefully pulling the zip of the tent door, I formed a tiny slit, through which a little snow, that had been resting on the zipper, fell. It had snowed in the night. I closed the door and shook it before daring to stick my head out. The Jimmies' tent emitted a faint bluey glow and a figure stood outside. Fresh snow lay at his feet and the only prints I could see were the ones that he had trampled – yesterday's were covered over. Gusts of wind threatened to bring fresh spindrift into the tent. I shuffled back inside. Simon and I moved sluggishly about our early rituals. Because the tent was so cramped we had twice already spilt water and now attached the pan containing the snow above the door flap by a small piece of redundant boot lace. The stove sat on the base of the tent with a short flexible tube leading to the gas cylinder which had spent the night in the bottom of my sleeping bag for warmth. We heard curses from the other tent – Hamish appeared to have lost his spoon in the fresh snow. He had already broken his plastic plate – that had become brittle in the cold – at the previous camp. Much worse, Ulric had lost his grip on his Karrimat in a gust of wind which carried it over the ridge and down the Kaberi Face. They were evidently already packing up. Their complicated three-man logistics usually meant their group got away first each morning. And that is what we had become – two independent groups.

Simon and I left the site about half an hour behind the others, walking towards the malevolent silhouette of the first sérac. We were grateful for the steps in the snow ahead of us. Their prints petered out, where a line of pin-pricks continued up a steep wall of sérac ice. Producing our short length of rope, we continued in two short pitches to a small cave where we found the last of the Jimmies about to follow the rope out and up to the left. We followed, turning the bulging ice on its left side, then climbing directly to a sharp crest of snow. It was already late enough to see without torchlight, when we had shuffled *à cheval* to the end of this fin. One thing was certain, this would not be our summit day, for above the clouds that boiled in the hidden depths of the cauldron of the Kaberi Face, we saw an ice-armed wind screaming over the summit, sending a white stream of snow and ice across the frame of our view. We were higher than we had previously ever been and deep snow lay underfoot. I counted six deep breaths before each double step; left . . . right . . . one . . . two . . . three . . . four . . . five . . . six . . . left . . . right . . . The slope of snow between us and the summit, 800 metres above, was constant in its angle and terrain, and this allowed me, once in a rhythm, to keep it. Except the higher we climbed, the more difficult it became to maintain the pace and occasionally I would collapse onto my ice axe and pant madly as if I had just run a hundred metres holding my breath.

Huge cornices threatened to swallow us into the sinister pit. Throughout the whole day the mist in the void on the right of our ridge never cleared. It was a great convective cell with light streams of air rising from the depths to the lip of the ridge but no further. It was the stronger wind blowing above the cauldron, armed with the snow from under our feet, that stung our cheeks and forced each of us to withdraw into our windsuit hoods and our own worlds. As before, on the first part of our climb at night, I pulled my balaclava over my mouth to protect it from the wind and to keep it moist. This time, however, in the daylight, I was wearing shades and as soon as I exhaled into the balaclava, my breath was deflected up across the glass where it immediately condensed. I tried retracting my lower lip and breathing over my chin and every other possible arrangement of balaclava and shades, but nothing worked. Such irrelevancies took on enormous importance on the side of the mountain.

As midday passed into the afternoon we were still a long way from the summit. I had just completed a long stint of trail-breaking and was exhausted. Liam took over, but he moved slowly, close to the ridge. The further we strayed from the crest the deeper the snow became until there came a point where we could make no progress and were forced back nearer the edge. Here was better snow, less of it, and on a hard base, but we risked cornices. Somewhere, about two or three metres from the crest, lay the compromise. Liam, at the front of the line, shovelled snow to bulldoze a trench where he thought that compromise should be. Those behind were not troubled by such thoughts – they simply followed silently. At about 7400 metres the slope levelled a little to an angle of about thirty degrees. We decided to bivouac and set about digging a platform for the tents. Had we realised that this task would take three hours, we might have been tempted to continue in the hope of reaching a naturally flat space. We were for the most part still engulfed in cloud and could not easily gauge the distance to the top. After three hours we had completed two tiny ledges in the snow. I do not remember ever being as tired. Each time I scooped a little snow in my arms and dragged it off the ledge, I dropped my chin onto my chest, eyes tightly squeezed shut, lungs desperate for breath and my headache fresh with pain with each ebb of blood. Simon sat above me with his mouth wide open and his chest heaving and pulling. We put our tent a little higher than the Jimmies' terrace and faced our door towards them.

Just before sundown, the clouds below and above vanished. It was a lonely spot. Masherbrum, monolithic and dominant, controlled the west. The sun was setting behind the long arm of its North Ridge, igniting the lingering clouds billowing up from behind. We had climbed high. Few peaks now broke the skyline – Masherbrum, K2, Broad Peak and the Gasherbrums. These were now our only companions – the other peaks had fallen away adding to the loneliness. Even Mustagh Tower had lost its former grandeur and melted into the background noise of the Karakoram. We had to search to see it.

But there was still a wind. The wall of the uphill side of our tent slowly caved in under the ever increasing weight of driven snow. This night I kept my windsuit and inner boots on. I had to, the thought of putting them on in the morning frightened me too much. Still I could not feel my toes. Cooking became impossible without the tent filling with spindrift which entered through even the smallest cracks in the entrance that we kept for ventilation. Temperatures had crashed, hoar frost had collected, life had become miserable. Sleep did not come. My mouth dried out as the rest of me got wetter. I writhed in my pit. This hideous place, Chogolisa. Had I really come this far, and all for this?

By five o'clock, four hours after the alarm, Simon and I managed each to drink about a litre of water. We emerged from our tent and pulled into the shells of our plastic boots. My fingers struggled with the stiff laces and stung with rage. The others had gone, their terrace was bare. We had heard the creases of their windsuits, and quiet mutterings. Then we had heard their breathing slowly fading up the slope. Then it had been quiet. Now I felt very alone and very cold. I studied the tiny thermometer clipped to the zip of my rucsac and announced to Simon it was minus 28°C. There was not a cloud in the sky, nor a breath of wind on that perfect dawn of 14th August, 1986. There could be no other summit day on our expedition, for I doubted if we had risen that morning to storms and descended to Base Camp, that we would have gathered the energy for a second try.

I looked up the slope to the three Jimmies. They barely moved. Above them the summit looked so near! I looked at our tent and wondered how much easier it would be to leave it and its contents and go for the summit lightweight and return that same day. When we had debated, months before, in which direction to attempt the traverse, I had opted south to north. This meant reaching the higher top first. I reasoned that if we had been too tired for the traverse, or if it should look too difficult, or bad weather threatened, then we could retreat in the knowledge that we had at least climbed the mountain. I recognised the beauty of the argument more clearly than ever now, only it wasn't beautiful – it was evil because it threatened to shake me from my conviction. Abandon the traverse! How easy the lightweight dash!

Suddenly lethargic and fatalistic, I faced the problems. My headtorch had died and Simon and I shared only one more canister of gas, enough for one more bivouac. Simon was supportive. It had been always the two of us and the three of them and now, with the others so far ahead that they were *incommunicado*, the point was driven home. Had my resolve weakened to wanting to retreat after the summit, I would have forced Simon to give up his traverse ambitions as well. What would he have thought of me then, to come all this way and to be denied? Yet it was also inconceivable, even at 7400 metres, to think of descent. The day was perfect, and the weather settled, we were fit, though tired, and almost on the summit. After impatiently stuffing our sleeping bags into the bottom of our sacks we dismantled the tent and split it between us. I took the skin, Simon the poles.

There was never any doubt that day that we would reach our summit. As ever, we moved at our own comfortable pace and I pulled ahead of Simon. He would not have wanted me to wait. He had his solitude and I had mine. I took time to look about me and to comprehend exactly where I was. I was surprised and overjoyed to see Nanga Parbat rising above the horizon over a hundred kilometres to the west. I had never dreamed of seeing so far. Not even when I reached the final exposed crest that led to the top did I feel the slightest flutter of wind. The summit lay just a hundred metres along the ridge. The Jimmies were there. I stopped to look, then turned my head slowly down to study Simon, a few minutes below me. A little tearful, I traversed the knife-edged apex of the ridge and at last stood on the summit. It was two minutes past eight. Chogolisa! I briefly hugged Hamish quite forgetting for a moment the huge drop on each side of us. Everyone smiled. Here on my first Himalayan summit, standing with friends, waiting for another, I had realised the fulfilment of an ambition, not merely the first part of our present expedition's objective, but a much wider desire. The summit of Chogolisa represented a place or state of mind that I had wanted to reach for all my life, a place that takes effort and where one cannot go further or better, and where the spiritual rewards are profound. Each mountain that I could see, and there were hundreds in each direction, represented a different goal, and every line of every mountain too. Not my goals. I doubted that I would climb on any of them soon, but somebody's, somewhere.

Simon arrived and we organised a group picture. Liam attached his camera to the head of his axe and pressed the self-timer. He had ten seconds to get into the shot. I wondered whether he could do it. Certainly I couldn't have. Six or eight paces without resting for at least as many breaths was an intriguing challenge. Liam never saw it that way. He cruised it – twice. I have never known a picture to be so emotionally charged. I look at it often and when I do am filled with a blend of sadness and joy.

Whilst Ulric and Hamish were very excitable in their own ways, Liam and Simon appeared far less emotional. Liam sat pensive, recumbent on the snow, gazing along the summit ridge or down one of the ridges that splayed out into the Karakoram. I kept my eyes above the snow, and on the starkly exposed forms of other mountains in our group. The line of mountains to the north looked like a huge train above the tramlines of moraine on the glacier. K2 was the front, its 600-metre funnel rising clear above the five perfectly spaced and evenly laden wagons. It seemed uncanny that Broad Peak and the four mighty Gasherbrums should all be the same height. Each rises 3000 metres above the glacier, 8000 metres above the sea; and there is only 140 metres between them. Behind me was the summit pyramid of Masherbrum, and way off in its own veil of cloud, Nanga Parbat.

Our objective lay to the north-east, the traverse to the other summit, Bride Peak. Its rocky summit was clearly discernible a kilometre distant. Warmed by the sunshine and psychologically lifted by the fact that we could go no higher, we started on the traverse with confidence. There was little discussion, just an understanding. I suppose each of us must have quickly questioned the pros and cons of the two options. The options were still the same: up or down, though the 'up' was now a metaphoric term. The choice 'which way down' might have been as accurate. Whatever, we all considered it and, as far as I can tell, we all chose the same way.

The traverse of the twin tops, from Chogolisa to Bride Peak, filled a short span of time but it was one of the most pleasant experiences of my life. At the end of each minute I had covered just over eight metres. Such a pace, below the summit, would have been painfully slow, but now it seemed remarkably appropriate. The powdery snow lay only a few centimetres thick above a firm base of ice and névé. There were no obstacles; no séracs to turn, no height to lose and gain and no cornices. Cutting the others out of my mind I slowly shuffled along hardly lifting my feet, except to swing them gently in front, disturbing the ageless snow and letting my mind slip away. Lovely girl. Bride Peak had become my friend. She bore no grudge. I added tolerance to her long list of lovable traits. We had struggled the day before, but she was positively doting on me now. I thought of the Koreans with their fixed ropes and rock-scarring pitons on K2. They were raping their mountain. I wonder whether they will enjoy their summit quite as much. Well, I supposed, looking across the vast expanse, a savage mountain might need a savage style. Chogolisa was a gentle peak and, as my eyes returned to the snow, I smiled in the knowledge that we were the only ones on her.

As the rocky profile of Bride Peak, the North-East summit, approached I noticed it looked hideously loose, and quite steep too. Surely not a sting in the tail! The climb that faced us was about twenty metres high. Shattered slaty rocks were piled on top of each other. It looked like a six-year-old boy had built it against the assurances of his architect mum and engineer dad that it would collapse. Some of the blocks rested in the snow on the ridge. They were too small to belay to and, as I bent over to inspect one, I noticed that the snow in which it sat was wet and also useless for an anchor. Two options again faced us – climb unroped to the top or don't bother. Ulric and I opted for the first. The others, unable to justify the obvious risks, bravely opted out. Ulric had surprised nobody by pushing himself to the front, and without a moment's delay started to scramble madly up the pile of choss, showering fragments of scree down the mountainside in the process. I wondered whether it was that Ulric thinks twice as quickly as normal people, or that he doesn't think at all. I set off soon after, but even before I came to the difficulties, Ulric had reached the top and was shouting down to me. My mind flashed to Whymper. As soon as *he* had arrived on the summit of the Matterhorn, he lobbed rocks down on the others. Ulric certainly had plenty of ammunition.

'It's all right, mate. No problem,' was all he said. I had learnt that a statement like that coming from Ulric was more or less meaningless. Just below the top, after a few easy but frightening manoeuvres that I wondered how I would reverse, I was forced to make a mantelshelf move. I was standing on a small but solid ledge with a huge incut hold for my hands. I wasn't in any risk of falling off.

'You've done it now,' came Ulric's advice. 'Big jugs on the left.'

Yes, but that seemed too easy. So I threw my foot onto the ledge and shuffled up pulling on my leg and hands together to make an inelegant belly flop onto the top. I was on the summit of Bride Peak. I was behaving like that six-year-old child.

'What the hell was that?'

'The highest heel-hook in history,' I remarked proudly. It probably wasn't.

The summit was a tiny rocky perch, enough for one person at a time.

61

Although in the past few hours I had grown blasé about the rushes of euphoria, I did manage another small tear on this summit too. I took a picture of Ulric in front of the train of Gasherbrums. He looked very pleased with himself. It was a beautiful and unhurried scene in which I had quite surprised myself, for I felt no urgency to descend. I could look right down the ridge to the col at 7000 metres. That was where we would camp – only 700 metres – that's not very far, I thought. A number of minutes passed before we wobbled down the rotten rock to the others.

Liam in particular had recognised the need to go down. A broth of clouds had appeared very suddenly below us and was licking up the North-East Ridge. Route-finding would be impaired. The ridge, making a couple of gentle wavelength turns into the steamy clouds, was clearly heavily corniced. Worse, the snow, Liam discovered, as he made the first long steps down, was dangerously wind-slabbed. He was breaking through a crust into powdery crud. The picnic was over. A minor epic was beginning.

It went like this. Our team work broke up. We waded, each again at our own pace, for five dreamy hours into the grey swirling soup. Liam, Hamish and I were leading, sometimes Liam, sometimes Hamish, sometimes me. We tried to keep the ridge in sight on our left, but with variable visibility we feared a couple of times that we had lost our way. I reminded myself that it was a cornice on this ridge that Buhl had strayed onto in 1957, and fallen, with it, to his death. Not too close I thought. If we missed the col, too far right, we would find ourselves at the bottom of the face well after dark and above a bergschrund of unknown size. Behind us our trench twisted upward. Simon and Ulric would be following, so we hoped. It was snowing now.

Suddenly, whilst leading, I heard a sudden deep thud. Behind me a crack in the snow thirty centimetres across had formed and extended across the slope for as far as I could see in the darkening gloom. Wind-slab! The breakline was just a metre above me, but the thought of wading upward, three steps up, two steps down, to reach the snow slope above repelled me. Then what? To traverse the slope above the fissure? All that effort without getting nearer the camp seemed worthless. My urgency had returned. I can't be arsed, I thought resignedly as I turned back down the slope, deciding to push on. I lacked energy and judgement. It was a dangerous condition. I made my first wallowing steps in the steep soft snow, half-expecting the slope to break with its avalanche behind me, and sweep me off and take me to my death. There was an uneasy silence. I continued terrified for another few seconds before my fear subsided and I plunged more confidently to the col half an hour later where I threw down my sack and sat on it, panting hard.

I was on level ground. The final light of the day faded and my headtorch did not function, so I sat feeling very lonely, hunched up tightly with my head in my hands, listening for the others. Liam arrived first, then Hamish a little later. It was about eight o'clock. The tents were erected. Simon arrived next but he had not seen Ulric. We got on with the chores of bivouac life, preparing drinks and pulling into our sleeping bags, now heavy and sodden. I somehow managed to convince myself that Ulric had arrived back and there was no cause for concern. Maybe I did this because I knew that his headtorch, like mine, was no longer working or that I remembered the wind-slab risk as near suicidal. It was nine o'clock before he appeared. I poked my head out of the entrance to the tent and saw his slim silhouette just ten metres away coming across the slope. He looked like a figure returning from hell, slumped and walking slowly towards us. His beard, heavy with ice and shining in our torchlight was drawn from his thin face and his arms hung limp, rocking gently. Here is his own account of his descent:

Once the euphoria of the summits wore off, weariness started to settle on me like a lead weight. As I staggered up to my neck in dangerously slabby snow, I got further and further behind the others. I donned my headtorch and followed the trench left by them until the situation became confused and I followed an avalanche runnel for fifty precious metres before I realised my mistake. In my shattered condition regaining the track cost me dear and I started crawling along what I hoped was the right track. Then once again I was uncertain where to go as the trench ahead seemed to bifurcate. Whistles and flashes of my headtorch were met with an indifferent silence. Anger and frustration welled up inside of me – I couldn't understand why nobody would help me and I couldn't bear the embarrassment of spending the night in the open only yards from the tent, just because I was incapable of following a two-foot deep trench in the snow. Then suddenly I spotted a dim glow just ahead of me. It was Hamish who was on his way back to help me with failing headtorch. Eventually after what seemed like hours I was ensconced in a warm pit with hot food (which I had to cook myself!) and a brew. Sleep came in mid chew.

That night Liam slept outside. The cramped conditions had finally got to him. I discovered that the Jimmies had also lost their second Karrimat, and that they were each lying on their rucsacs for insulation. I had not had any sensation in my toes for three days and I badly wanted down. Everyone hoped that this would be the last night on the mountain.

63

The morning was beautiful and, without brewing up, Simon and I left at around 5.30, for once before the Jimmies. Simon had at first decided to 'stay and keep the others company' but, as I nodded a 'see you later' and started off unperturbed, he had followed.

Simon and I had had what might have appeared to be a strained relationship on the mountain, speaking very little to each other and then only about the climb. But perhaps this was more of an unconscious defence mechanism. We had shared a small dome tent on the walk-in and at Base Camp and an even smaller tent now. We were missing our privacy. As we left, Liam who was stirring from what must have been a good sleep, assured us he would be coming soon. We could see right down to the basin below the face we had previously descended. There was, indeed, a huge bergschrund but in good visibility there would be no problem negotiating a safe route now. I could see that by traversing around the back of the Ice Dome, we could as expected reach the slopes that we had previously been on. I broke trail all the way to the familiar slopes, with Simon keeping his distance behind me, in his own world, his eyes on his feet.

Liam caught us up at noon. Simon and he waited for the others, and I pushed on for Base Camp, thinking of my toes and not of the glacier and the sun at its highest and hottest. I arrived at camp at 6.40. Gulzar and Mohammed Ali made a big fuss of me. Mohammed had just finished preparing a meal for himself and Gulzar and selflessly gave me his portion. I relaxed properly for the first time in months, relieved and profoundly happy.

6

A mixture of moods

I wallowed in Base Camp's superfluity. In the morning Mohammed Ali brought parathas and tea to my tent, shaking the flysheet to wake me up. It was colder now than when we had arrived in July, and I stayed in my tent, wrapped warmly in my sleeping bag. I could no longer lie out like a cold-blooded lizard in the daytime sun. Through the sound of autumnal winds rattling our polythene kitchen shelter, I could discern the slap of Mohammed Ali's hands as he turned the chapatis. I marvelled at the prospect of drinking a gallon of tea. All I needed was to collect water and rest it over the kerosene flame. On the mountain it had taken hours to melt the snow necessary for a single cup of water. Back in Britain, I mused, I could flick a switch for the same effect. And we were heading that way soon, I thought with satisfaction. But my mind kept drifting back to our climb, following each twist of the descent. I had been frightened on the mountain but I was becoming much more so now.

Mohammed and Gulzar declared that they were going to the Pakistani Gasherbrum II Base Camp to celebrate the Islamic New Year, which made it easier to have a celebration of our own without guilt. Mindful of their beliefs, we had kept the beer a secret from them. In the evening we would be able to consume it openly. Left alone, I began to worry about the others. But they arrived in the afternoon and, as I expected, had something to say about my line of descent.

'By the way, you were sticking your neck out back there, mate,' Hamish said. He was commenting on the bottomless footprints they had followed on the final glacier descending to Base Camp, a huge, black, icy-still abyss beneath each one.

I shuddered. 'Well, it was a little dumb,' I felt like apologising. It might make the memory less embarrassing to live with. I had been impatient and didn't want to stay on the hill another day. There had been no gas left and I couldn't feel my toes. Liam and Simon had said

I should stay 'just one more night'. Even though I knew that they were right and that the glacier was dangerously broken and deadly under the afternoon sun, I had left them all and pushed for Base Camp, making those nightmare tracks. I would take the risk – 'just this once'. I had meandered on the glacier. Once I had thought of going back but I had not been able to face the prospect of re-crossing crevasses. I, too, had seen through my steps, and recognised the risks. Once or twice I had crawled on the snow bridges, trying to spread my weight over the soft snow. I assured myself that fewer dangers lay ahead than behind. My doggedness had taken me on.

At last I came to the long ice slope which I remembered from our recce. It descended at an angle of some fifty degrees to the Upper Baltoro, from where only a tired but safe struggle through the moraines would have led to camp. I turned to face the slope and started immediately to front-point downwards. The clear green water ice was polished like marble and was about as hard. There were small fragments of rock embedded in it, around which the ice had melted a little. I put my crampon points there but they were blunt and skated beneath my tired legs, penetrating just three or four millimetres. After a few hundred kicks the rhythm jarred and I grew tired, my calf muscles suddenly very hot. I was very exposed and delicately poised. After all there *were* only three tiny picks of steel holding me to a slope that swept for 300 metres with cruel uniformity into jumbled séracs. There were lots of potential graves down there, I thought. Resting was impossible, so I kept on going, cursing the heat and wishing I had stopped at the top of the slope, just for one minute, to take off some clothes. I had not hesitated and I had paid again for my impatience.

I had looked up and down the slope to measure my progress. Looking up once to the steep wall above I noticed a small dusty cloud immediately above me that seemed to have exploded from nothing and was growing and thinning. Moments later the sound reached me – a familiar, cracking, rock-grating sound. Then had come the cold horror of realisation. The cloud was rock dust! Stonefall! Holy shit. Stonefall! This was it! I had one free arm and I put it over my head, leaning in as best I could to the slope. There was nothing else to do. Just one rock would have been enough to unbalance me or rip my claws from the icy slide, gravity would have done the rest; I would have been racing, faster and faster still, wheeling and turning down the ice and the instant I touched the smooth walls of the deep freeze I would have died, if lucky, and never be found. The first fragments whistled past me, on each side.

'You stupid bastard,' my lips trembled; all else was gripped with fear.

A rock hit me – a small rock – on my rucsac just a few centimetres from my head, but the rest had passed me by and only when I heard the bigger ones impact on the glacier below did I dare look up. Everything was still again; except my legs which shook uncontrollably.

Now, with my blistering toes immersed in warm water and a book and a mug of beer shared between my hands, I had not the remotest desire to walk uphill again. I had waited patiently, a little nervously perhaps, for the others to arrive. Now that we were all together we celebrated our success, with beer from our Happy Barrel, still fermenting as we poured it down.

It would not have occurred to me to do any more climbing on this expedition, had the Scots not suggested Broad Peak. Simon and I were alike in dismissing the idea, partly because we had no formal permission and partly because he and I were injured. Simon had damaged his knee leaping a crevasse on the Upper Baltoro just a few hundred metres from camp, which, like my frostbite, prohibited any further climbing. I for one welcomed my injury as it gave me a clear conscience to decline the attempt. I doubt that I would have easily said no otherwise, even though my heart wouldn't have been in it. A more mature climber, not to mention politician, would not have needed such an excuse.

The Jimmies were keen. Broad Peak at 8048 metres is the twelfth highest peak in the world. There was logic behind their plan. They were perfectly acclimatised, not over-thin and very fit and determined. When we put it to Gulzar on his return he blew his top, as he had every right to do. As the authorities were keen on having things written down, we wrote a letter to the Ministry with a copy for Gulzar. He signed both copies before we gave the Ministry's letter to a Balti mail runner who left in double stages for the capital. The letter pledged £1400 as a peak fee and absolved Gulzar from blame by stating that he had not been party to the attempt. Gulzar decided to stay at the Concordia Army post – a tin hut and a radio – while the Scots were on the mountain. He would also visit them at the Broad Peak Base Camp.

Once more Hamish, Liam and Ulric set about scouring their equipment for ways to reduce it. I wasn't totally surprised therefore when they announced that they weren't taking a rope. It seems crazy now but it didn't then.

'There are some fixed ropes in place,' they agreed, 'and we can solo the rest.'

Solo in this context means unroped and, as invariably happens when unroped in the mountains, a team is split up and the climbers are alone in every sense. I watched them busying themselves with gear and food for their attempt. They would leave for Broad Peak within three days of returning from Chogolisa. As I looked on, I tried to fathom from where they had gained their energy, Liam in particular.

Simon and I had already agreed that we didn't want to wait in camp for them whilst they were climbing. We didn't even want to see them leave for the mountain. My frostbite, although not serious – more of a nip than a bite – deserved attention, at least a warmer climate. We decided that if we couldn't arrange a separate debriefing at the Ministry and get on the next flight home, we would wait for the others in Islamabad. The prospect of a week in the capital city was decidedly more inviting than a week on the glacier.

For me the expedition was over. We had come and done what we had set out to do. I wanted to walk out from the mountain, clear in that knowledge, happy and content in our achievement, not as an annex of an expedition that climbed Broad Peak. Broad Peak was their business, not mine. Secretly I anticipated feeling very jealous if they did make the summit; fearing my own climb of Chogolisa would be diminished by their ascent of a bigger, steeper mountain. I could hear people saying, 'They climbed Chogolisa to acclimatise and then the three Scots did the climb.' Had that been the expedition's objective it would have been different. Perhaps I would not even have managed to traverse Chogolisa, had Broad Peak been my most important thought. I quickly decided that I wanted no part of their plans. However, I would not have dreamed of standing in their way. Simon and I, recognising their ambition, did what we could to offer support, if only moral, and then packed one heavy sack each for the walk out to Skardu. Gulzar, I could tell, dearly wanted to come with us, but his sense of professional duty prevented him. He said he would stay, for a few days at least.

On 19th August it was time for us all to leave. We had previously lit a huge bonfire for our rubbish and thrown all the tin cans and foil in a crevasse. As we sifted through the remains, Gulzar and Mohammed left for Concordia. Simon and I were next and, wishing the Jimmies luck, we walked up above camp onto the moraine strip. We sat for a moment watching the others gaily throwing our surplus kerosene on the fire. There was a haze of smoke and heat rising from the flames and a light dusting of snow on the ground. We waved a ski stick each and turned to go. At Concordia we stopped and gazed at the huge bulk of Broad Peak and the 3650 metres of rock and ice between us and the summit. Hamish and Ulric caught us up and headed north up the Godwin Austen Glacier. We decided not to wait for Liam a few hundred metres behind, we nodded a 'see you later' and turned towards home. Within an hour we had reached the Army post where a couple of miserable-looking soldiers, sitting by the entrance of their tin hut, too small even to stand up in, threw us a pathetic glance. As a posting, Concordia is a hell hole and these two knew it. What on God's earth are you guys doing here, I wondered, looking at one of them. His eyes were lifeless behind his drawn face, and I could not imagine a response. How many disbelieving stares have these soldiers had to put up with over the years? In winter many die here of cold, and some, those posted on the Conway Saddle overlooking the Siachen Glacier in India, of oedema.

Simon and I spoke very little. On the way in we had met climbers in groups, bound together by their obligation to the morale of the expedition. Now we were meeting climbers on their own or in non-talkative pairs, walking quickly, heads down, minds on home, ears in headphones. Some of their team would have already returned, some would still be climbing on a last ditch effort, or as an encore to success. Some might never go home. Conversations, I have found, at this stage of an expedition, are fewer, but they are rarely awkward or contrived. People speak only when they want to, and make no apologies if they don't. Simon and I did not have much to say.

We walked as far as Goro, where there was another Army post. The inhabitants of this were no more cheerful than their colleagues at Concordia. An Australian team's liaison officer was there. He told us that there had been a disaster on K2 and that there had been many deaths and successes too. I wondered how he measured success. He had no details. I immediately remembered Rouse, agitated, standing by the barometer willing the needle to move.

In the night it snowed. Noises outside were muffled by the weight of snow on the sides of the tent. We slept well enough. In the morning the snow became rain. It ruined everything. The lovely white now dripped grey on the hard slate, and the pitiful soldiers stayed in their box. We left in the middle of the morning when we gave up hope for an end to the rain, which was just as well, as it never came. There was nothing to see above the level of the moraine, no markers even to gauge our progress towards Urdokas. I would have liked a final view of some of the peaks, though I realised that even if it cleared we would not see Chogolisa again. Mercifully the slaty rocks were lying flat and something of a path had been formed. In winter the glacier would shift and hide itself under deep snow. Next year, the first long line of shade-bespectacled porters, wading in the snow under the bright spring sun, will not be able to find the path and a new route for the season will be formed. Cairns, built in previous years, remain buried under snow long after the first expeditions

69

arrive. When exposed like follies they are often hundreds of metres from the new path.

At Urdokas we met an expedition from St Mary's Hospital in London. They were climbing on Lobsang Spire, in memory of Pete Thexton, an ex-student of the hospital who had died on Broad Peak in 1983, but who had previously climbed a fine new route on the Spire. Their own expedition had been successful and they were waiting for porters to come so they could break camp. They told us of the disaster on K2. Rouse was dead. So too was Mrufka the Polish 'Ant'. Julie Tullis had died, and two more Austrians. It was little consolation that both Al and Julie had reached the top. On descent they had all been pinned to the ridge above 8000 metres in the same stormy period that had grounded us at camp before the traverse. After three days Julie had died and after six the others set off down. Al was delirious and too tired even to move. The others except the two oldest, Kurt Diemberger and Willi Bauer, collapsed one by one in the snow. In all there were thirteen deaths on K2 in 1986.

Looking about me in the morning I recognised some of the boulders that we had climbed on five weeks previously. My favourite problem now formed the wall of the kitchen. The weather was better and we could see right up the glacier to Broad Peak. I like Urdokas. It is a kind of gateway, a place on the way in to rest. Its quickly thinning green grass is the last a climber will see until here again on the way out.

Thexton's younger brother Mike was at Urdokas, filming for the expedition. Afterwards he wanted to walk up to Broad Peak to pay his respects. I admired Mike's resolve, his need to come to the mountains to grieve. It was three years since Pete had died, of oedema very high on the mountain. When he died he was swathed in a tent and tossed down a crevasse. He is, as Mike says, preserved in the cold. Ageless even. 'You, thirty still, become my younger brother,' he wrote. It was an intriguing thought, and one which I liked – it seemed positive. A couple of weeks later Mike spent two days on his knees with a gun at his head, held hostage in a Pan Am 747 on Karachi Airport runway. We live in a peculiar world.

We left camp together, Mike turning right, and Simon and I left, at the bottom of the scree and grass descending onto the moraine. In three days Mike reached Broad Peak, whilst Simon and I, descending through thick air beyond the Baltoro snout, tilting gently downward out of the mountains, reached the narrowing of the Braldu Gorge. At Dasso, the roadhead where we arranged for a jeep to take us to Skardu, we met Hamsa Ali with eight porters setting out for Base Camp, as previously arranged. He had some mail, all of it with good news from home. This was perhaps the best moment of the trip; physical effort, which at the beginning had been invigorating, was now no more than a necessary slog, and I was glad to be rid of it. Yet I felt lean and healthy, though in reality I was certainly not. More importantly I felt an enormous sense of personal achievement, and could see that Simon did too. I saw interest in the most mundane things, and the good in the bad. Most valuable of all, the expedition, not just the traverse of Chogolisa, had immeasurably raised my self-confidence.

But had I analysed at the time why I was so happy, I would have also had to deduce that I had become quite selfish. Simon and I were still operating independently, looking after ourselves before each other. On the walk-out Simon had dislocated his knee three or four times. He had been in great discomfort and was now worried about what might be his prognosis, but all I can remember was how it slowed us both down. Why, also, had Simon and I abandoned the others, in particular our Liaison Officer who had probably never wanted to be at Chogolisa in the first place? And why were we now prepared to leave the country before the expedition was fully reunited? My frostbite was hardly that serious. I was pursuing my own wishes at the exclusion of others, but I didn't register the fact. It was a thick-skinned quality that ensured my contentment.

In Skardu we discovered to our delight an American-style hamburger joint that did 'Club Sandwich and Fries', served with a cold Coke. We ate as many as were necessary to feel ill. Another restaurant, which had opened in the seven weeks we had been in the mountains, had called itself MacDonalds and had tried to emulate the Big Mac, mistakenly thinking that even if they succeeded people from the West would want to eat it.

Incredibly, we managed to book two seats on the next flight to Islamabad, on 31st August. This time we would fly in a Fokker Friendship. Because the Fokker is a propeller plane it has a flight path ceiling of 5000 metres which means it must fly through very mountainous scenery below the level of many of the summits and above the Indus River, whose valley it cannot turn in nor escape from. The pilot has to rely on someone at the other end of the valley to say that the weather will be clear for the next two hours. It is not uncommon for a flight from Islamabad to Skardu, or Gilgit 200 miles to the west, to be delayed by up to a week, especially in winter. The problem of navigation and particularly of visibility on landing is less pronounced flying *from* Skardu, but as a plane cannot leave before it arrives it means that there are normally many more passengers than seats on flights. The prospect of a twenty-four-hour truck ride along the Karakoram Highway keeps most passengers waiting at airports until the very last minute before deadlines of connecting flights from Islamabad force them to take the road.

The evening before our flight was due to leave, Gulzar had still not appeared, nor the lads from Broad Peak. I scribbled a note for them. The jeep for the airfield came just after dawn. The morning was quiet and calm. Looking back at Skardu through the dust we were throwing up from the winding road, I felt very sure that we would not return; at least not for a few years. Yet I had only to wait a few days. Whilst boarding, I was aware of a man in uniform talking to Simon, a few metres behind me in the queue. He had run across the tarmac to speak to him and I waited by the stairs for Simon to catch me up.

'What did he want?' I asked. 'Did you take a photograph you shouldn't have?'

'I'll tell you on the plane,' Simon replied.

We found a couple of seats and I kicked off my boots and settled into the first cushioned seat for nearly two months. The enjoyment was to be short-lived.

'What were you going to tell me?' I turned to Simon. He hesitated and was looking terribly shocked. 'Simon?'

'Liam's dead, Fanny.'

I believed it the instant he told me. It was so matter-of-fact. But I asked him to repeat what he had said and as he did so his words fixed me to my seat. The doors closed, and the plane shook down the runway and took off, climbing steeply above Skardu and turning tightly towards Nanga Parbat.

Liam, the soldier said, had 'fallen into China' and I presumed that he was lying at the bottom of the East Face of Broad Peak, accessible from Concordia only by a long and difficult traverse around the north side of the mountain over the 6200-metre Sella Saddle, and across the North Gasherbrum Glacier to the bottom of the face. Nobody has ever been there, and the area is so vast that there would be next to no possibility of finding his body. It is very unlikely that he will ever be found, and as I sat with my eyes fixed on Nanga Parbat, the aeroplane engines humming in the background, I wondered whether that was a good or a bad thing.

I imagined Liam, the strongest, trail-breaking, pushing towards the summit, pulling it down with each slow step. The soldier's brief statement of fact produced hundreds of images in my mind of Liam, and assumptions of what had happened. Certainly, I realised, they must have been on the summit ridge for that is the boundary with China. I assumed, correctly, that Liam had fallen whilst ascending. In retrospect I wonder why it did not occur to me that they might all have reached the top and Liam fallen on their way down.

The flight gave us both time to think, not only of Liam but also to decide what we should do with the news. We went straight to the Ministry to have it confirmed. Muneeruddin was shocked. He knew nothing about it. But his biggest concern was not Liam's death but the fact that three climbers had been on the mountain without adequate paperwork.

'Where is your Liaison Officer?' he demanded.

'On the Baltoro,' I stammered. Actually I didn't even know that.

'Why were your team on Broad Peak, you had not the permissions. *Where is Captain Jamal!*' He was furious, understandably.

Simon stood motionless and said nothing. I could see that he was trying not to hit the man. The Ministry wanted a statement. I didn't know anything. I wrote one anyway. Everybody signed. We were achieving nothing. Muneeruddin kept on shouting, we could not calm him down. We left.

It was the last day in August, hot and dry. As we left the offices of the Ministry and stepped onto the white pavements I could feel the elements etch into me like never before. The sun burned and tore into me, screwing my eyes. Momentarily I felt sick, and hugely depressed. A great weight had been clamped to my back.

'Little shits. Bastards.' It was all I could say.

Simon and I took stock. We could not have the death confirmed, so could not tell Liam's family, though the dreadful thought of them reading about it in a newspaper almost drove us to the telephone at once. We had seen British newspapers and how they had covered the K2 story. I wondered whether they would greet Liam's death with indifference or sensationalism. And how reliable was the source? After all, Muneeruddin had not been told. Had the soldier confused our expedition with another? No, he had known who we were; and he had used Liam's name. We decided to alert Britain, but not Liam's parents directly. We rang a mutual friend, Jeremy Adams, in London and asked him to telephone the Foreign Office, which he did, stressing the unconfirmed nature of the report. For the first time I really feared the power of the press. We explained to Jeremy that we would endeavour to return immediately to Skardu to have the death confirmed beyond doubt. Then, we agreed, we would send a telegram to Liam's parents and confirm the death to John Haig, the Second Secretary at the British Embassy in Islamabad and a friend of many climbers. There were no flights to Skardu so we took a flight to Gilgit, and a bus from there. The journey was painfully slow and as each hour passed I wondered how far the ripples had travelled.

In Skardu we rushed to see Alfredi, the Government tourism liaison man for the Northern Areas and he verified the news. Liam had certainly died. Hamish had sent a note with the pilot of an Army helicopter. We telephoned John Haig and sent our telegram. There was nothing now more to do, but wait patiently for the others to arrive. My mind returned frequently to Liam and Broad Peak. Two weeks previously, leaving Base Camp, I had shut myself off from their attempt and now, for different reasons, I tried hard to focus on it. I did not reflect on our achievement on Chogolisa. Simon and I never really allowed ourselves to celebrate that success, except perhaps in the one brief day in Skardu that we enjoyed before flying to Islamabad.

Hamish, Ulric, Gulzar, Mohammed Ali and Hamsa Ali arrived on 3rd September. They were happy to be down and they grinned out at us as they rode up the driveway of the K2 Motel in their jeep. Gulzar was especially pleased and he took my hand and shook it energetically. I was pleased to see him too. Hamish and Ulric told us what had happened on the mountain. They had climbed very quickly, in two days reaching the col between the main and the middle summits at about 7800 metres. The next morning they had left their tent, sleeping bags and stove to make a lightweight push for the summit. At about twelve o'clock Hamish and Liam were some ten minutes ahead of Ulric on the summit ridge approaching 8000 metres. In just one hour they would have been on the summit. In poor visibility Liam had strayed onto a huge cornice overhanging the East Face which had then given way under his weight, throwing him down the Chinese side of the mountain. Hamish had narrowly avoided falling too and, had they been roped, it is likely that he would also have been killed. Hamish had then waited for Ulric before the pair of them immediately descended. Liam's fate that summer had been horribly similar to that of Hermann Buhl in 1957. He had already climbed Broad Peak with Kurt Diemberger. Attempting Chogolisa a week later, he fell through a cornice to his death. The link between these two beautiful yet unforgiving mountains is burned into my mind forever and I am always reminded of Liam when I think of Broad Peak or Chogolisa.

As expected, there were no flights to Islamabad, so after selling or giving away most of our gear, we boarded a jeep and set off towards Gilgit and the Karakoram Highway. It was a strange thing but, although we were shocked, the shadow of Liam's death upon us did not make us unhappy at first. Instead we were closer as friends and more supportive.

74

Any tensions and miseries between us were centrally collected and then expelled. Sadly, they bore down on Gulzar. The Government tourism official, Alfredi, came to see us off. Hamsa Ali was there too. Gulzar stated that his place for the entire journey was in the front of the jeep with the driver, and no amount of travel sickness from the 'members' would move him from that seat. Normally we might not have worried about letting Gulzar have his way but we knew that he had taken the stand boldly instead of slyly, as was his nature, because of Alfredi's presence. He badly needed to make an impression and to restore his dignity, but we denied him even of that.

'Gulzar! That is very selfish of you,' Hamish said. 'We will rotate on a fair basis.'

'I am a Captain in the Pakistani Army!' he demanded, almost crying. We quickly dropped the subject – its pathos embarrassed everyone. Poor Gulzar, he had been cut off from his peers for two long months and slowly through the expedition his authority had been undermined and his self-esteem had been eroded by people who did not share his certainties or values.

The first hundred miles of the journey followed a dirt track that clung to a steep-sided rubble slope above the Indus. Sitting on the left side of the jeep allowed me on many corners to look vertically down at the smashed, some smoky black, remains of other jeeps and trucks along the side of the turbulent white river, a hundred metres below. Our driver gave the convincing impression that he really couldn't care less if we made our destination or not. If he was nervous then the naswar (marijuana) under his tongue certainly offered a cure. Once we were forced to stop at a landslide and bail out, while our driver edged the jeep across the shifting scree before the terrifying journey continued. Ulric, almost predictably, throve on it, hanging off the back, one hand clinging to the rail, the other to his camera. A broad grin swept his face.

Our debriefing at the Ministry in Rawalpindi was thankfully brisk and Muneeruddin was very courteous. The necessary protocol changed hands, and the royalty for Broad Peak was paid from our $4000 helicopter bond. We also, at last, said farewell to Gulzar which consisted of us shaking hands and him turning quickly away and boarding a taxi that he had instructed to wait. I was sad that we could not have parted on better terms. The taxi was lost at the end of the street as it merged into the city's traffic.

We took a cab to the British Embassy Club for a beer. That evening we were, for the first time, able to relax and talk openly as an exclusive group. Liam's absence was obvious and the conversation turned to him.

I had never seen Ulric so outspoken. Relaxing at last, he was able to grieve.

'There were cornices like the one Liam was on all over Chogolisa. *Christ . . .*' his voice had wavered on a high note and I saw his eyes were wet. '. . . We must have fucking *camped* on one that big!'

I glanced at Hamish, listening sedately, to Ulric's outburst. I could not hope fully to comprehend what had been forged between these two when they returned from the summit ridge of Broad Peak. Hamish's long thin face finished at a scruffy hairy chin. His beard, I had observed over the period of the previous week, was actually falling out. Yet his eyes, sunken and weathered, still possessed an inextinguishable spirit. I looked back at Ulric, who now sat pensive, eyes glazed, staring at a point beyond the bottom of his glass. These are powerful images and I am glad I have them, for I will always remember Liam through Hamish and Ulric. I know them better now, but I doubt I will ever feel as close to them as on that evening in September in Islamabad.

Three days later we arrived back in Britain. I drove with my parents to their house in West Sussex. The country lanes were tight and winding. Our dog, an energetic border collie, jumped wildly around me. I took a shower and shaved. The food that I ate was wonderful, the bed that I slept in cool and clean. I had not prepared myself for this. I had assumed that arriving home to Britain, I would be able to slip easily into its way of life. But this was not the case. Three months had passed, though it felt like an era. Something very definite had happened to me and I felt quite different as a person; as if a spirit that had once lain dormant had been thrown into life.

7

A fatal accident

Falling
Texture of the wind crashing
Into a million facets of
me;
Am I the wind?
Or was it always there
Can I catch it?
Get ahead of it into the stillness?

Within a week of arriving home from Pakistan I started work in Manchester at the British Mountaineering Council. On my way there I attended Alan Rouse's memorial service in Sheffield. The church was packed and the service extremely moving. As expected, a party was organised rather spontaneously at the punk-style suburban semi of Joe Simpson and John Stevenson. Within its bare rooms music pumped the atmosphere, people were shouting to be heard, bottles and beer cans mounted underfoot. The air was thick with cigarette smoke. John sacrificed his wardrobe for a huge bonfire in the back garden. The flames licked dangerously high and seemed each minute to be on the verge of spreading to the house. The wardrobe's components were thrown onto the fire from an upstairs bedroom window.

Dennis Gray, the General Secretary of the BMC, was there. When I had telephoned him earlier he had enquired whether I had found a doss in Manchester, and I was able, as we stood in the glow of the fire, to tell him that such a place had been located. Next thing I needed, he informed me, was a reliable car. As I was broke, Dennis, presumably under the influence of copious drink, offered to give me a loan from BMC funds,

77

and some advice on where to go to get my car. He told me to ring the Professor.

'Who's that?'

'The Professor? Who's the Professor?' He paused for effect. 'Jim *Perrin*!' he announced in glee. 'Star of stage, screen and labour exchange.' I was beginning to regret asking. Perrin was, according to Dennis, 'always wheeling and dealing in the second-hand car market'.

I took the chance and rang him a few days later from my office.

'Oh splendid,' said Perrin in what I took, mistakenly, to be a pseudo-posh voice, 'the new laddie at the BMC.'

'Yes, that's right. Um, I hear you could help me get a car.'

'Certainly, young fellow. How much have you got?' He sounded like he relished the idea. I told him I had about £1000. 'Right, bring the lot, cash, in your back pocket and we'll go to Belle Vue. We'll get something, don't you worry.'

He was right. We did get *something*. I was £850 the poorer and a Volkswagen Derby the richer. When I bought the car I couldn't lock the driver door, so I had to lean over the passenger side to lock it. When the passenger door handle fell off, I couldn't lock either door. So I put my valuables in the boot until I snapped the key in its rusty lock. After one week the dash lights failed; after another, the glove compartment door fell off. The first time it rained I discovered the car leaked, which explained why I sometimes arrived at work with my trousers still tucked into my socks.

'Come on your bike, Andy?' was Dennis's quip.

I got my arms wet as well when it rained, leaning out of the window to operate the windscreen wipers manually. On the third week I was awoken by a call at two a.m. from the Manchester University security guard who had been patrolling the car park that the BMC use.

'Are you the owner of the Silver Derby, SPT 970V?'

'Yes?' It was the one night I had left it at the office.

'Well, I've got some bad news for you. Someone's ripped your door open and smashed it up a bit inside, stolen your radio and stuff. A bit messy. I've shut the doors. Want me to leave it?'

I thanked him and went back to sleep, cursing. In the morning I went to inspect the damage. It was exactly as I had left it.

I nursed the car through another two years and a new engine. When I scrapped it, I got £50 but most of all I was glad to get it off my hands. The education had cost me about £2000.

As National Officer I was responsible for servicing a number of voluntary committees concerned with climbing walls, equipment, expeditions, etc. and through these I met some interesting characters, and some thoroughly baffling ones as well. Many of the issues that were discussed, particularly at the Management Committee were politically highly charged and for some it was the prospect of a good argument, as much as the issues, that brought them to the forum. None more so than Ken Wilson. Ken had a preposterously high regard for his own opinion and the passion with which he argued, his powers of expression and his point blank refusal to back down invariably led him into the final throes of each debate on, as he put it, 'weighty matters of doctrine'.

'Climbing is about anarchism – it's fundamentally irresponsible and disordered,' he would say. This statement I saw as a wish rather than a belief but it formed the core of most his arguments against, for instance, qualifications and structured competitions. Regardless of what he said, there would always be someone who felt they had to disagree. Too often that person was Dennis. Both would claim to have the views of the climbing population behind them. To take Ken on was to risk being worn out emotionally, for his tenacity was remarkable.

'If you can't stand the heat,' he would bellow in protest, 'then get out the kitchen!'

Both were clever, and politically stubborn but, sadly, I saw that the clashes of their characters over-shadowed the real debate, causing a huge waste of time. It was difficult for me, at first, to put their arguments into the context of the real climbing world.

The Technical Committee, among its other duties, such as the setting of standards for certain items of equipment, investigated design and manufacturing faults consumers reported to it. I saw this as the Council's most worthwhile committee. Its profile was low and its discussions thorough, and it brought professionalism from industry with it. Its diligence uncovered many blatant failings. One of our meetings was attended by a man who had fallen twenty metres off an ice wall and broken his leg when his crampons had failed. He brought the offending article with him. His matter came late on the agenda and after about five hours of other discussions about stress-raisers in ice axe picks and the phenomena of karabiner-keeper oscillations and their relation to the forthcoming EEC standard, he started to look bored. After another hour he had presented his story under cross-examination. Then he listened for a further two hours whilst the committee deliberated. His look of boredom turned to bewilderment. The meeting had lasted ten hours and had been, as Fred Hall, a member of the committee, noted, 'more of an ordeal than his fall'.

Another favourite for debate was the sit harness versus body harness

79

dialogue. A sit harness was lighter, more comfortable; a body harness less likely to break the wearer's back. One manufacturer claimed that even with a heavy rucsac on, hanging upside down, it was impossible to fall out of their sit harness.

'That's great,' retorted Fred. 'Much better dead on the rope than on the ground!'

Thankfully, I was able to climb frequently, even if for only a few hours in an afternoon by driving out into the Peak District. London had offered no such opportunities. Sometimes I devoted part of my working day to climbing. As I worked many evenings and weekends I felt justified in this. Anyway my job and my play drew closer together as sometimes I was confronted by work matters whilst visiting climbing areas in my own time. This did not bother me at first, in fact I welcomed it. From the day I had started work I attempted to fill my whole life with my job or its related activities and I adopted an impossible schedule, driving a thousand miles a week visiting climbing walls and their prospective suppliers. Had the events of the approaching New Year not stopped me, I feel sure that something else would have done.

John Taylor and I met up, soon after I arrived home from Pakistan. He had spent the summer in Chamonix with a friend from Stirling, Iain Small – 'another vegan weirdo' – and they had climbed many impressive lines. His one regret of the summer was that he hadn't climbed on the Grande Jorasses, the area's most striking mountain, and we agreed to visit Chamonix in the winter to do just that. First, for the New Year, we decided to climb together in Scotland.

I coaxed my car up to Stirling on 30th December where I picked him up, and we slid down the Glencoe road. We planned to climb on Ben Nevis the following day, and then go on to Aviemore in the Cairngorms for Hogmanay. We stopped at a layby in the valley at about 2.30 p.m., and walked briskly up to Stob Coire nan Lochan, each soloing a short Grade III gully, before returning at dusk to the car. It had been a spontaneous day. We stayed that night at the Clachaig Inn. Mal Duff had hired the chalet from the inn as a base for his guiding operations, and he happily let us sleep on a spare double bunk. That night John, who in the summer had turned vegan to rid his skin of eczema, provided an enormous bean stew, more than enough for dinner. In the Alps all of his bivouac food had been pre-cooked and he had resisted any type of milk chocolate or meat or cheese product as snacks. I admired his discipline, knowing that I could never have managed it. It was a simple relaxed evening and we sat around the chalet with Mal and Andy Black all evening. Then we slept soundly.

80

(Above) John in August 1985 on the summit of Les Droites (4000m) in the Mont Blanc massif, the Grandes Jorasses behind. (Below) Conway's Great White Roof, Chogolisa (7665m), viewed from K2 Base Camp. Bride Peak (7654m), the North-East summit, is on the left, with the higher top on the right. The traverse is from right to left.

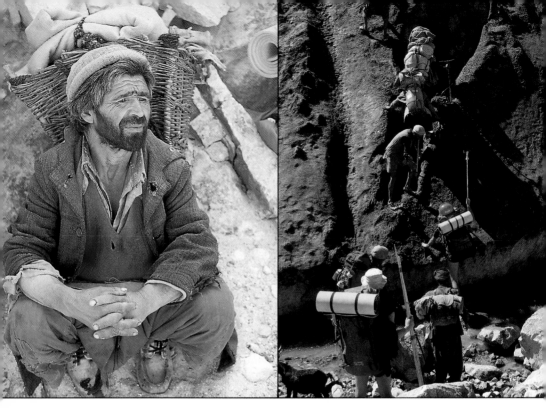

(ABOVE LEFT) Haji Ghulam s/o Mohammed, at fifty our oldest Balti porter, rests between Paiju and Liliwa on the walk-in to Chogolisa. (ABOVE RIGHT) Porters and climbers negotiating an ice pitch on the snout of the Biafo Glacier a few hours above Askole. Rosi Ali and our goat await their turn. (BELOW) The Baltoro Glacier snout, which has a thickness of over 300 metres, viewed from Paiju. The Cathedral and Lobsang groups form the distant skyline.

(ABOVE) The North-West Face of Chogolisa viewed from the head of the Vigne Glacier, with the South-West summit far above. Our route of ascent follows a diagonal line right from the left side of the face to the col at 6800 metres and then the South-West Ridge. (BELOW) Andy and Simon at about 7300 metres on the South-West Ridge. The summit is just visible in fast moving clouds above.

Summit day on Chogolisa, 14th August, 1986. Hamish (ABOVE) approaching the South-West summit with Nanga Parbat (8125m) visible 100 kilometres distant and (BELOW) enjoying perfect conditions on the traverse, looking to the rocky summit of Bride Peak. Hidden Peak (8068m) punctures the skyline on the left. Baltoro Kangri is on the right.

The electronic whimpering of the alarm woke me. Inside the room was darkness. It was before dawn on New Year's Eve. The alarm was out of reach – as I had intended – so I actually had to get up to turn the wretched thing off. I crawled back across the floor into bed, listening to John stirring. He was awake and not happy for it. I hated early starts; the rain outside, hammering on the glass, enhanced the relative comfort of our beds.

'Don't you think we ought to get up?' John's voice penetrated my delirious contentment. I realised that I was nodding off.

'What time is it?' More groping for the alarm. 'Six fifteen. Yes, let's go,' I said with as much conviction as I could.

We lurched about the cold rooms collecting our things. The dark wet exterior was blurred through the misted glass. Mal and Andy had already risen when we finally emerged from the chalet and inserted ourselves timidly into the rotting damp upholstery of my car. We drove through the cheerless morning to Fort William and parked at the Golf Course. I turned the engine off and it was suddenly very quiet. My eyelids shut lightly.

I awoke. Mal was banging on the window. We slumped from our vehicle to theirs for the drive up the Forestry road. Inside their Land-Rover I fell asleep again, my head knocking fitfully against the window. We jolted to a halt at the dam and the engine was cut. Pavlov-dog-like I opened my eyes. Still dark. How uncivilised! The wind was stronger here. I fell into an ambulatory doze, as I trudged through the unfrozen bogs towards the CIC hut in the centre of the corrie, stopping frequently to adjust my layers of clothes. At the hut John insisted on having several brews of tea; a friend of his was staying there. It was light at last.

We decided to climb Observatory Ridge, a classic climb on the right of the Orion Face, the top of which was hidden in cloud. We had no wish to tax ourselves – just to exist contently for a day on the mountain. The Orion Face was plastered white and its gullies choked with snow, though none of it of much use to a climber. The mountain's winter dress nevertheless held our gaze. For one hour we cut our path strenuously through the snow, towards the buttress, occasionally looking back to the dark figures of other climbers spreading, ant-like, from the hut. We wove our way, very slowly and enjoyably up the buttress, turning most obstacles with ease, roping for one short difficult section and then moving together up the face. The weather was poor, there were no vistas to enjoy, yet despite this the day was fun, relaxed. The climbing in itself was enough for that. We finally arrived on the summit plateau at about three o'clock and made our way, via John's compass, through the mist to the observatory shelter, where we demolished the remainder of our food.

We did not converse. The wind was strong enough to snatch our words and the white-out conditions enough to feed a thin line of anxiety between us. We acted. The best way off the mountain would be down Red Burn, rather than via Number Four Gully which descends to the hut. We had no reason to return there. We shortened the rope between us; I took the coils, winding them over my shoulder. John removed his helmet and put it, with his hammer, inside his rucsac. Despite wearing all my clothes, I felt chilled, and uncomfortable against the persistent attack of airborne ice and spindrift. We paced a hundred metres south, then walked on another bearing to the west, which we thought, mistakenly, would bring us out at the top of Red Burn. Our bearing was incorrect for after about a kilometre we entered steeper slopes falling to the left, the top of Five Finger Gully. We decided to contour the slope. My feet were breaking through a light cover of snow as I moved from rock to rock. I stopped to let John catch up and we conferred over our position. 'Keep contouring' was our final sentence on the matter. Moving ahead again I felt the rope tug gently behind. John was there. We resumed, neither hurried nor concerned. Half a minute passed.

Suddenly I was jerked violently onto my side and pulled quickly down the snow. It took only an instant to realise what was happening, by which time it was too late to react. My body was pressed onto the slope, accelerating, helpless against the speed. I was not frightened, only surprised at the swiftness of it all. I closed my eyes and relaxed. This was my instinctive reaction. Then I was airborne. I waited, screwing my eyes a little, tighter thinking, 'When will it come?' Crash! My eyes lit up. The hard stone smacked against my chest. Then, groaning, sliding still, I blacked out.

A rock had already pierced John's fragile skull before we came to rest. The gully had chewed us and spat us out at the bottom. It was dark when I came to. The wind had died and the night air was crisp and sharp and clear. I crawled painlessly up the snow slope to John, lying with his head down the slope; very still. I leaned over him. Where are we, John? I thought. But I was alone for John had gone away. Sagging on his body I tried, but failed, to fathom where I was. We must have fallen, I concluded at last. An avalanche. More time passed. It didn't concern me. Comfortable now. Warm too. Sit here a while, I thought, and look out beneath the clouds. I was not frightened.

Then I heard voices to my left, across the slope, and I saw torchlight.

Instincts again took over. Suddenly anxious, I shouted as loudly as I could. Again and again I summoned them to respond. They called back, acknowledging, reassuring, but still I shouted. All at once a wave of relief flooded over me; I grasped what had happened and where I was. A figure approached. It was Andy Black looking momentarily very shocked.

'John?' the figure spoke.

'Andy,' I said, wearily, meaning me, not him.

'John?' He nodded his head towards the snow-swept body.

'He's dead,' I said. I could not have known.

Andy examined the body of my friend carefully. Then he ransacked his rucsac for clothes and dressed me in them. Mal arrived too, and they tried to move me. The fall had broken one leg, and badly sprained both my wrists. I was delirious through shock, and unable to help myself, or them. Mal ran down to the valley for the Lochaber Rescue Team, leaving Andy to nurse me.

'What degree did you do?' he asked me, knowing the answer.

'Geology.'

'Where did you do it?'

I said, 'London.'

He asked me questions for as long as he could think of them. For him, the waiting before the helicopter arrived was fraught. He sat, for five hours, nursing and coaxing me, knowing that I might have died at any time. My lungs had been punctured by a broken rib and were filling slowly with blood and my delirious state confused the otherwise obvious symptoms of hypothermia. I was dangerously cold, but I did not feel it. I did not shiver or complain. Though the conditions on the ground appeared settled, in the air it was extremely windy and it was only on a last ditch attempt that the RAF chopper and Lochaber team member, Iain Sykes, managed to reach me. Andy must have seen the helicopter struggling to make its approach and realised, if it failed, that it was unlikely that I would survive long enough for the back-up party, already walking up from Glen Nevis, to arrive.

Details are blurred but I vaguely remember the waiting. Five hours passed in the space of one. Andy had trussed me up in apparently hundreds of layers of clothes which made me feel terribly undignified. No sooner had I heard the chopper arrive, faint in the mist above me, than Iain was leaning over me and talking gently while winching me to safety. The ordeal had been painless. It was four minutes to midnight when I was finally swung out above the slope and pulled into the chopper where we celebrated New Year. I was glad that Andy came with me, too. Iain produced a dram of whisky and I think I smiled momentarily then.

John also travelled in the chopper and at Fort William we parted company for the last time.

Doctors and nurses ran around me for hours. I was grateful. A tube was inserted through the wall of my chest into my lungs and I watched the curious sight of blood rise within it and empty into a large beaker resting on the floor. The doctor filled syringe after syringe of fluid from my knee. My wrists were largely ignored. Then I was allowed to sleep. Two climbers, a mountain rescue team, the RAF, and the doctors and nurses of a hospital had worked selflessly to save my life. My gratitude to them is profound.

The next morning I had my first visitors, the newspaper people. There were several mountain incidents over Hogmanay it seemed. The Ward Sister dealt with them. I received many letters and the highlight of each day was opening them. Predictably, most were written in soft and comforting tones, but others, particularly from John's closer friends, were very direct, and as a result, much more moving. Tommy Curtis described John as a 'brick of a man. It really is a fucking bitch.' He wrote on the way to Jordan, where he was on a PhD assignment on their sewers. 'I work in shit,' he explained. He told me that he had an apartment there, and a maid who, he said, could look after me should I fancy a fortnight of recuperation. It was just the sort of spontaneous offer that John would have made. His letter made me laugh and cry; it was perfect. Though laughing was physically painful, I found I could easily do it, when prompted.

John's parents, John and Kath, drove from their home in Leicester, and paid me a visit. I had met them briefly before, so as they approached I recognised them. They looked worn but strong. I said to them 'Sorry' and burst into tears. I was still crying when they left an hour later. I wondered what they thought of me. Why should I live, and John die? I wore a helmet, yes, but why did John take his off, and I leave mine on? John, I remembered, was always more careful. Was I always more lucky?

With John on the Droites I had laybacked up a huge flake of rock two metres high, levering it off. I had fallen and the flake had become tangled in the rope. As I fell I flicked the rope clear and the rock had bounced down the mountain past John.

'*Attention! Attention!*' he had called after it. And then turning to me hanging on the rope, he had smiled and said, 'You lucky sod.'

Yes. Maybe I was. Maybe I always have been.

I still see John's parents. They have never questioned my own fortune, or John's misfortune on that occasion. At first we talked solely of John, relating stories of him. I discovered that in the last two years of his life, his parents had not really known him fully. He rarely visited home or talked with them about his climbing, reluctant to worry them. Yet to me he talked of home many times and how, for instance, he hoped his parents would be proud of him when he got his degree; the sort of statement that passes easily between friends, but uncomfortably between parent and child. It had seemed so unimportant then. I couldn't remember when I had last told my parents, if ever, that I loved them, yet I didn't doubt that, had I been killed too, they would have known that I did. Later the Taylors and I were able to talk about other things, though John will always be our common bond and the *raison d'être* for our friendship.

Although I had liked and respected Liam enormously, my reaction to his death on Broad Peak was to become as mentally detached as possible. It was, I suppose, my psychological defence, and it unsettled me that I should be able to come to terms with his accident so easily. John, however, was my best friend and losing him hurt me very much, though I did feel strangely grateful or privileged, that I should have been with him at the end. In the next few months I learnt what it means to grieve, primarily because I initially failed to. Within just three weeks I had overcome my physical injuries enough to return to work, and I threw all my energies in that direction in an attempt to put the accident to the back of my mind. I had organised for the BMC a visit of a group of Polish climbers to Scotland and ludicrously I decided to lead the meet myself. I was exhausted and distorted and unable to walk without crutches though, even with these, my wrists prevented me from travelling far. Predictably the whole fortnight was a shambles, which depressed and agitated me even more. So I filled my time with work. The more I did, the more I created for myself. I had entered a vicious spiral of emotional decay, and I grew hugely depressed and uncertain. Lesley Smithson, the office manager of the BMC, kindly took me in to her house, and each day she drove me to and from work, caring for me where I could not manage for myself. Her patience was endless. I attended physiotherapy at Wythenshawe where an empathetic Mrs Dodd, whose husband was a climber, drove me through a punishing schedule of exercises for my knee. Lesley loaned me a bag of peas for the swelling. Despite my doctor advising me against rock climbing 'for at least a year', Mrs Dodd positively encouraged me and she set me a target date of May to be fit enough again to get back into the hills. By May I was leading at Extreme standard again, and in June I led my first ever E5 rock climb, in the slate quarries of Llanberis.

It became very important for me to climb on snow and ice again, to

85

prove to myself that we had been only unlucky and that, with care, mountaineering can be an acceptably safe and spiritually rewarding pursuit. Thus, I was grateful when Mark Dixon agreed to spend three weeks of the summer with me in the Alps.

The Alps that June were virtually unclimbable due to the horrible weather. We spent most of our time climbing in the Dolomites or on smaller limestone cliffs, tucked warmly into a holiday mode. Our time together was fun, if unadventurous, and sufficient to convince me that climbing was certainly worthwhile. It marked the turning point of my depression, and I started to look forward again to visiting the mountains.

8

Bonington, Menlungtse and the yeti

It was around this time, in the spring of 1987 that Chris Bonington and Jim Fotheringham, with two Norwegian climbers Odd Eliassen and Bjorn Myrer-Lund were on Menlungtse, an unclimbed and by all accounts extremely difficult mountain in the Rolwaling Himal which straddles the Nepal/Tibet border. Menlungtse, 7181 metres, had never been officially attempted, despite being in close proximity to other more popular peaks, such as Cho Oyu, Gauri Sankar and even Everest. The reason is that the peak lies wholly in Tibet, and cannot be attempted from Nepal, at least not legally. Up to that year the Chinese authorities had kept Menlungtse off their permission list, so even politically it was a difficult mountain to climb. Chris had written to the Chinese Mountaineering Association in Beijing to ask them to make an exception. Their response had hardly been encouraging, for the CMA said they had never heard of it. Menlungtse, as a name, was invented by Eric Shipton and Michael Ward after visiting it during the Everest reconnaissance expedition of 1951. Of course the mountain had a Tibetan name, Jobo Garu, and when Chris replied to Beijing with this slightly amended application they agreed. Even for him, for there are few as politically agile, this had been a major coup.

Chris was the Vice-President of the BMC at that time, and so I had come to know him. Undoubtedly the most famous of all British climbers, he was fantastically experienced, not just in the bulk of climbing that he had done but in its variety. In the 'fifties he had been a leading rock-climber, in the 'sixties a leading alpinist and young Himalayan achiever, and in the 'seventies a leading expeditioner with several epoch-making climbs to his credit, both as leader and climber, not least the South-West Face of Everest, and the first ascent of the Ogre. In the 'eighties he had continued to climb at the forefront, making ascents of Kongur in the Xinjiang Province of China in 1981 and at last Everest itself in 1985. I could see that he was immensely proud and satisfied with these adventures, but equally I could see that he would dearly love to collect them all again.

My own picture of Chris had been of a very hairy, rather overbearing man, and it was difficult for me to change that perception at first. But he could be quite sartorial at times, when his hair was cut and his beard controlled. He was also very approachable, once he dropped a public front that I suspected he had developed more through necessity than desire. What impressed me most of all was how he grew suddenly excited, childlike even, with the prospect of some climbing, no matter where and for how long. I had to remind myself sometimes that he was older than my father. For me his raw enthusiasm, as much as his achievements, gave him his credibility and it was, I thought, appropriate that he should be the public's mountaineering symbol as well as its spokesman.

Menlungtse is a granite mountain, guarded on all sides by either its steep ramparts of rock or horribly convoluted mushrooms of corniced snow or sérac ice. In 1979 from the Eastern summit of Gauri Sankar Peter Boardman had described Menlungtse as a 'mighty white obelisk of snow and pale pink granite, whose shape matched that of the Matterhorn from the East'. It was, he had added, 'the loveliest vision of all'. Chris's team was attempting a spur of mixed rock and ice that descends from the West summit of the mountain in the hope that from there they could quite easily traverse to the Eastern, higher summit. Photographs of the mountain taken by Doug Scott from Xixabangma in 1982 suggested that this should be possible. After some hard technical climbing in unsettled weather they failed to penetrate the steep 500-metre granite headwall at the top of their route. Descending after one attempt, Bonington nearly killed himself when an anchor failed and he somersaulted backward, reacting quickly to grab another rope from another anchor to stop his downward slide.

It is true that Chris has been fortunate in his thirty years as mountaineer not to have died in the mountains. It would be naïve to think that he has survived solely because he is in some way more careful and skilful than others, though this of course is often the case. Simply, he has been very lucky, and humble too. He knows that his skull is just as fragile as any other's. He has also been unlucky with so many friends killed – Estcourt, Burke, Clough, Boardman, Tasker – on his expeditions. Compared to Doug Scott's more numerous expeditions Chris's have seen much more grief. This of course has played a part, albeit small, in making them more widely known, for the press do dwell on the dangers and tragedies in climbing more than on the successes. This is inevitable, but at least it usually means the media seek some informed comment to flesh out their reporting, rather than blundering on themselves. The danger of climbing is, after all, the main factor that separates those who choose to go to the mountains from those who choose not to. If one is to communicate mountaineering to the masses accurately then one should not avoid the facts of death.

After Chris and Jim and their friends had retreated from the west side of Menlungtse, they traversed to beneath the main summit and considered the East Ridge. This would have been one of John Taylor's lines, had he seen it – a powerful, dominant, yet elegant single crest that climbs forcibly and directly to the highest point of the mountain. Alas, the climbing on this ridge also looked prohibitively difficult and uncertain beneath its shining white mane of unstable snow. Bonington himself did not see the ridge from close to; only Jim and Odd had been sufficiently near to assess it, but they were unreserved in their assurances of its difficulty, and they collectively decided against trying it.

At the base of this ridge, Odd and Jim had photographed some unusual tracks in the snow. They appeared to be prints of a biped extending for some distance over the snow and moraine. A local Tibetan, on being told of the tracks, immediately ascribed them to the chuti, a small yeti. Although under close questioning none of the villagers would admit to ever seeing a chuti, they were impressively convincing. Curiously enough, it was near the same spot that Shipton and Ward had taken their classic photograph in 1951, depicting an obvious line of footprints that they too attributed to the yeti. For Bonington, this coincidence was far too intriguing to ignore, and in the next year he sent the press, and at times himself, into an excitable frenzy. He immediately set about organising a return, and was granted permission again for Menlungtse for the follow-ing year, 1988. More than anything he wanted to climb the mountain, but also, it seemed from certain angles, he wanted to find the yeti. Certainly it provided a rich vein of interest for sponsorship. He dubbed his forthcoming project 'Menlungtse and the search for the Yeti'.

In Britain he mentioned his plans to me once; the yeti did not feature in this conversation about returning to Menlungtse with Jim Fotheringham, perhaps because he surmised, correctly, that I would have thought he had gone barmy. I was envious, but did not say as much. I already had a project of my own, but for a year later. I had received permission for an attempt on a traverse of Makalu, the world's fifth summit, for the autumn of 1989. As it would have most likely meant leaving my employment, I had not talked of it widely, certainly not to Chris, effectively my boss. I had booked it long in advance simply to give myself something to look forward to. It had seemed necessary at the time, after John's death, when I had felt least motivated and most miserable. Once booked, however, I began to view the expedition with some excitement. I, and Mike Woolridge with whom I shared the permit, had gathered a team of ten climbers, all willing to contribute towards the peak fee and go onto the permission list. Hamish and Ulric were among them, also Victor Saunders. Then one day in October I found a message on my desk to ring Chris.

'Andy, have you any plans for next spring?'

I hadn't. 'Working I suppose – maybe I'll do the Alps in the summer, or a quick trip to Pakistan.'

'Do you fancy a trip with me? I mean to Menlungtse?'

I was gobsmacked. 'Oh right . . . well . . . um, sure!'

Jim Fotheringham, it seemed, doubted he could find a *locum tenens* for his dental practice in Brampton in the Lake District and had reluctantly dropped out. I tried to sound as keen as possible. I felt I had succeeded.

'You don't need to decide yet,' Chris said. 'I'll bring some pictures down to Management Committee on Wednesday. Maybe you can find a couple of hours in the afternoon. We can go cragging, and chat about it.'

We went to Cheedale and climbed Sirplum, a huge and strenuous roof climb on enormous holds in a wild position. I had never enjoyed a rock climb so much. I swung myself out across the overhanging rock, hanging out like a bat, lacing my ropes through numerous runners and looking back along the arching slack of rope towards Chris. He moved quickly across the roof when it was his turn to follow, to appear at the belay a little puffed and red in the face, as I had been, from the physical exertion, but disposing of the pitch with no trouble at all. Driving back to the meeting he expanded on the expedition. It was obvious to me that he wanted to lead the entire trip from the front, and for the time being at least I was happy to listen attentively to his plans. To reach Menlungtse we would travel via Kathmandu in Nepal to cross the border into Tibet at Friendship Bridge on the main Kathmandu-Lhasa road, a road which neither country seem able to keep entirely open, due to landslides. From Tingri, a tiny settlement on the Tibetan plain, we would engage yaks to take us south over the Fusi La, the Himalayan divide, and descend the Rongshar Gorge to a village called Chang bu Jiang. From here we would walk up the Menlung Chu to yak pastures below the West Face of the mountain. The journey via Kathmandu was greatly complicated by the fact that Menlungtse, being Tibetan, had to be approached from the north. Nevertheless the journey to Tingri through Nepal was a great deal shorter and cheaper than the alternative of flying to Lhasa via Beijing and then travelling overland by jeep to the same point. Chris described the mountain to me in generous terms. He said that the East Ridge, direct to the main summit, would probably be the best route. Later I talked to Jim who said that the East Ridge was much too hard.

'I've seen it. *He* hasn't,' he told me.

Chris and I also discussed the timing for the expedition which he wanted to be open-ended, starting at the end of March. As the monsoon was bound to arrive in June, that effectively marked the farthest time limit, though the effect of the monsoon as it breaks is always difficult to assess. It is sometimes possible to climb, particularly on the highest mountains, quite successfully during the monsoon season, though the Governments of Nepal and China do not fully recognise the summer as a climbing season. We also spoke of the yeti. It would be fun to look for it he said.

Going in search of the yeti made me think about its existence. I wasn't a cynic, so much as a plain disbeliever. I believe in UFOs but not spaceships. By their very definition there have been hundreds of sightings of UFOs, that is indisputable. But I need evidence, not conjecture, to convince myself of visitors to our planet from outer space. Similarly there have been unidentified sightings of bear-like animals in Himalayan forests, unusual tracks in snow and unfamiliar noises. Yet of all the hundreds of expeditions to the Himalaya, yeti-hunting or not, there has not been, for me, a single convincing piece of photographic evidence pointing to the existence of the yeti, other perhaps than Shipton's evocative picture from 1951. Even this has been accused by Ed Hillary and others of being doctored. If it was a practical joke, then it is a very successful one. As I see it, to believe seriously in a yeti as a tall hairy upright abominable snowman one needs a sense of humour much more than a rational mind.

When Vic Saunders was climbing in Bhutan, on the first ascent of Jitchu Drake, he mentioned to their Sirdar, Kharma, that Bonington was in search of the yeti.

Kharma said, 'Well, he's wasting his time going to Tibet.'

'Why?' asked Vic.

'There's one in Madras Zoo – I've seen it.'

I wondered how Chris felt about the yeti. Certainly it was his friend, a friend to all of us. Nobody but the climbers was interested in Menlungtse, but on the strength of the interest in the yeti the BBC were sending a team from the natural history unit with us, and a reporter and photographer from the *Mail on Sunday* were coming too. William Hill, the bookmakers, were accepting bets on us finding the beast. The odds fell from 150 to 1 to 66 to 1 in the months leading up to our departure which reflected the British public's sense of fun and eccentricity. Between these three organisations Chris had virtually secured full sponsorship for the expedition. Had he found the yeti in 1987 at Menlungtse, Chris admits that he would have been ethically torn between broadcasting his discovery to the world and 'leaving the poor old yeti to live in peace'. If we found it in 1988 such an option would be taken from us. I could see that he hoped we never found it, though to this day I still cannot decide whether Chris has ever actually believed that the yeti might exist.

Chris gave an interview on Radio 2 one day which I heard by chance on my car radio. It was so outrageous I almost pulled to the side of the road. Chris acknowledged that the yeti had never been sighted.

'Doesn't that suggest it doesn't exist?' the interviewer asked flatly.

'Certainly not,' said Chris. 'What it suggests is that the yeti has an acute sixth sense, that always tells it when it is in danger. We were once together, we and the yeti, perhaps around the time of Neanderthal Man. We developed motive skills and practical forms of intelligence; the yeti developed ESP. *That* is why it has never been sighted.'

Chris was now the President-Elect of the BMC and he joked that he might have his title stripped from him in view of the fact that more and more people were saying that he had at last flipped. 'Too many days at altitude,' they joked, 'premature senility.' Most of the climbing world, however, thought that he had found a brilliant scam for raising money, and admired how he readily made a fool of himself without embarrassment for the cause.

The climbing team for Menlungtse consisted of two Americans, David Breashears and Steve Shea, and two Britons, Chris and me. A proven high-altitude cameraman, David had twice been to the summit of Everest, and each time brought back film footage. He was also well known for his ice-climbing prowess and with Jeff Lowe had pioneered a desperate climb on Kwandwe in the Khumbu Himal of Nepal. He was probably the most suitably experienced and strongest climber on our expedition and he immeasurably boosted the odds of our team reaching the summit. His fellow countryman, Steve Shea, was less experienced in the Himalaya but no less so overall and was technically brilliant, particularly on ice and mixed ground. David lived in Boston whilst Steve lived in Jackson, Wyoming, amid the Grand Tetons where he was able to keep superlatively fit. I was very much looking forward to meeting them both.

Chris had also invited Charlie Clarke and Jess Stock as support. Charlie is a consultant neurologist at St Bartholomew's in London, where he voluntarily ran the Mountain Medicine Data Centre, an invaluable source of advice for expeditions of all sizes and types. Charlie himself was something of an authority on high-altitude physiology and had recently been elected as the president of the Medical Commission of the Union Internationale des Associations d'Alpinisme, the world body for mountaineering. As such, Charlie gave us more than a hint of confidence.

Once at a pre-departure meeting at Chris's house I confessed I had overlooked my tetanus jab. Within two minutes Charlie had been to his car and fetched the necessary equipment.

'Roll your sleeve up, then.'

I am the world's worst coward for needles.

'Right, this won't hurt.'

But he was wrong. It did and to make matters worse, he slapped and punched my arm as soon as he had removed the needle. Like most doctors, I doubted that Charlie would have much time for minor miseries or whinging.

The BBC were there to film our meeting and stage a discussion about the yeti.

'What do you think, Charlie?' Chris asked, appealing to the camera.

'The yeti? I don't believe in it; of course I don't.'

John-Paul, the programme producer, could not have dreamed of a worse response. I warmed to Charlie immediately.

Jess came as a logistics manager and a trouble shooter. Chris presumably reckoned that he needed a break from that side of things once on the trip. It would allow him to relax and put himself in the right frame of mind for climbing. Jess had founded Europa Sports, a ski and climbing equipment distributor based in Kendal, and had recently sold up and entered into an early retirement of sorts. So he had bags of time and experience to offer. Jess was not our treasurer, as he once reminded me, he was our 'financial controller'. He lived half his life in Chamonix, and half in Kendal or in his Audi Quattro somewhere in between. He made hundreds of telephone calls from all those places.

John-Paul Davidson (producer), Nigel Meakin (cameraman) and Arthur Chesterman (sound recordist) made up the BBC entourage, whilst Iain Walker (assistant editor) and David O'Neil (photographer) represented the *Mail on Sunday*. It occurred to the newspaper as departure loomed that they would need a courier on hand at Base Camp to ferry their film and written copy back across Tibet and Nepal to Kathmandu where they could be faxed or 'DHL'ed' to London. Alan Hinkes, a Newcastle-based climber put himself forward and was duly appointed.

I already knew Hinkes. He worked for Berghaus, the clothing and equipment manufacturer and distributor who supplied the Menlungtse venture. He was their technical consultant, along with Brian Hall and Chris, and it was virtually impossible to think of him without also thinking of his firm. Physically he was strong and formidable, with sunken cheeks and a square-cut jaw. He had a unique personality, outwardly vivacious yet remarkably blunt and thick-skinned. At times he appeared to be quite insensitive in the manner in which he scattered off-hand remarks, but equally he was rarely hurt or offended by those tossed in his direction. If he said something you knew it was true, or at least he believed it was true. It was as if he was incapable of deviousness. This quality of almost childlike simplicity made him accessible to all who wished to get to know him and a valuable friend.

As a climber he was remarkably audacious and much more determined than technical. He had already climbed on several expeditions in the Himalaya and in the last summer had established a bold new route on Xixabangma, an 8000-metre peak in Tibet. He was also a talented photographer, a self-taught skill. As with his climbing, his doggedness, as much as his keen eye for a picture ensured he always achieved good results.

The BMC gave me unpaid leave for the trip, for which I was very grateful, and I was able to work right up to the weekend before we left. Apart from organising delivery of some of our equipment there was really very little for me to do.

Alan and I spent the night before departure at Victor's in London and in the morning attended a press conference at the Natural History Museum. Ian Bishop, the Curator, sat with Chris facing a wall of press and television. In front of them was a William Hill billboard: 66 to 1 – Bonington Yeti Hunt. Ian Bishop was to be the arbitrator for the bet, though he didn't look as though he was revelling in his duties. 'Photographs won't prove anything,' he had said, to the delight of the bookmakers who stood to be near bankrupted if we brought back the yeti.

The media were having a field day. I made the mistake of straying a bit near. 'Excuse me. Do you mind,' said one reporter, fighting his way to the front. Charlie, who was in a suit, not just for the conference but the entire journey to Nepal, remarked to me that this was the best bit;

being invited to a press conference and then being asked to get out of the way.

This was certainly a different type of expeditioning to what I had experienced before. In its planning we had met frequently and minutes and notes were produced. Each of us signed a contract, detailing copyright of photographs, press statement timings, etc. I found these formalities unfamiliar but inoffensive. Everywhere we went Bonington was recognised. I could see that this was sometimes useful but it must also have been quite tiresome for Chris.

Pakistan International Airways upgraded our tickets to first class in exchange for a small press conference and an opportunity to make a fuss of someone, which they lavishly succeeded in doing. Despite being a Muslim airline, they allowed us to take wine and beer on board. In fact they bought it for us.

Representatives of Safeway, who had freely provided, packaged and airfreighted all our food to Kathmandu in ready yakload-sized boxes, came to the airport to see us off. Charlie, as quartermaster, had chosen all of the food at Safeway in Enfield, enlisting the help of ten store assistants each with a trolley. Safeway's earnest young researcher, Sue Anderson, who had given each of us a food diary as part of a nutritional study, accompanied him through the aisles. She could not miss the opportunity of discussing first hand with the doctor just what he thought the climbers should eat in preparation for the mountain. It was with some dismay, but quiet understanding, therefore, that she witnessed Charlie direct the store assistants towards the alcohol counter where he filled a good number of trolleys with cartons of wine.

'These carry very high calorific value,' he had assured her.

We changed flights at Karachi, which even in March seemed as hot as I had remembered it, finally arriving in Kathmandu on 31st March, midday. Jess, David and Steve had already been in Kathmandu for one week organising our food and visas for onward travel into Tibet. I spent the rest of the day on the roof of our hotel, the Tibetan Guest House on the fringe of Thamel, the most tourist-populated district of the city. From here I could see across the whole metropolis and beyond to the outlying hills, Nagarjun, Shiva Puri and even to some of the Himalayan mountains in the north. Dust hung over the town producing on our first night a stunning red sunset behind the silhouetted stupa of the Swaymbunath temple.

Kathmandu is a charming place and much more civilised and fun than I had expected, in its range of interesting shops, restaurants and places to visit. It has become a designer resort – popular, accessible and

convenient but also ethnic and unkempt. The strikingly different re-
ligions of Hinduism and Buddhism exist side by side harmoniously here.

'We've been speed hiking on that one,' Steve told me, pointing to
Nagarjun, a forested hill overlooking the city. It looked large and
imposing in the failing light. 'Yeap. Forty-five minutes from the gate at
the bottom.' Patently, he was as fit as I had been warned, for during the
following days in Kathmandu, the best I ever managed on Nagarjun was
fifty-one minutes.

Steve Shea was a laid back, ingenuous and hugely entertaining Vietnam
veteran, with an infinite anthology of colloquial American. 'Watch out
for the dogpie on your sneakers,' was his first advice to me on Kathmandu
when we had arrived at the airport.

Once, whilst climbing in Yosemite Valley in California, Steve had met
a couple of Newcastle climbers, Kevin Maclean and Dave Macdonald,
and had been amused and confused by their Geordie dialect. The arrival
in Kathmandu of Hinkes therefore set Steve into a great excitement as
he tried to imitate his accent. In fact Hinkes isn't a true Geordie at all,
but an ex-pat Yorkshireman exiled in Newcastle, and Steve's efforts
sounded much more convincing than Hinkes's. At times Steve's behaviour certainly belied his forty years.

Steve and David were close friends, though quite different on initial
acquaintance. David had a slightly tense air of professional seriousness
about him and a much more deliberate and careful manner. He was, if
anything, fitter than Steve, with his slighter and younger frame, and was
casually smart, clean-shaven with a neat short hairstyle. Steve, who
seemed to wear whatever first came to hand each morning, had grown
a wiry beard which was greying at the sides. A long beaked baseball cap
usually concealed his hair. Both wore simple wire framed shades, and
Steve was normally chewing something.

Once we had procured all the remaining supplies and engaged in
some filming with the BBC team, we relaxed and waited for our China
visas to materialise and for instructions to come through from the CMA
in Beijing on when to go to the border to meet our Liaison Officer and
interpreter. We had already enlisted two Nepalis to work as cooks with
us in Tibet. These were Krishna, a Rai from Sheduwa in the Arun Valley
near Makalu and Nima, a Sherpa from Beding in the Rolwaling Himal,
just a few miles over the border from Menlungtse. Krishna in particular
was typical of what expeditions have come to expect of their Sirdars. He
was relentlessly willing and felt that he couldn't ever do enough to help.
He was a small, powerful man, socially confident, and effervescent. In
his village, which I visited the following year, there is a marked social

(ABOVE) A view from Base Camp of the headwall on the West Face of Menlungtse, with four climbers at about 6600 metres on the first attempt below the elusive ice gully. The eventual line of ascent takes the headwall direct on the centre-left of the picture. (BELOW LEFT) A young Tibetan girl living at over 4000 metres in the village of Tingri, the roadhead on the approach to Menlungtse. (BELOW RIGHT) Inside the desecrated Chue gompa near Chang bu Jiang in the Rongshar Gorge of Tibet.

The West Face of Menlungtse;
Alan (ABOVE) on hard ice, at 6300 metres and (BELOW) starting the headwall at 6700 metres.

Andy at 6950 metres, leading the final pitch of the West Face.
The route takes the obvious gash above.

(Above) Andy in evening light on 23rd May, 1988 on the summit ridge of Menlungtse West (7023m). Cho Oyu (8201m) and Gyachung Kang (7952m) behind. (Below) Andy and Alan back at the base of the ridge after climbing to the West summit.

divide between the Sherpa and Rai or Chettree communities. I found the Sherpas quite patronising of the Rai, though Krishna's strength of character had obviously not allowed him to be down-trodden by such attitudes. Nima was also willing, though more in reaction to than prediction of our needs, a quiet, gentle man, slight and good looking.

On 3rd April, Chris received a telex from the Chinese. It threw the future of the whole expedition into doubt.

ATTN MR BONINGTON,
WE'RE SORRY TO INFORM U YR LO N INTERPRETER R UNABLE TO MEET U AT XANGMU ON TIME. BECAUSE OF SOME REASON NOW IT'S INCONVENIENT FOR U TO CLIMB MENLUNGTZE, SURELY WE'VE DOING OUT BEST TO CARRY OUT OUR FORMER AGREEMENT, BUT THIS TAKES SOME TIME. THE REASON WE SENT U THIS TLX IS THAT WE HAVE TO, N EXPECT YR UNDERSTANDING. CMA.

Chris was suddenly under pressure. He did not doubt that the problem was a political one, and he and indeed the whole expedition were a pawn in a greater game. He threw a telex back at them pleading with them to reconsider and then sat to think. The CMA responded with a telex which ended:

. . . CMA WOULD ACCEPT AN APPLICATION TO CLIMB XIXABANGMA.

'Xixabangma,' remarked Shea, 'is as high as shit can be stacked.'
Hinkes had climbed it. No further comments were passed.
That advice, the CMA's not Steve's, suggested that it was the Tibetans who were prohibiting our visit. Although Tibet had its own Mountaineering Council, permission for Xixabangma had always been issued from Beijing, likewise for Everest. But there was obviously no formal agreement regarding Menlungtse. The number of unclimbed mountains in the world was declining, and their commodity value consequently increasing. Due to the political restraints of the past, many of the remaining unclimbed peaks lay in Tibet. The question was not whether the Chinese *could* force the permission through but whether they *wanted* to.

Chris publicised our predicament astutely. He even managed a live interview with the BBC's Breakfast Time programme. All he said was that the CMA had a heavy administrative burden but he believed, as had always happened in the past, they would sort it out and soon be in a position to issue our permit. At the same time he kept telexing Beijing to let them know that he had the international media poised for a story, which was true and that we were loaded and ready to move. Chris had also spoken to his old friend David Wilson, Governor of Hong Kong, about our problem, and arranged for our military attaché in Beijing to visit the CMA and send us an impression of the situation. One way or another Chris was sure to force their hand. Something was going to happen.

There was nothing more to do in Kathmandu, but wait. It became a prison of sorts and with that new uncharitable feeling I started to become conscious of the other side of the city; primarily that it was filthy. We used to go to a snack shack in Thamel for breakfast, passing on the way a big yellow rubbish dumper that the hotels used to dispose of their garbage. We had christened it the Kathmandu Breakfast Club as each morning we could see people sitting inside eating whatever they could find. The stench was powerful.

'Hmm, smells good,' quirked Shea.

My mood seemed to be controlling what I noticed in the streets. Each day of waiting, the dust levels in the city seemed to get worse and worse. Black dry snot collected in my nostrils.

On the 11th Chris's infectious smile returned. The CMA had advised us to go to the border. The telex promised no more than that, but it provided a fresh backcloth for the waiting. The telex had come at the eleventh hour, for our inbuilt contingency week had been fully used up. Before we left, we attended a puja, a Buddhist blessing at Boudhanath in Kathmandu for our safe return from the mountains. It was a beautiful occasion, that touched me deeply. The lama gave us each a knotted piece of string. The knot contained a prayer. I wore it religiously for the next two months.

9

Stealing across Tibet

There had been a landslide, a big one, the year before, and eight kilometres of the road to the border were down between Lamosangu and Barabise, so at eleven o'clock we disembarked from our truck and hired porters to carry our loads to the point where the road continued. Another truck at the other side would take us to the border. For the truck-owners of Barabise the landslide had been a prayer answered. They could charge what they liked for the remaining few kilometres' drive to the border, and as far as they were concerned the engineers could struggle for all their worth; they weren't bothered if they never managed to reopen the road.

By the time we reached Barabise it was too late to move on to the border, so we were forced to stay the night. The town consisted of two hundred metres of shops and houses along each side of the main road. It was outrageously squalid, but it did sell beer at a suitably inflated price. But what the heck, Iain Walker was paying, so we all perched ourselves on the balcony of our guesthouse and got drunk. Another round of beers had just been opened when an earthquake suddenly shuddered through the town. My reaction was hardly textbook – I ran into the building. The others contemplated jumping into the street but managed to postpone their take off until the shaking subsided. Whatever, we had spilled our drinks.

The street then filled with people, whooping, cheering and laughing at our stunned reaction. David looked unperturbed. 'Ha, sure, no problem. Happens every day.' Some of us were less convinced. John-Paul Davidson chose this moment to give me a small necklace of red coral that he wanted me to leave on the summit of Menlungtse. He had just married.

'You old romantic. But I'm flattered,' I said.

JP didn't understand why. He looked forlorn and I didn't need to be

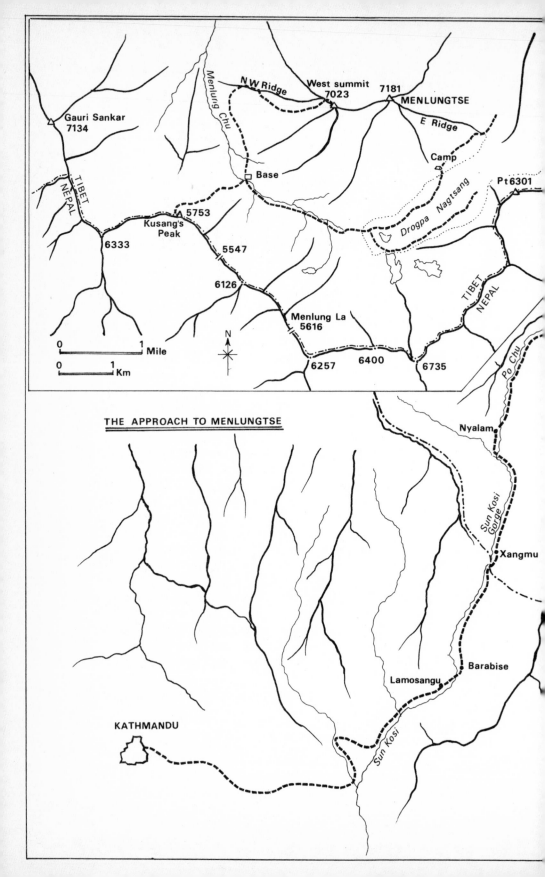

THE APPROACH TO MENLUNGTSE

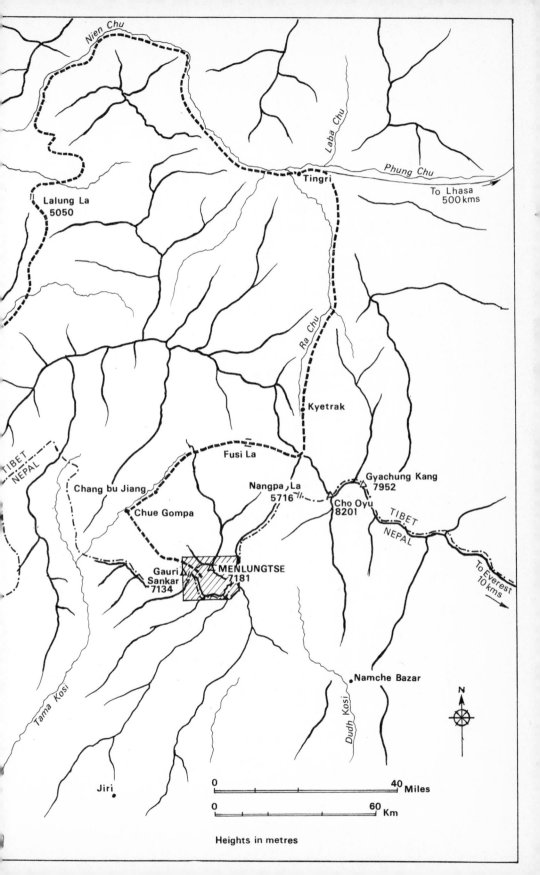

Nien Chu

Lalung La
5050

Laba Chu

Tingri

Phung Chu

To Lhasa
500 kms

Ra Chu

Kyetrak

TIBET
NEPAL

Fusi La

Chang bu Jiang

Nangpa La
5716

Gyachung Kang
7952

Chue Gompa

Cho Oyu
8201

TIBET

NEPAL

Gauri
Sankar
7134

MENLUNGTSE
7181

To Everest
10 kms

Namche Bazar

N

Tama Kosi

Dudh Kosi

Jiri

0   40 Miles

0   60 Km

Heights in metres

psychic to see that he was pining badly. 'Flattered that you think that I'm going to get up,' I explained. I was touched by JP's request, though I later discovered that Margaret, his wife, had never even seen the necklace.

By 10 o'clock the next day we reached the border which consisted of a thick white line painted across the road halfway across the Friendship Bridge that spans the Sun Kosi river. The once grand bridge post on the Chinese side of the river was a mess. Glass and plaster lay scattered about, and its guardians looked bored. Typical, I was to learn, of Chinese soldiers a very long way from home.

Our interpreter was there; Fan Xiachan from Beijing; a young and very excitable man, in his twenties, with a slight build, a warm round face, gleaming white teeth and a generous shock of jet black hair.

'Hello,' he said, 'I am Fanshawe An.'

'What?'

'Yes. I am student. From Beijing.'

To my relief he avoided further confusion between us by offering Francis as an anglicised version of his name. He informed us that our Liaison Officer, a Tibetan official from Lhasa, had been forbidden to join us. Francis wore a constant expression of urgency and panic and I did wonder whether the Tibetan authorities knew that we were on the border of their country at all. Francis, with Chris in tow, hurried off up the hill to Xangmu, the Chinee frontier town, some two kilometres distant. Chris had taken a bottle of White Horse Scotch with him to the border, though I doubted that he would drink it himself. It was, however, intriguing that we didn't see them again for the remainder of the day or night. The rest of us sat about on the loads, distinctive red boxes, red duffels or plastic-coated and sealed cardboard boxes of Safeway food, finally rolling out our mats and sleeping bags when we gave up hope of moving that night.

In the morning we had clearance to proceed, even though the Chinese border officials had no record of our party. Chris returned full of praise for Francis who, as we were to discover, knew exactly how to deal with the authorities. Francis came from a family of academics; both his parents were professors and he had recently married the daughter of a general; he had not only inherited brains, he had also never been refused anything. Simply, he never took no for an answer. His rather manic giggles and squeals of excitement sometimes gave the impression that he thought we were all part of a huge game, but thankfully, I mused, one that we were sure to win, with Francis on our side. It was clear that no amount of political nonsense could suppress *him*.

The road to Xangmu was also blocked, so we needed to employ another batch of porters to ferry our equipment for a few hundred metres steeply up the hill behind the bridge, cutting across several switchbacks in the offending road before reaching a waiting truck on the far side of the landslide. The porters, all Nepali, had appeared from nowhere. Some made three or four journeys up and down the path. One had a fistful of yen and asked Charlie to change it for rupees. Charlie obliged but gave the man a really mean rate of exchange. I was appalled.

At the truck half a dozen young Chinese soldiers were supposed to be working on the road but enthusiasm for their task was lacking. There was a small playful puppy with them for which they threw sticks. One of the soldiers offered the puppy something. It was a lit cigarette. The small dog licked at the cigarette, yelped and bit the soldier's hand in fright, who then proceeded to kick it across the road. Instinctively I stepped forward and remonstrated in angry English to be met by a circle of deadpan expressions. Were they psychopaths or imbeciles? I retreated.

At Xangmu we crossed the border into Tibet without incident and had a meal in the hotel especially built for the tourist trade that had been expected to boom. They'll need roads first, I thought. The hotel was typical of what we would come to expect in Tibet. It was both enormous and empty, once grand but now run down and plain. The rooms were bare and cold. Despite the abundance of hot-water taps, there was no water, hot or cold, virtually no electricity, and the toilets were revolting. Cigarette butts littered the corridors, missing the cheap plastic waste paper bins. The restaurant offered a standard meal of boiled rice or a bowl of Maggi noodles, ubiquitous in Asia and imported from the industrial hinterland of China, several thousand kilometres to the east. I decided to follow Francis's lead and opt for the rice with a glass of water as a chaser. Francis threw it down with typical Chinese chin-to-bowl gusto.

'Hurry, now. We must go at once,' he said mid-swallow.

All of our restaurant food and board expenses in Tibet, were on credit from the CMA. Francis simply signed a chit which then made its way to Beijing for payment. It was thus necessary for Chris at least to return home via Beijing, where we could settle our accounts.

A mini-coach was waiting for us, along with a truck for our equipment and within two minutes Hinkes had managed to plaster both vehicles in Berghaus stickers. For the first few kilometres along the impressive Sun Kosi Gorge, I rode with Steve and Dave on top of the truck.

Above Xangmu the road got off to a hazardous start across a huge scar in the landscape, another landslide, a kilometre wide. This time the

103

slope was red mud and boulders. The Chinese, we were not encouraged to learn, had not bothered to build a decent road across this section because it was swept away so often during heavy rain. I eyed the black clouds above nervously. The truck inched its way along a narrow ledge and across runnels down which my imagination saw a seething torrent of boulders and trucks somersaulting towards the river, a tiny white thread a thousand metres below us. The driver seemed to be hesitating as he squeezed his three-metre-wide truck along the three-metres-and-ten-centimetres-wide road. Then he stopped and asked us to get off. He didn't need to ask twice. I leapt from my perch and ran for it.

Above the gorge we started our slow climb onto the Tibetan Plain and a five-hour drive to Nyalam. As we climbed the vegetation thinned until a point where the dull greens of scrub and grass faded to virtually nothing. Scree, dust, rubble, sand-banked rivers and a light dusting of snow on the higher ground marked this inert terrain. The hillsides were painted in dull hues of brown and grey and drew a smooth and rounded skyline. We had gained three kilometres of altitude since Barabise. Inevitably, the headaches and dizziness of altitude sickness set in. Charlie had prepared us for this and for those who wished (I hadn't) had prescribed a course of Acetazolamide, commonly known as Diamox, which has proved itself to be effective in helping the body acclimatise.

We bumped the truck and bus into a large empty purpose-built parking space at Nyalam in front of a long, white desolate-looking building. This would be our overnight stop. Behind the town rose stunningly beautiful white peaks, reminiscent of the Chamonix Aiguilles, except some of these were over 6000 metres high. Their sharp profiles, like a child would draw a mountain, contrasted abruptly with the more rounded foreground. Behind those peaks lay Xixabangma. It was from here that Doug Scott, Alex MacIntyre, Roger Baxter-Jones and friends approached the mountain in 1982 when they climbed their impressive new route on the South-West Face. They had seen excellent views of Menlungtse on that occasion, though from Nyalam any hopes of seeing larger, more distant mountains were quickly dashed. The next day, however, we were to climb higher to Tingri over the Lalung La at 5050 metres and we hoped that from there, at least, we would be able to see Menlungtse and the larger peaks flanking it, Cho Oyu and Gyachung Kang.

The view of the mountain peaks behind Nyalam was much too magnificent for the town which itself was dust and concrete dressed with rubbish and excrement. It resembled a deserted spaghetti Western film set. The dark sinister Tibetans stood silently in their bulky yak-skin jackets and trousers and gazed at us. The skins had been turned inside out, and their tailoring was basic. Their own skin was grey from dust and ingrained dirt. They held utterly blank expressions and even when the wind gusted and I could feel my own body react to the cold, not even their eyelids flinched. These were hard and long suffering people; their history dictated that.

It was difficult to imagine, in such a stagnant place, that there was once bloodshed on a horrific scale. It is clear that over a million Tibetans were killed as a result of the Chinese occupation throughout the last forty years. Most died during the clashes of Mao's People's Liberation Army and the Tibetan rebellion in the 1950s when the Dalai Lama fled but the killings had continued during the 1960s as the Red Army controlled the so called 'democratic reforms' in the Cultural Revolution. Such annihilation amounted to about twenty per cent of the entire Tibetan population, and even today it is difficult to find a Tibetan who has not lost at least one member of his or her family at the hands of the Chinese. The attempted destruction of the Buddhist religion is also staggering. Today there are less than one per cent of the pre-occupation monasteries and shrines still standing.

I wondered how Francis felt about these facts. During the Cultural Revolution his parents, both academics, had been subjected to compulsory and sustained periods of heavy manual labour. I did not doubt that he found their treatment absurdly illogical if not wholly barbaric, but what I was unsure of was his regard on a personal level for the Tibetans. Interestingly, Francis was a religious person, a Christian, and I suspected that he would have more empathy for the Tibetans than most contemporary atheist Chinese. But Francis's demanding and temperamental manner concealed his feelings, so too did his reluctance to divulge his political views.

In the evening we visited what is undoubtedly Nyalam's only restaurant. The menu said noodles, or would have done had there been one. This is what we were told we could eat. The compound where we stayed was damp and cold with rodents' droppings on the floor and beds. Yet I felt, as on the Chogolisa expedition, enormously content, and there was no other place that I wanted to be in.

Early the next morning we started our lonely climb to even greater heights, my head still thumping from the current altitude. I reminded myself that Ken Rawlinson, a climber from the Newcastle area on an expedition to Everest in 1984 had developed oedema in the Tingri basin, where we were heading, and that the team had been unable to evacuate him as that would have meant driving him back up over the Lalung La.

Ken only just survived, but many of the others in the team had thought that he was probably going to die, Alan Hinkes one of them. My own insurance was Dr Charlie Clarke, who had sat himself in the truck for the journey. He looked subdued by the altitude, but not ill. Next to him Steve Shea looked grim, especially so wearing one of his disposable industrial dust masks.

The atmosphere of Tibet was powerful. Nigel Meakin, the BBC man, spent much of his journey looking through his camera lens. There were so few features, yet so much to absorb. We passed small dry-stone-walled settlements on the road. Sun-bleached prayer flags fluttered against the tall posts to which they were attached. Irrigation here had nurtured a splash of green, reeds tall and rocking in the breeze. We also passed more black cloaked Tibetan men and women, some with yaks on the end of a rope, who smiled as we passed and waved their sticks at us serenely. Some shouldered wooden ploughs, though I could not see what they were growing. Their ears were studded with colour; greeny blue of turquoise and red of coral. Their yaks were also colourfully decorated and as they fell forward with each heavy step, bells around their necks hidden under thick rough hair jangled melodically. My initially unfavourable impressions of Tibet were quickly being dispelled.

Our road climbed near the dwindling waters of the Po Chu, one of the main feeder tributaries of the Sun Kosi. After the col, the road would lose height, whilst following the course of the Nien Chu that drained to the north and then east. It would be tempting to assume that the col, indeed the whole Himalayan chain, provided a watershed between those rivers that flow south to the mighty deltas of the Indian and Arabian Oceans and those that bleed to the north, to the Pacific or Arctic Oceans. But it is an extraordinary fact of the geography of Asia that the major rivers of the Indian subcontinent have their source to the *north* of the great Himalayan chain, that is so often, mistakenly, likened to a barrier. Indeed most of these rivers have their origins here in Tibet, which in view of the desert climate, and hence rather modest precipitation, is even more remarkable.

The Indus makes an incredible westward sweep penetrating through the Himalaya in Indian Kashmir, a natural extension of Tibet, and on to Baltistan. Symbolically, at least, these waters have carried Buddhism; Skardu was once Buddhist, but is now Islamic. The Indus cuts a deep gorge around Nanga Parbat and flows to Karachi to debouch into the Arabian Sea. Similarly the Brahmaputra, which is fed by the Tsangpo, in turn fed by the Nien Chu on the other side of our col, had forcibly cut a deep gorge around another sentinel at the other end of the

Himalaya, Namcha Barwa, at 7756 metres the highest and most coveted unclimbed mountain in the world. From here the river flows to the Bay of Bengal. The Ganges and Sutlej take an even more audacious line, slashing directly through the Himalaya. It is, for me, a strangely comforting thought, that such an awesome natural wonder as the highest chain of mountains in the world can not suppress the water that brings life to millions of Indian people.

For these rivers to follow such a difficult and unobvious route, one has to assume that they have a history older than the Himalaya, and that the incredibly deep gorges are a result of the fierce erosion of water cutting down simultaneously as the land rose, like the Grand Canyon in the United States. There is little doubt that the Himalaya was formed when the continent of India, as a result of continental drift and plate tectonics, collided around fifty million years ago with the Asian continent. Compression of the boundary sediments that had no escape route downward into the earth's crust piled up, folded and faulted, and were uplifted to form a monstrous ridge, much higher even than the present nine kilometres elevation of the Himalaya. The upper slopes of Everest house shallow sea sediments, some are relict river delta deposits. During this monumental struggle the Asian continent overrode the Indian continent, thus raising the height of the area yet further. Tibet, as I was witnessing, was an impressively lofty place.

John-Paul had an expression, 'in the can'. It represented a state of satisfaction that came each time he recorded something and sealed it out of harm's way in the canister. No matter what disaster struck, he knew that he had something at least to take back to London to edit. The more he had 'in the can' the happier JP became, and it explained why he became happier and happier as each day of filming passed. Hence it was no surprise that he leapt from his seat when we approached the Lalung La to organise some more filming.

'Stop! Stop!' he screamed.

He and his cameraman and sound recordist bailed out and set up to film the passing of the truck. The truck driver, in his innocence, did not know that to look at the camera while it was running was a sin, worse than using exposed film as toilet paper. Charlie, in the passenger seat, did his best to communicate to the driver that he should look straight ahead. However, the sight of the producer leaping on the spot behind the tripod waving his arms frantically to convey the same message was too intriguing for our Tibetan driver who stared in pitiful disbelief at JP.

'Cut! Cut!' JP screamed.

107

JP asked the driver to reverse the truck down the hill and repeat the exercise. But the second time no lessons had been learnt.

'Cut! Cut!'

All this was happening at 5000 metres while I sat in the minibus, that JP thankfully didn't want to film, holding my throbbing head as gently as I could in my hands in an effort not to move it. Eventually the driver got bored, and finding JP very childish decided to ignore him.

'At last!' cried JP into the recording microphone.

'Cut! Cut!' cried Arthur, the sound recordist.

From the col we looked out on an array of high Himalayan mountains. Xixabangma was most obvious, monolithic and starkly beautiful to the west. To the south our horizon was jagged like broken glass, gleaming in the sun. David Breashears tried to pick out the peaks: Cho Oyu, Menlungtse, Gauri Sankar; but I could not recognise any of them. The problem was not the view, nor David, but me. The altitude had overpowered me.

David O'Neil, the photographer for the *Mail on Sunday*, declared he wanted a group picture of us walking in line, whilst he would try to frame us all in a picture with the mountains behind.

'This is a road, David!' Chris said. 'What would we be doing walking on a bloody road when we've got a bus?'

In order to make the notion less absurd, David asked us to put rucsacs on and each carry ski sticks. The photo would silhouette us against the backdrop and the road, he assured us, would not show in the photograph. I could barely walk, let alone carry a rucsac and walk in pace with the others. Steve was worse and could barely stand up.

'Chris at the front,' David directed, 'all else filing behind.'

Not only was it high where our photographer wanted to arrange his shot, but on the most exposed point of the entire journey; it was also deathly cold. A sharp wind ripped across the plateau and over the col, tearing through the madly flapping prayer flags. In order to keep warm I had to run on the spot, except I couldn't because even the slightest exercise sent hammers in my head into spasms of gay abandon and my lungs gasping for breath, a phenomenon that Shea had inelegantly termed 'sucking wind'.

Through my distress I had to admire David, for his fitness was remarkable. A professional who knew exactly what his newspaper wanted, in his mind's eye he had already laid out the front page of the next fortnight's edition, and he ran around the lunar boulders juggling his Nikon lens as if at Billy Smart's Circus at sea level. When he had us organised, a feat in itself, he shouted, 'Okay, walk,' and we all tried to look as natural as possible, as if we had walked on roads like this all the way from Kathmandu. David lay twenty metres away in the dust with a long lens like a game stalker with a gun and disposed of a roll of film through his autowind.

'Again,' he shouted.

In Tingri he developed the films and showed us the negatives. The pictures *were* brilliant and were in fact used in the newspaper with the caption 'marching to Base Camp', or something to that effect. 'Getting his shot' was nothing new for David. In order to get a picture of Lester Piggott in jail he had once spent several hours up a tree waiting for the man to come into view. But his greatest picture of all was going to be of the yeti. For this he had devised a sophisticated trip-wire mechanism that he was going to put in place between three trees in the yeti's favourite habitat, the rhododendron forest. If the taut cotton threads were so much as breathed on the cameras would be sent into a frenzy of excitement, flash guns and motor winds and all. A whole film would be exposed in about ten seconds. The speed at which the yeti could run would determine the size of its retreating arse in each frame.

Tingri, at about 4350 metres, was a welcome place for our next night halt. There should have been ninety yaks ready there for the next stage of our journey. There were none. It reinforced my personal hunch that the Tibetan authorities were clueless as to our whereabouts, as did Francis's renewed excitement and *en passant* comments such as 'Keep out of sight' and 'Stay in the compound'. Accommodation in Tingri was a military camp that we shared with about thirty rather miserable looking soldiers. A wall surrounded the small assembly of buildings with an iron gate, that was locked at night. Charlie immediately took over the compound kitchen and with Krishna and Nima set about preparing what was to be a superb meal.

Most sizeable settlements in Tibet, I was learning, were characterised by a discord of harsh concrete barracks, such as these, and the rather more ethnic, though equally unattractive housing of the indigenous Tibetans. Ruins of only partially destroyed monasteries crowning the villages were not uncommon sights also.

The soldiers here lived at a similar altitude to the Baltoro garrison in Pakistan, though the difference in their environments was extreme. We were nestled up against the base of a small rocky hill. The plain in front of us stretched for several miles out across a desolate valley. The plain, partially a dry bog, was fed by three rivers, the Nien Chu, Laba Chu and Ra Chu and because of this was well drained. The area was carpeted with grass and scrub, a continuous cloth of pale green. Above the plain rose Everest. Ours was the exclusive view that the pre-war British expeditions had enjoyed. The upper slopes of the mountain were dark, still devoid of snow after being stripped by the winter jet stream winds. Contrary to most mountains, I smirked, thinking I had made a great discovery, many of the Himalayan giants are white in summer and black in winter. Two of our team had been to the summit; Chris and David Breashears, whilst another four had been on its slopes, including one of our BBC crew, Arthur Chesterman, who was sound recordist on the South-West Face in 1975. Equally impressive, Cho Oyu, the world's sixth summit, also rose above our plain, its huge unclimbed North Face staring blankly at us.

Chris and Francis prepared their yak-procuring plan and would leave in the morning on a two-day tour of local settlements and their headmen. The White Horse Scotch was once more to be crucial in their negotiations. We could see that on Everest the weather was perfect. No plume stretched from its summit. Menlungtse would be having the same fine conditions. How long could this weather last? Thoughts like this are common on expeditions. Rather than be thankful for the currently settled weather I became impatient to be where I could capitalise on it. I argued with myself that a season can only have so many fine days and that more now meant less later. Nonsense, of course.

Tingri was not exactly our roadhead. The yaks from this place would travel unladen for sixty kilometres to a point beyond Kyetrak at about 4700 metres where it is common for expeditions to Cho Oyu to site their Base Camp. We could make this journey in the truck in two shifts. From there we would begin our walk over the Fusi La at about 5200 metres to the small village, Chang bu Jiang at barely 3000 metres in the Rongshar valley which drains southward, eventually crossing the border into Nepal to feed the Sun Kosi. If there were no political obstacles, it would be so easy to reach Chang bu Jiang from the south, perhaps in only three days from the village of Charikot on the road to Jiri. In fact there is a road of sorts that extends all the way to Chang bu Jiang. It was laid by the Chinese during the Sino-Indian border dispute of 1962–3 when a small garrison was built in the village. The road is only negotiable for two months a year, during the summer, when the warm monsoon rains are sufficient to wash enough snow from the Fusi La for a tractor to force a way through. The route that we were about to follow was in fact a busy trading route, taken by hundreds of yaks carrying wood from the low lying forests around Chang bu Jiang for building in the barren wastes of Tibet.

We waited an entire day in Tingri. Hinkes and I found a shop. Above the door a notice said: WELCOME TO DANDAS SHOP. LAST SHOP BEFORE EVEREST. We bought some sweets and gave them to the myriad kids in return for photographs of them. In the afternoon I walked out on my own onto the plain and took some shots of Everest. The day was hot and the grass dry so I lay myself out and slept for a few luxurious hours. My headache had passed, and I was able to absorb unreservedly the aura of my vast and silent surroundings.

10

With yaks to Base Camp

Chris and Francis had been successful. In a single day they had acquired eighty-nine yaks to make the journey as far as Chang bu Jiang, where we would use the local fleet to take us to Base Camp. The yaks, with their herdsmen, had already set out for the Cho Oyu Base Camp. In the morning on the 16th, half-laden with gear and people, the truck left Tingri of the first of two shifts, carrying the BBC team of three, Alan, and the climbing team of four. Predictably, JP insisted that we stop frequently to film events. The driver, fast becoming a film star, needed no rehearsals now and rose to the occasion, weaving across streams and ditches, sometimes stopping to inspect the ground ahead with as much diligence as a cricketer inspecting his wicket. Quite often we drove for kilometres at a time without seeing the road. And not once did he look at the camera.

'What a team!' cried JP.

Straight ahead Cho Oyu grew bigger as each kilometre passed. On its right lay the Nangpa La, a huge trough that parted the mountains. Less than thirty kilometres beyond was Namche Bazar, the famous Sherpa village in the heart of the Khumbu. We were almost back in Nepal.

Even before we reached the site of the Cho Oyu Base Camp, snow had appeared on the ground and in places drifted across our route. Worried that he might over-commit his truck, the driver at last stopped and we bailed out. We were about ten kilometres from the Nangpa La, about six from the Fusi La, on the right. Jobo Rapsam, an elegant snowy peak of 6750 metres rose behind the Fusi La. It occurred to me, as we erected tents for sleeping and the cook tent for Krishna and Nima, that we had not seen any yaks since leaving Tingri. Chris was confident that they would appear the next day, so I did not let their absence worry me. It was decidedly cold and a sharp wind, unobstructed by the landscape, flapped over the tents. We were at about 4700 metres and I found it difficult to sleep. It was satisfying to think that for this night, and the next two, we would be at altitudes higher even than at Base Camp.

The next morning, with still no sight of the yaks, Steve and I climbed up above our camp onto a rocky knoll for some bouldering and scrambling, and for a view back down towards Tingri. We reached the top after about an hour. The moves on the rock were just difficult enough to merit caution. Now, from the summit, we realised there was no easier way down, and I was suddenly conscious of how much more difficult it is to climb down than up, especially in a pair of sneakers. The effort of climbing had proved exhausting.

'I'm maxed,' said Shea, which meant he was tired.

We found a chorton, a Tibetan-built cairn of stones, neatly constructed with a collection of battered tall reeds splaying out decoratively from its top. Weathered prayer flags lay here too. I wondered how often this place was visited and when the last person had stood here. Looking towards Tingri we could see yaks, spread out in a small black moving smear on the valley floor. We stayed for a few minutes sheltered from the wind by the chorton looking up at Cho Oyu and admired how a mountain so huge could also be so graceful. In the afternoon the yaks arrived. Their herders, about fifteen in number, erected tents, two pieces of cloth draped over a simple frame of sticks, and sat inside them to cook. Their diet was simple, minute quantities of yak butter tea, smoked yak meat and tsampa, a homogenous compound of maize and highland barley. They made tsampa balls in large numbers and shared them with their animals, three each for the yaks and one each for themselves. For a flame they burned yak dung. The smoke filled the tents and drifted through their matted black hair and yak-skin clothing. Their herd dispersed far across the terrain and I wondered how long it would take them to round them all up again.

In the morning we distributed loads to the yak herders who became fantastically argumentative. Francis was by no means conversational in Tibetan. Nima and Krishna understood some Tibetan, but their English was too simple and slow to communicate what was being said reliably. The herdsmen knew no Sherpa or Nepali. As each party found that they could not be understood, the level of noise rose. The herdsmen started to wave their arms, and bang their hands down heavily onto the boxes or the ground. Occasionally one of the herders marched over from the group and picked up a box, pretending to be labouring with its weight and dropped it from a great height for effect. I noticed that most of the yaks were so far away that they were indistinguishable.

At two o'clock, after four hours of bartering, a deal was struck.

Everyone dispersed. Jess was left standing, suddenly alone, where he had stood for the entire negotiation. He looked around disbelievingly.

'Where are they?' he said.

'What?'

'The bloody yaks!'

It took the herders two hours to round up their animals and another hour to load them with our gear. I noticed that the negotiations had given the herders strength, for they appeared to handle the loads with considerably more ease than before. Indeed some were able to toss the boxes on to their backs and run for hundreds of metres after their unwilling yaks. It was mid-afternoon before we left and it made no difference to the herders that they had agreed with Jess to camp that night beyond the Fusi La. Two hours of slow walking would be quite enough for that day.

We followed the road up onto a large terrace, about two kilometres from the Fusi La. Steve and I arrived to find many of the yaks being unloaded and Jess sitting on the grass looking depressed. I didn't share his concern and was very happy to stop for the night. JP had blessed me with the camera tripod which he had overlooked finding a porter for. Its weight alone had exhausted me. My headache had returned and also for the first time I felt a little nauseous. With relief I watched the first of the tents being erected.

The views to Cho Oyu and into Nepal through the Nangpa La were the finest I had seen. Hinkes and I climbed up a small slope above the camp for uninterrupted views but the exertion left me speechless and I screwed up my face with the pain of complaint from my head. When I did not appear at the cook tent for dinner, Chris brought me a drink of tea and some food.

'Got to look after my climbing partner,' he said, handing me a drink of something hot. He was squatting in the doorway. 'How are you?'

'Fine,' came the automatic reply.

We had never actually discussed climbing partners, or whether indeed we would climb in pairs at all, but his assumption was a fair one. I was touched by his concern, even though his pampering made me feel pathetic. Outside the tent a reddish hue painted the bleak panorama with an unearthly glow in keeping with an ever more illuminating journey. Doped with Panadol, I slept fitfully through the night.

My health improved over the next three days as we dipped over the pass and descended towards Chang bu Jiang. The pass was exposed to a stinging wind coming from the south. Prayer flags flapped madly. I walked backwards, leaning into the current. The herders threw me a curious glance. Their own bodies were contorted by the wind, but their faces were dead pan, composed and unsuffering. As we descended from the pass the wind subsided and we waded through snow inelegantly. Some of the yaks plunged up to their bellies and recovered with an explosion of energy. Further on, the cover became thin again. Lichen appeared on the rocks and grasses lay low in sheltered niches. The walking was effortless. As David commented, it was 'great to open up'.

On the 20th Chris and Francis covered two stages of walking in one day, organising our second batch of yaks and herders. The rest of us ambled along at the yak's constant three kilometres per hour pace, slowly adjusting to the greener landscape, a result of lower altitude and a wetter climate. Despite the improvement in terrain as we descended, the yaks never seemed to pick up speed. Nor were they allowed to falter. If one did, a rock, thrown with superb accuracy, would jolt it into action and send our loads winging into the air. We passed high cliffs in the valley, thousand-metre sentinels of granite. David and Steve enjoyed picking lines for climbing, craning their necks and pointing high into the sky.

Chang bu Jiang was a beautiful terraced village above the river. Tight pathways meandered about its stone-built houses and juniper bushes. We erected our sleeping and cooking tents on a dusty flat area and also put up our mess tent, a bright blue and yellow five-metre geodesic dome. For the three hundred or so villagers it might as well have been a spaceship. For some we were the first Westerners they had ever seen. The young children were most inquisitive, at times annoyingly so. Chris made the mistake of producing his Polaroid camera and taking a few pictures. Soon he had the whole village clambering around him. Many of the women offered to go to bed with him in exchange for a picture, often communicating their proposition graphically, and pulling him with all their strength.

'Ladies, please!' said the debonair Bonington. 'One at a time!' Except, one at a time, would have meant next month before we made it to Base Camp. I was amazed.

'What do they see in the old knacker?' I said to Hinkes's back. He was already walking towards Chris.

'Let me have a go with that thing,' he pleaded.

This was Sherpa life. Although Tibetan, this village, its crops, its architecture, its people's promiscuity, were typical of many Sherpa villages in Nepal, whose border was just a few kilometres downstream. We all welcomed the opportunity of seeing inside the homes of these warm people, accepting their hospitality and drinking their chang, a milky-coloured alcoholic drink, fermented from millet. Most of us got very drunk.

115

Chris and Jess were gathering the necessary yaks for the final stages to Base Camp, helped by a villager Chris had met the previous year. Kusang had left the village when he was old enough, before the Sino-Indian war, to go to Calcutta where his uncle owned a small shop, and where he learnt English. In around 1970 he received a letter to say his mother was very ill and he returned to Chang bu Jiang, where he married. Of his five children, two had died at birth and another as a young infant. His new baby son, just a few months old, over whom he doted constantly, was also looking very frail and weak. However, his eighteen-year-old daughter was fit and strong and eventually came with us to Base Camp.

To reach Base Camp we would first descend for two kilometres to the Chue gompa, another vandalised monastery at the confluence of the Menlung Chu and the Rongshar Chu. Climbing up beside the Menlung Chu, we would reach summer yak pastures below the West Face of Menlungtse in three days.

I produced my rock boots and took to some of the numerous boulders. David and Steve came with me, and on most problems David, in his sneakers, got the better of me. JP, Nigel and Arthur came too and, after filming David swarming up an overhanging fist crack, they filmed me, close up, pretending to be looking up at David on the rock and shouting encouragement.

'Go for it!' they made me say. 'Scope it out! *Yes!* Just one more move and it's all over.'

'You feel like a prat, don't you,' Steve said when we had finished.

In the afternoon Steve and I walked down to the Chue gompa. Chris had warned us of what to expect. This monastery had been remote enough to avoid total destruction during the rebellion and Cultural Revolution years. Instead of clinical and absolute eradication, the Chue gompa has been vandalised on a rather casual basis, though the same forces of indoctrination were responsible. The result is even more soul-wrenching. It stands on a high perch above the confluence of waters and commands an impressive view down the Rongshar Gorge to the frontier with Nepal. It is surrounded by vertical cliffs, a thousand metres tall. In its heyday, perhaps two hundred monks would have lived here. Today the Chue gompa is a pathetic sight. Its dignity stolen, it is a meek and poignant reminder of the crass arrogance of those who take power and then abuse it.

From a few hundred metres we could see that the framework of the temple was still intact, suggesting something of its former majesty, but as we approached we began to see the effects of the vandalism. Apart from its inner sanctum, the gompa, it was hollow, and its wooden beams

116

were black charcoal. Rubble was strewn all about, beautiful thanka paintings were splintered and smashed. A school, now deserted, had been built beside the temple and we walked across its yard to reach the monastery. We passed a pile of prayer-engraved slates, most of which had been broken. We looked at the devastation and at each other. Stepping carefully over the ruins, as I made my way towards the gompa, I felt a very strong sense of loss. We hesitated at the door, eventually taking a deep breath and venturing inside. I wondered whether I should remove my shoes. My heart missed a beat. Steve was speechless.

The main Buddha was gone. Presumably the soldiers had taken it for its gold, pearls and other jewels. This was the only value that they recognised. Beside the Buddha throne were figures of others, reincarnate lamas. Their straw-filled bodies were riddled with bullet holes. Some had been ripped from their stances and lay face-down on the floor at our feet. Others had been mutilated with an axe. I tried to put myself in the minds of those who had last seen the gompa in its former beauty before committing it to its present death. It was strange to remember that these people were themselves probably Tibetan. I tried very hard to let myself cry, but I could not. I gathered my grief and did not expel it.

Outside we were met by an old man. Once a monk at the temple, he now lived in the old school. He did not say anything, but looked deeply into our eyes. He clutched a small necklace of wooden beads. His own eyes were glazed with tears, but also with a kind of hope.

'We're very sorry,' Steve said remorsefully and gently, as I had never heard him speak. He held out his hands, to show that we meant no harm. The man pointed to the ruins and then threw his hands down together to simulate the passing of the soldiers, so explicitly that it might have happened yesterday. This was a powerful moment. I could feel my chest tightening.

'This is intense,' Steve said, with wet eyes. Then we left.

It took us an hour to reach Chang bu Jiang. Symbolically for me, the rest of the day was cold and wet, heavy clouds had rolled up the valley.

The others were sorting and counting the loads. Hinkes was pouring paraffin on a fire to burn our rubbish. Tibetan hands were darting into the flame when he turned his back. Charlie looked depressed. One of the boxes was missing. All of the Bath Oliver biscuits had been stolen from under our noses. Charlie had a passion for these. They were, as he told us authoritatively, 'the best expedition biscuit available'.

'He was a failed medical student, you know,' Charlie had said in Tingri.

'Who?'

117

'Doctor Oliver. That's why he took to biscuit-making.'

'Then why was he a doctor?'

He did not know why.

Iain Walker was depressed too. Charlie had examined a teenage girl in the village who was weaker and sadder than the others, and diagnosed a hole in her heart. He doubted that she would live very long, though a simple operation in London could have saved her. Iain suggested that we bring her home.

'She is extremely weak,' Charlie told him. 'The altitude of the Fusi La might kill her.'

'Then we can find another way, a helicopter.'

'There are hundreds of people in Nepal like her, thousands even.'

Charlie was being too dispassionate for Iain's satisfaction. 'I'll cable my editor. Maybe the paper will pay.' And so he did. Hinkes's first dispatch from Base Camp would contain a letter to the *Mail on Sunday*, 'seeking advice' on this matter. Iain had not been deterred by Charlie's clinical cold water.

In the morning the epic began. Ninety yaks, their herders and hundreds of kids gathered around our site. Jess had a masterplan of marrying loads to animals, and the next hour would see it implemented. The tension mounted. We were paranoid. Hinkes, Steve and I were appointed guards. We decided to cordon off the area with one of the ropes. The herders pushed and shoved. In the hub of the chaos was Jess, with a clipboard, Chris, the village Headman, Kusang translating, Francis translating, JP, Nigel and Arthur filming, David with his Nikons. On the fringe of the crowd a fight flared up. One of the herders had thrown a stone at a yak, but not his own. The owner had laid in. Punches were flying. Their wives stepped in. They were angry. The men froze.

'I don't blame you, mate!' Alan said to himself. 'I wouldn't mess with *her*.'

Kusang wanted to please us, so was negotiating as much as translating. The villagers felt betrayed. Tempers blazed further. Hands came thumping down on boxes. Standing on a boulder, with an air of detachment, watching all of this, I found the scene slightly comical. Until I noticed that the rope had been cut.

'Look at what these buggers have done!' I called to Hinkes.

'The *little* toe-rags!' he exclaimed.

Yet out of chaos came order. Laden yaks began to migrate from the village. Jess had triumphed, though the yak herders had not been totally outdone. As Jess said into Nigel's camera, 'They're really friendly happy people . . . And then they shaft you.'

At the Chue gompa we turned left and headed uphill again. We passed yaks coming the other way burdened with wood, eventually destined for Tingri and beyond. The path was narrow, the drop on the right into the Menlung Chu steep. In places tangled rhododendron threatened to trip us up. We stopped to camp in a clearing. On the other side of the river, above the forest, snow slopes swept cleanly upward into cloud.

'What are those slopes attached to?' I asked Chris.

'That's Gauri Sankar.'

'We're almost there then!'

'Yes,' he said calmly.

That afternoon through the clouds we glimpsed Menlungtse itself. It looked outrageously steep. Its sight threw our purpose back into focus. So this is why we have come so far, I thought to myself. We could not see the main summit, but the lower, West summit, ahead, easily fixed my gaze. It was so tall, and elegant! So much rock!

'It's awesome,' David Breashears muttered with stunned breath.

Though our interest was in the other summit and the East Ridge, I studied the headwall of the West Face with prolonged interest. Our view swept obliquely across it. Chris had awakened to his childlike excitement and scurried to where I had the telescope rigged.

'There's a way through that,' I told him. The headwall of the West Face was the obstacle to the West summit, and the reason why Chris had suggested the direct route to the East summit on the other side. 'The rock is riddled with ice smears and chimneys. It'll definitely go!'

'Let me see, let me see.' Bonington found it difficult to curb his excitement, as he pressed his eye against the glass. His mouth opened a little with his concentration. 'Umm. Yes indeed! Maybe you're right. Maybe that *is* the key.'

'But the East Ridge is okay?' I said, looking for confirmation.

'Yes, yes. I think it's better.' He tried, but failed, to sound convincing. 'I think we should have a look at it first.'

I slept lightly that night, anxious to hurry to the base of the mountain and soak up its views and possibilities. In the morning I was up and out of camp more quickly than usual, and by midday I had left the forest and was moving swiftly among the scrub towards Garu, the site of the previous year's Base Camp. I marvelled at the mountain. Its North-West Face came into view and was fantastically impressive, a pyramidal smooth granite wall, near impossible to climb. The West Face, on the right, consisted of steep rock buttresses, separated by snow-filled gullies, leading to a formidable band of séracs at half-height. From these a relentless sweep of smooth green glistening ice led in about 800 metres

119

to the final steepening 300-metre high headwall of granite, absolutely vertical at its top. The West summit was perched neatly above on the right. On the left the East summit winked at me. It was below the level of the West summit, though only because it was two kilometres behind. I was looking across the North Face of the mountain. I could not see it all but what I saw immediately below the summit was representative; a jungle of séracs and fluted snow, a playground for avalanches. On every angle the mountain was steep and impressively defended.

Next morning there was snow on the ground, too much for the yaks to move and risk snow blindness. Steve, David and Chris used the day to progress to the upper meadows below the West Face and decide on the exact position for our Base Camp. I crossed the valley and climbed as high as I could on Gauri Sankar's lower slopes to look in more detail at the headwall of the West Face. I had become very attracted to it. At about 4700 metres I stopped and sat on the slope facing Menlungtse. Even before I had stopped panting, I directed the binoculars on the mountain. My jaw dropped. Running right through the headwall was a continuous smear of ice.

'Incredible!' I said out loud. 'That has *got* to be the route.'

I looked about, momentarily embarrassed. I was quite alone. Below me, riding thermals above the tiny collection of tents was a huge lammergeier, almost three metres from wingtip to wingtip. My eyes followed it upwards, until it was above me circling higher and higher. I did not see it flap its wings. I jumped to my feet and skipped back to camp. It had been a fruitful sojourn.

11

A fruitful inspection

On 27th April we established Base Camp, a small village of dome tents beneath the West Face. We chose a flat grassy site affording beautiful views to Menlungtse, Gauri Sankar and smaller peaks flanking the Menlung La. By way of the Menlung La, Nima could have reached Beding, his own Nepalese village, in a single day.

Kusang and Dung, who the BBC had employed in Chang bu Jiang to help with their filming, strung out prayer flags between the two highest projecting boulders and gathered us together for another puja. I concentrated very hard on the ceremony, throwing the rice I was given as high in the air as I could. This, I thought, might increase our chances of success. The event was less sophisticated than in the Boudhanath Temple but, if anything, it was more atmospheric and meaningful with the mountain looming up behind us.

Charlie had just completed the final touches to the interior layout of his tent, home for the next few weeks, when the first avalanche came roaring off the West Face.

'Fuck my boots!' he exclaimed, scampering from his tent.

A sérac immediately above us on the face had collapsed. The billowing plume grew and grew. Its power fixed me to the spot. Cracking and booming it came. Nima and Krishna darted from their cook tent. Everyone was watching now, trying to gauge its threat, deciding whether or not to run for it. To panic and scarper would not look cool – on the other hand, it could be sensible. After a few seconds I had convinced myself that it would not reach us, and began to enjoy the spectacle. So had everyone else. Half a minute passed before the air was silent again, and a thin veil of icy mist came sweeping through camp and tranquillity returned. An hour later Charlie's tent had disappeared. He had moved home to behind a boulder at the back of our village.

Next morning, on the 28th, Charlie announced, by way of self-

121

deprecation, that he had been lost the previous night for half an hour trying to walk the fifty metres back to his tent through the mist and darkness from the metre-deep toilet that Hinkes had dug. I admired his devotion to team morale. He also declared that he had brought a homebrew beer kit. He and Iain kicked it into action, much to everyone's approval. Over a kilogramme of sugar was used as fuel.

'Two to three weeks,' he informed us.

'Just about the time you'll be returning, Hinkes,' I said to Alan. 'We'll have a piss up when you arrive with our letters.'

The weather was perfect and a beautiful unclimbed mountain rose up above us. It was a mountain that Alan did not doubt we would climb. Now he had to return to Kathmandu. Being salaried by the *Mail on Sunday* was of little consolation. Here was a prize that he was turning his back on. He had always known that it was not his for the taking, but nevertheless he was jealous. He made no bones about that, as he shouldered his twenty-five-kilo sack and set off, carrying letters home, copy for the newspaper, films and personal luggage. He walked non-stop, passing through Chang bu Jiang that day and up the steepening track onto the snow beneath the Fusi La by moonlight. The next day he reached the site of the Cho Oyu camp. It was deserted. He stopped for a few hours before putting his head down and pounding the remaining seventy kilometres to Tingri in a single push. Hinkes was no slouch.

My greatest wish was to see the East Ridge. To reach a decent viewpoint, we would have to walk for only a few hours around the south side of the mountain. Chris, Steve, David and I agreed to leave on a recce the next day.

'Let's use today to acclimatise some more,' Chris had suggested. 'Then tomorrow we can leave early and return the same day.' Nobody could argue with his logic.

Charlie decreed that we could use hill food whilst on this recce. He prepared a high-altitude picnic of the most wonderful fare: pâté, Primula cheese, oatcakes, chocolate. No matter how inventive Krishna and Nima were, they could not have curbed my fondness for these western luxuries. We left before dawn, heading for the snout of the glacier at the end of our meadow. Above, we found that we could easily traverse across it to a terrace on the south side, the true left bank. From here we walked quickly towards its far end. In profile was the East Ridge that Bonington, in a weak moment, had said was our best chance of success. I reserved judgement until later.

Other views were opening up. We could see the Dingjung La, where Shipton and Ward had first seen Menlungtse. Immediately above us was a stunning little peak, simply Point 6301 on the map. On the left we could see down onto the glacier; ice and water, rock and dust. We stopped at the end of the terrace. I was panting from the exertion.

'Who's got the bins?' David inquired.

Chris had. He was looking at the ridge. 'Uumm' he muttered uneasily. Then he passed them to David.

'Chris, it's ridiculous! We can't climb that!'

'It does look a bit hard.'

'Hard! Look at it, it's falling to bits!' He gave the glasses to Steve, and to me in turn.

The crest of the ridge was a serrated knife-edge of apparently soft and unstable snow. It was heavily corniced. On the only side of the ridge that we could see, smooth granite, too steep to hold snow, swept relentlessly for over a thousand metres. It did not merit our further investigation. I remembered what Jim Fotheringham had said about this ridge and found it strange that Chris should have been so confident.

'It's got to be the West Face,' I opined.

'And then the traverse,' David finished it off.

I remembered Doug Scott's pictures from Xixabangma that suggested the traverse between the summits would be mostly on snow with few technical problems.

Chris had already been thinking. 'We can't be sure, but it does, yes, look hopeful,' he said deliberately. 'Let's go onto the frontier ridge behind camp to acclimatise. We'll get a better look at the face. There, up there.' He pointed to the ridge that came down from the eastern shoulder of Gauri Sankar. 'If we like it, great. If we don't, let's look again behind that ridge.' He looked back at the East Ridge.

'Sounds great,' Steve said positively. He was always fast to voice his approval about things he liked. It made those who he was addressing feel comfortable.

We walked briskly back to camp, excited that we had formulated a plan of action. Behind camp there was a small bump at about 5800 metres on the frontier ridge. Chris studied it through his binoculars. 'Why don't we climb that? It'll be a first ascent! We'll christen it Kusang's Peak,' he decreed.

The BBC could not stay at Base Camp very long. The delays in Kathmandu had crippled their schedule. They were planning to leave in a few days and spend some time with Charlie in the forests of the Menlung Chu. Their task was not to find the yeti, or even to look for it, but to make a film about trying. JP appeared to have the whole film script written in his head before we even arrived at camp. The more attention he paid to filming, the further he divorced himself from what his viewers thought he was doing, at least his more gullible ones. He had already filmed Kathmandu, the walk-in and around Base Camp. Now he needed more yeti-hunting footage. He had filmed some yeti-searching, with Charlie collecting faeces on the meadow.

'Ah, I wonder what this can be,' Charlie had said, right on cue, bending down to place a large turd into a plastic freezer bag. 'Lucky I didn't stand in it.'

JP found some intriguing tracks in the snow above camp. He had taken Kusang along for a closer look. These he couldn't ignore. He badly wanted these in the can.

'What are these tracks, Kusang?' JP had said, panting from the altitude. Kusang appeared dumbfounded. 'They're not *big* prints are they?' Kusang seemed to be pondering and examining the tracks, JP willing him on. 'Definitely not yak or snow leopard, are they?'

'No, these are from chuti.'

'And what is a chuti?'

'A chuti is a small yeti.'

'A small yeti,' said JP. 'Well, I never!'

On Menlungtse, David would carry his small Bell and Howell 16mm camera for high-altitude footage, so all that the BBC really needed now was to film us, looking purposefully at the mountain and then packing our rucsacs, pretending to leave on our climb. They also asked each of us to say a few words into the camera about our hopes and fears. JP's half-joking suggestion that he film us on Kusang's Peak and screen it as if on the lower slopes of Menlungtse, was dismissed as 'unethical' by Chris.

They filmed Chris, Steve, David and me leaving for Kusang's Peak. JP, Nigel and Arthur were above us as they started to film. Upon reaching a large, but avoidable patch of snow, Chris and the Americans had gone around the side. I had gone straight on. After ten metres I was floundering up to my thighs. Nigel turned the camera on me. This will make great viewing, he thought. I could feel the lens zooming in. I started to grin. What? Embarrassed? Me? Ha, don't be ridiculous! I thought about going back, but that, I concluded would make me look even more stupid. What would the viewers think? So I soldiered on. Next thing, I was in a pitiful struggle up to my waist. JP was rubbing his hands in glee. Every time I stood up, the snow under my feet collapsed and I fell back onto the seat of my pants. It was as good as a scene from *Fawlty Towers*. My boots and clothes were full of snow. JP was willing Nigel on. 'Keep filming!' I eventually crawled and staggered out of the snow.

'Okay, how much?' I joked with JP.

'What for?'

'You know, how much? You're the editor, right?'

'Oh, I doubt I'll put *that* in. This is a serious programme!'

We decided to camp quite high on the lower slopes and then in the early morning climb our modest summit, returning all the way back down to Base Camp during the rest of the day. We carried twenty kilos. After three hours we reached a suitably flat site for the tents at about 5200 metres. Menlungtse stunned me with its beauty, bathed in Alpenglow. Our tents were customised versions of the ones I had used on Chogolisa – single skin Gore-tex Mountain Geminis. They had poles on the inside that could be erected, if necessary, while both people were inside the tent. They also had an optional snowhole entrance which offered greater space inside for storing rucsacs or stretching legs. Nevertheless two people were a tight fit and, as tent partners, Chris and I were having our teething problems.

'Why are you so restless? Can't you sleep?' Chris demanded.

'No, I can't.'

'Well just lie still then. Or if you must fidget, keep it on your side of the tent.'

We slept in opposing directions, head to feet. It gave us more room. It also diluted the shock of my first experience of Chris's snoring. On the walk-in it had guaranteed him a tent to himself, when Jess, after first trying ear-plugs, had fled.

'Oh, was I snoring? Sorry, mate,' he said cheerfully, in the morning. 'Don't be afraid to give me a shove in the night. I won't wake up.'

Pity, I thought. 'Yes, I might just do that.'

We left at two in the morning. Chris and I were ahead of the Americans. We groped up the snow slopes, weaving in and out of rocky outcrops. We were roped, though moving together. Soon I had led us onto a rocky buttress. We slowed down and David and Steve caught us up.

'It looked easy from Base Camp.'

'It is,' David said, addressing a pool of light above him. 'There's a snow slope up this way!' He paused. 'And which of you guys was snoring last night?'

I reversed the pitch, and we recoiled the ropes and followed on behind the others, who had continued on the snow, taking their turn at trail-breaking.

We continued on elegant snow flutings and occasionally steep ice up towards the frontier ridge with Nepal. When dawn came we were

125

The upper 1200 metres of the route to the West summit of Menlungtse.
The route up to 5800 metres is hidden behind the North-West Ridge.

rewarded with impressive views over the Rolwaling ranges. I was surprised and pleased at how much height we had gained. Some mixed climbing on the ridge itself led us to the top of our rocky bump at 5753 metres. There were no clouds in the Menlung valley, though plenty in Nepal, and our view to the West Face of Menlungtse was unobstructed. It was still shaded. The technical problems of climbing appeared to rest in the upper section, the granite headwall and the bare green ice beneath. I knew what that ice would be like, hard, brittle and requiring constant and strenuous front-pointing. What we wanted to avoid most of all was unnecessary traversing on that ice. Therefore route-finding below it was crucial, as we needed to approach the weakness on the headwall, the icy gully that I had already studied, from directly beneath.

We were roughly level with a band of séracs running across the face at mid-height. There seemed to be a kind of terrace above these, and we guessed that we could easily traverse at that level. Thus it was possible, we deduced, to reach the centre of the face, immediately below the headwall, by moving across from the North-West Ridge on the left. As there was an obvious shelf on the ridge at that height, this seemed to be a logical move. Certainly we did not want ever to climb beneath the séracs, which had already proved themselves to be unstable. We assumed that we could climb the ridge to the shelf. David was studying the face discerningly. For reference purposes, he proposed some nomenclature.

'Let's call that shelf on the left the Promontory.'

'Sure thing,' agreed Steve.

I wondered, did the word have a different meaning in America. I didn't risk exposing my ignorance, so kept quiet. We were all watching the face carefully now. Above the terrace there were more séracs, though much less threatening.

'Rather than go up the ridge to avoid those upper séracs,' David paused, '. . . we should make the traverse right from the Promontory and then go up that central line between them.' He was referring to a strip of steep snow, about fifty metres across, that seemed to be unbroken by crevasses or séracs. It led right up onto the upper ice.

'Central Highway,' proposed Steve.

'Great,' agreed David.

What were these guys trying to do? I thought. Climb the face, or name its features? David predicted that we would find a decent site for our tents in one of the last crevasses, behind a sérac, before the green ice. So far so good. From there?

'Shall we go for that gully?' I asked. 'The one in the headwall?' We could see that that line would commit us to some traversing on the ice, but not enough, I thought, to offset the advantage that the gully line presented.

'We can assume that,' Chris said, getting nods from the others. 'Then we can ditch the gear and go lightweight to the main summit and back.' It had been so easy to say.

David returned to the present. 'Let's get down before the snow melts.' We heeled and glissaded our way back to the tents. With heavier sacks we carefully descended to Base Camp. The BBC were just about to leave. I was glad that we were able to see them off. I was going to miss them all.

'See you,' JP said to me. 'I hope you get up.'

'If I do, I'll leave your beads.'

'Good. Then you can come and stay with me and Margaret, and you can tell us about it.'

'I'd love to.' We hadn't discussed what to do if I didn't get up. I decided that in that scenario I would leave the beads somewhere on the mountain anyway.

David O'Neil, the *Mail on Sunday* photographer, also left to spend a few days in the forests on his way home, searching seriously for the yeti, though he was less of a believer in its existence now, than when we had left London.

Jess was thinking of returning with the BBC. Whereas the climbers still had their task ahead of them, Jess had already achieved the bulk of his when the team had arrived at Base Camp, and I could see that the prospect of the next few weeks without projects to manage or problems to solve would be hard for him to come to terms with. We encouraged him to stay but tried to make him feel that he would not be letting us down by leaving. Over the next few days, he decided to stay.

Of the media entourage, we were left with just Iain, the *Mail on Sunday* journalist. Iain was probably the person, outside the team, who was having the most fun. He was genuinely contented in the mountains and isolated with the expedition. This was interesting, considering that he was not already a keen walker, climber, or outdoor enthusiast. His personality was warm and amiable, much helped by his soft Scottish accent. I enjoyed talking to him about his perception of our mountain and the way in which we, the climbers, were reacting to it. If it had not been obvious to Iain before, it certainly was now that our interest lay with the mountain, not the yeti and, whilst maintaining a concern for the latter, he became increasingly involved in Menlungtse, offering to

128

help carry supplies to the base of the mountain. Ultimately, through his backing, he was to help shape the eventual outcome of our expedition.

On 3rd May, everyone at camp, except Francis, Nima and Krishna, set out together towards the base of the North-West Ridge. Iain, Charlie and Jess had offered to carry some of our climbing kit to the base of the route, including our hill tents and stoves. Steve and David intended to make a recce of the first 600 metres of ridge up to the Promontory. They would fix all our ropes, about 360 metres in all, and leave our hardware, including about twenty ice screws, at the top. The idea was to provide a springboard to reach the Promontory comfortably in a day. Chris and I planned to climb to the top of a small peak overlooking the base of the proposed route. Everyone intended to return later that day. Soon after leaving camp I felt the need to relieve myself. I stopped immediately below the face and waited a while to let the others get ahead and around a corner out of sight. A minute later with my trousers around my ankles I heard a sérac peel off the face.

'*Avalanche!*' I screamed. With no time to lose I jumped up and promptly fell flat on my face. '*Aahh!*' I had failed to pull my trousers up. I could not make strides longer than a few centimetres. I heard the roar above me. '*No, No!*' I was really panicking now. I saw burial as the only option. At least let me have my trousers up when they find me, I thought. A flock of bharal, Tibetan blue sheep, had exploded into frenzy, as if a snow leopard had suddenly materialised among them. They darted in all directions. Above I saw the billowing cloud of white snow.

'*Ooowa!*' I started to run. 'Rucsac!' I ran back a few paces and grabbed my sack, like a fool who grabs valuables when fleeing from a house fire. I threw it onto my back and, looking straight ahead, sprinted for what I thought was my life. After half a minute I stopped and turned around. The noise had almost died. The avalanche had been small. Where the sheep had been there was a dusting of snow, but there had never been any chance that the snow could have reached me. 'Still,' I said to myself smugly, quite forgetting that I would have looked like a complete clown to anyone watching, 'you can never be too careful.'

'What are you talking about?' the others said when I caught them up.

'Did you not hear it? A bloody great thing!'

'Yes, we're sure, Andy. Wiped out camp did it?'

'Honestly, a **really** big avalanche.'

When I got back to camp five hours later I asked Francis and Nima if they had seen it. They had, but the others continued to disbelieve me or think that I was wildly exaggerating.

129

From our highpoint of that day Chris and I had seen the line that David and Steve were following. A long snowy couloir of snow and ice led in about 200 metres onto a huge cone of snow. On the left a bottomless gully led through a narrow gap between séracs and finally on to the Promontory. In order to reach this gully it appeared to be necessary to make a long diagonal abseil from the top of the snow cone. Overall it had looked a promising route.

We had returned to Base later in the morning, expecting to move up to the bottom of the mountain the next day. Charlie and Iain arrived at camp at about two o'clock looking very weathered. They told us of an interminable scree slope that they had climbed to a levelling where they left the tents. Jess had stayed with the Americans to help carry gear higher on the mountain and at eight o'clock they arrived, exhausted. They had managed to reach the cone of snow, where they had left the remainder of the rope for fixing. David meticulously described the nature of the snow, the rock and the climbing. He had not seen into the upper gully, as Chris and I had, but instinctively he knew that from the cone it would be better to explore that way, even if initially by abseil, than to force a direct line up the rocky ground above. They were tired from their efforts and wanted a rest day. It should have been obvious from this fact alone that we were not yet ready for a serious attempt. David and Steve were normally so fit that a day's hard effort at relatively low altitude would not make them so tired. We agreed that after a short rest we would return to the ridge, with Chris and me fixing the remainder of the ropes and returning to its base. The day after that we would begin our climb.

David would be filming and, for that purpose, he had several film cartridges, each weighing about 500 grammes which he distributed among us. He would carry the camera. Chris and I as one pair, and David and Steve as another, each shared a Sony Professional Walkman into which we planned to record our thoughts, and other noises consistent with climbing at altitude, such as the crunching of axes in ice, clicking of karabiners and heavy breathing. The weight of these items was equivalent to about two or three days' food and gas. On 5th May, just after dawn, Chris and I left Base Camp. On the tiny path to the bottom of the ridge Chris added a couple of rocks to a small cairn I had previously not remembered seeing.

'Cairns are not allowed,' I said to him.

'What?' He sounded bemused.

'Cairns.'

'Says who?'

'The BMC. The Access and Conservation Committee. They make a mess of the countryside. You're the President.' I had put him on the spot.

'These are Tibetan,' he said flatly. 'These are ethnic cairns.'

Such a response was typical of Chris. If he needed a get-out, then he could be relied upon to find one.

'You ought to be a diplomat.'

'I already am,' he reminded me.

We struggled wearily up the scree to the cache of gear. After a brief rest we continued to the face and pulled ourselves up the ropes. The day was indecisive, not snowing nor warming us with sunshine. The angle of the terrain was steeper than I had imagined, fifty-degree rock slabs, overlain with snow. A broken trail where the others had abseiled down two days previously was still visible. After climbing for 200 metres, we came to the base of the cone of snow where we found more rope for fixing. I led out a long pitch up the cone to its top where it rested against a vertical granite wall. We placed a nut and a piton and abseiled down the vertical step of rock falling away to the left. We dropped about forty metres and found a good belay on the ice beneath. The abseil had felt committing, particularly in the gathering mist. Chris led out the remainder of the rope, fifty metres, and we secured our climbing rope for above. Even though we had no real weight in our rucsacs, I felt exhausted by the effort. We jumared our way back up the rock step and then slid down the ropes. It was eight o'clock before we reached the tents. David and Steve had been there, waiting, for many hours and David came up to the base of the ropes to meet us with a flask of tea.

'We were getting worried about you guys!' he said, as we heeled back down the snow to the tents. The next day we would start on our adventure.

12

The Promontory, Central Highway and beyond

It did not snow in the night. Nor had the wind disturbed our sleep. The morning of 7th May was clear and the gentle wind fresh and welcoming. Nothing could prevent our departure. We left soon after dawn. Although the Promontory, at 5800 metres, was only 700 metres above, 300 metres from the top of our ropes, we knew that the final icy couloir beyond the abseil would be a sun trap in the afternoon. Chris and I were unable to keep up and the Americans pulled ahead of us. It did not matter for each pair was self-sufficient, at least in ascent. We climbed on a single sixty-metre length of rope. When abseiling we planned to tie the two ropes together and descend as a four.

Despite our weariness we reached the snow cone in a fraction of the time it had taken us the day before and in clear weather the abseil down the fixed rope on the rock step was much less intimidating. Looking up from our previous highpoint, the séracs below the Promontory were gleaming in the sun. The couloir itself was shaded.

'About an hour, Chris?'

'What, the sun? Yes, we had better keep going.'

The inevitability of the approaching ovenlike heat gave us a little spurt of energy to accelerate our progress. We exchanged leads for five pitches, up to and over a short steep section of hard green water ice at the narrows between sérac and rock. At around eleven o'clock the sun swung into the gully. Within minutes the heat had us panting. The glare from the snow was intense. Up above Steve was making a rising rightward traverse across the gully wall onto the ridge, just forty metres below the campsite. The ice was hard, requiring several blows of his axes. When he reached the ridge he fixed the rope. David waited for Chris and me to arrive and we jumared up to Steve. A beautiful pitch of steep ice climbing up a thin

132

blade of a sérac, then took us to a small basin depression on the Promontory – a perfect level tent site for the night. David filmed me as I staggered up the final few metres of levelling snow. I was too weary to act.

Once we had erected the tents Chris crawled inside ours and lay out to sleep. David, Steve and I, warmed by the sun, sat on our rucsacs and kept the stoves purring producing drinks, every fourth of which we passed in to Chris. From this altitude we were able to see above the ridge of Kusang's Peak to the Nepalese Rolwaling. Clouds filled the Nepalese valleys but the mountains were clear.

I sensed that Chris was depressed and that he blamed himself, possibly his age, for his fatigue. I wondered if he felt that Menlungtse was one of his last big projects. On Everest in 1985, at the age of fifty, with Sherpa support and bottled oxygen, he had, for about a fortnight, become the oldest person ever to have reached the top. It had been a timely triumph. When Reinhold Messner had climbed Lhotse and Makalu, to become the first person ever to climb all the 8000-metre peaks, he had chosen their normal routes. By the same token, Chris had adopted the easiest style possible on Everest. Messner wanted to win a race against other climbers, whilst Chris had sensed his own opponent – time. Now lying in a tent on the Promontory, Chris was suffering, so he thought, from the effects of age. He loved the mountains so much and the challenges that they held. Now he was coming to terms with the realisation that climbs like Menlungtse would be more and more difficult. In fact the truth was much kinder. We were *all* tired, an effect of heavy sacks and a strenuous day in a suntrap.

In order to reduce weight we decided to leave some equipment on the Promontory, and retrieve it on the way down. We disposed of two snow stakes and some ice screws and one or two gas canisters each. I also jettisoned some spare clothing. We ate a large meal that night, conscious that what we ate now we would not need to carry – at least not in our rucsacs.

The weather continued to be settled in the morning. Chris and I set out as soon as it was light and climbed up another fin of sérac ice and onto the top of the hanging glacier that we had seen from Kusang's Peak. There were no difficulties here and we moved together quickly and easily with ten metres of rope between us. There were few visible crevasses in the snow and we were able to take a direct line towards the wide scoop that led upwards into the centre of the face. This was the Central Highway. Chris's spirits were greatly improved and his enthusiasm had returned. We completed the traverse and kicked a line

133

of steps in the steep névé snow of Central Highway. After each few metres of ascent I stopped and looked around me. Now, above the terrace, we could enjoy the exposure. Our footprints from the Promontory were individually indiscernible. They had become just a thin black line. Two splashes of colour were moving slowly along it. The terrace itself looked smaller and it blended into the face to which it belonged. We were a thousand metres above the valley, even further from the top of the face. Looking up and across the ice I could not see a single reprieve in the angle of the slope. By the middle of the morning the sun had climbed high enough behind the West summit to cast its direct light obliquely across the face, leaving the headwall of the mountain in shade.

We came to a large crevasse that extended across the face, invisible from below. A snow bridge led across it to a steep wall of water ice. Chris crossed to the far side of the abyss and took a belay, our first of the day, beneath a slim groove that formed a weakness in the wall. I stemmed across the groove, its ice shining under the sun. The moves were fantastic. David and Steve had followed our exact route and were almost at the snow bridge by the time Chris had joined me above the cliff. We continued up to the left of a column of rather temporary looking séracs, above which we hoped to find another good camping spot. We were at about 6200 metres, virtually onto the green icefield. The snow beneath us was little more than a veneer above the harder ice and the angle of climbing had suddenly reared up. Above the séracs we could see only a constant shining surface, a flawless shield of ice. We climbed carefully upward, following the snow as much as possible. In places the cover waned to nothing and we would have no option but to claw our way nervously up the ice, standing on the ends of our frontpoints, just a few millimetres penetrating, tapping with our ice axes with as much force as we dared. At times like this, the exposure was fervently felt.

For three pitches we tiptoed upward. Chris arrived at the top of the séracs first, and traversed across to them. This was the final pitch of the day and one that had him whooping with delight. I followed, smiling broadly, a reaction to Chris's infectious euphoria. He leaned out from his ice screw and disposed of a roll of film, like I imagined David Bailey takes photographs of models. He had good reason to be happy. The day's climbing had been superb, the weather was settled, and the setting quite remarkable. The séracs had peeled slowly off the face and enlarged a crevasse which had slowly filled as sloughs of snow came off the icy face above. The crevasse presented us with a spacious and sheltered campsite. Above the lip of the ice wall that overhung it lay hundreds of metres of green ice, unblemished like a huge ice rink turned on its side.

134

'Tomorrow's climbing looks formidable.' I stated the obvious.

Chris looked up the ice and nodded his agreement. Then he glanced down to look for the others. But he couldn't see them. His grin had gone.

'Where are Dave and Steve?' he said.

'I thought they were behind us.'

'Well, they're not there. Surely they must have done that groove pitch by now.'

'Yes, I saw them. They must have gone another way.'

'But *this* is the bivouac site. They *have* to come this way.' Chris appeared to be very angry. He was suddenly fatalistic, imagining that we would not rendezvous and have our climb jeopardised. 'The bloody wankers! Why couldn't they follow us?'

It was two o'clock. We pitched our tent and put on a brew.

'Excuse me. Can you help us? We're looking for a couple of climbers, Messrs Bonington and Fanshawe!' David had appeared twenty metres away at the other end of the crevasse.

'David!' said Chris, much relieved. 'How are you?'

'Oh, fine. But none the better for the barrage of ice that you guys were showering on us! Bloody great dinner plates of it.'

We had forced them to veer right and find their own way up to the crevasse. But they had known exactly which way to come through complicated broken ground. It had been typical of David's uncanny feel for the mountains.

'Let's lead out one of the ropes tonight onto this ice. In the morning we can jumar up and carry on,' suggested Chris, keen to maximise the time that we had to spare. David filmed Chris working his way up the ice. Each time he kicked with his feet he released tiny shards of ice which slid down the slope tinkling as they came, like a breeze through a chandelier. Even without a rucsac his progress was painfully slow to watch. At last he ran out all the rope.

'Twenty feet!' I had shouted. A minute later, 'Ten feet!'

He placed two ice screws and abseiled down to join us. 'Gosh, that ice is *bloody* hard,' he said in his Sandhurst voice.

'Better make an early start then, if we're going to get through that headwall,' I added, hopefully.

I found it hard to sleep that night. My mouth was irritatingly dry, and despite drinking about three litres that day I felt dehydrated. Panadol did little to relieve my headache. Chris was not snoring but he muttered fitfully in his sleep and I resented him that pleasure. Come alarm time at three o'clock, I was more tired than the previous night. Chris

135

and I had an arrangement that, as he was usually more alert in the morning, he would do all the cooking and preparing of drinks whilst I lay relaxing. In the evening the reverse would occur. Certainly the tent was too small for both occupants to move simultaneously. I lay semi-comatose, whilst Chris sat upright at his end of the tent, tending the stove that hung from the ceiling. The wind outside carried spindrift, so we kept the entrance closed. Thus we were being gassed and suffocated as well. Frost built up on the inside walls so that each time Chris moved and the tent shook, ice rained into my hair. My sleeping bag offered a kind of damp warmth. It was one of the most unpleasant times in the entire expedition.

David and Steve left before us, and reached the top of the rope as it began to get light. Then they set off up the icefield above, rising slightly rightward. Surprisingly we could not see the gully from below. We had no real fix on it, but hoped that as we went higher and further right we would begin to recognise some of the features of the headwall. Chris and I decided to take a slightly lower line to the right, following an unlikely streak of snow that clung rather dubiously to the ice. It gave us better footholds, though we still needed to penetrate our axes through to the ice to get a decent purchase. It was decidedly cold. At each belay, David leaned out from his ice screw and swung his feet below him like a pendulum in an attempt to get circulation into his toes. Against the backcloth of an uncompromising headwall the two climbers above me, inching their way across the flawless ice, made a memorable sight. Their boots, like eagle's claws, projected perpendicularly from the slope; each held in place by two tiny picks of steel.

A crevasse loomed above, with a slight overlap of ice above it. There was a small sérac on the left. From the previous camp we had assumed it was much smaller, barely a rugosity on the surface of the shield, perhaps a hundred metres above. Yet we had been climbing for three hours and still not reached it. When we did, late in the morning, there was enough room in the crevasse to sit down and we met up with Steve and David. I gazed up at the headwall. It looked from here only fractionally nearer than from the previous camp.

'Deceptive,' I said.

'Uum . . . bummer,' agreed Shea.

Chris was looking in another direction. 'There's a storm coming.' He had been watching the Nepalese side of the frontier ridge below us. 'There's been clouds building up all morning.'

'That's normal,' David said.

'*Those* aren't normal!' Chris pointed to anvil-topped cumulus nimbus,

136

way out towards Kathmandu. 'I'm telling you. I've been watching them. They're coming for sure.'

During the previous year on Menlungtse Chris had endured a very strong storm that had threatened to flatten his and Jim Fotheringham's tent while their companions' tent had been torn to shreds. All four were able to retreat quickly in the morning but, had the storm continued unabated, the final outcome might have been very different. I could see that Chris was frightened by the prospect of a repeat experience.

'I know just how quickly the weather can change,' he said with real urgency. 'Let's dig in while we can.'

By digging in, he meant enlarging the crevasse enough for us all to bivouac. However, David found a better site for us twenty metres above and within an hour we were all fully ensconced on a flat ledge about five metres wide. In one direction it petered out, in the other it sloped steeply down into a large crevasse. A wall of ice rose above the ledge. The other side of the ledge, where it fell away down the West Face, had a small lip to it. Practically invisible from below, there was in fact room for two tents comfortably and, best of all, we could walk around on this small haven unroped in perfect safety. 'It's unreal!' commented Steve.

Chris did not let himself lose sight of the clouds, that I now had to admit were looking threatening. We pitched the tent and then packed a wall of snow around it about half a metre high. Once we had done that we sat out in the sun, almost enjoying the exhibition on the other side of Kusang's Peak. A gigantic wave of white cloud welled up and advanced. Like dry ice from a beaker it spilled over the frontier ridge and poured down the eastern slopes. Base Camp, a tiny cluster of tents on the valley floor, was smothered. Some of the anvils in the far distance were up to ten kilometres high. Yet until Gauri Sankar, opposite, was obscured by cloud, it was hard to believe that the clouds were anything more than a spectacle. The security of our tent site allowed me to be so irrational and, in Chris's eyes perhaps, happily naïve. The tidal surge halted soon after. We had watched the whole show, bathed ourselves in constant sunlight.

We were now at over 6500 metres and Steve looked suddenly weary, more so than the rest of us. He belayed David who ran out both our ropes up the ice for 120 metres towards the headwall. Still we could not agree on the whereabouts of the gully, in the end deciding to head for the uppermost bay of ice nudging into the headwall. I was unconvinced, but bowed to the majority rather ungraciously.

In the morning of 10th May we started, pulling steeply up the ropes with jumars as handholds, crampons scratching on the metal sheet of

137

ice. Although there were no clouds in the sky there was a strong wind which glided silently across the smooth ice. My legs felt hollow with cold, my feet and hands were stinging. As soon as the first of the Americans had reached the top of the second rope, Chris and I started out on new ground. Again, we found the occasional smear of snow and followed these where we could. But after only two more pitches we were faced with only hard green ice between us and the headwall, quickly growing and surrounding us. Suddenly I felt its power, that awesome sweep of verticality that we had come to climb. When it was my turn to lead a pitch, I glanced quickly up, looking for the gully of ice, before slowly picking my way upward. Two high placements of my ice axe and hammer . . . kick . . . kick . . . kick. I walked up the ice for another metre, scanning it for the slightest indentations. My calf muscles were on fire. At the top I tied off the rope to an ice screw and signalled for Chris to follow. He simply jumared up the rope. I watched the screw flexing each time he pulled up, then glanced uneasily at the valley floor over 1500 metres below. My eyes were invariably drawn to the headwall, still shaded, dark and imposing.

'Shit!' It was Chris.

I looked down, and watched him skidding on the ice, accelerating. He was falling! My heart started to thump before I realised what had happened. He was in no danger. He had been clumsy and his feet had skated on the ice. The rope had followed a diagonal line, so that he had lost his grip and started to pendulum. He drew an arc below me, sliding helplessly on the polished slope. When he came to rest directly beneath me, he kicked his feet into the ice with venom and resumed, jumaring up towards me, without a word. Silently we exchanged leads at the belay and he continued towards the bay. David and Steve were not far behind.

After five pitches, I led into the bay. It was already midday. Fangs of granite drooped down on each side of me. The bottom edge of the headwall became indistinct. To left and right I could look down on smooth slabs of granite. The wall from below appeared almost to be overhanging, impending bastions of granite, as smooth as marble, impossible to climb. I swept my gaze across the huge amphitheatre. There were fewer fissures in the rock than I had expected, and less glints of ice. My heart sank. I searched for the gully but did not see it.

'This must be the wrong bay!' I called back to Chris. By traversing above a string of rocky islands that came down from the headwall, I figured that we could easily enter into the next recess. I was sure that we were off route. David had caught us up. He was on Chris's stance

138

and they were talking. I heard them mention the East Ridge. I could not understand why.

'Let's look at the next bay,' I shouted again. They continued to talk. Chris waved his arm as if to say be quiet. I let them converse a little longer. Then it dawned on me that they were discussing retreat. I grew suddenly angry.

'Oh, come on! Let's at least give it a try!' I could not disguise my anger. 'We haven't even got to the gully yet.'

Chris turned and exploded. 'Andy, just fuck off will you!'

Stunned into silence, I placed a screw and leaned back on it. Chris began to jumar up the rope towards me.

'Well?' I said tersely when he arrived at my stance.

'Andy. Just cool it!' There was a pregnant pause. 'Steve's knackered. David reckons we should go down.'

'Do you?'

'Well, I'm not sure . . .'

I had to admit that I was very tired. I also had to concede that we were poorly prepared for this route. Our sacks had been too heavy, partly because of the filming gear, and we were insufficiently acclimatised. It did make some sense if we could rely on the weather, to go down, relax and then come up for a second try. But also I felt strongly that we had not given ourselves a proper chance. How difficult, for instance, was the ice gully? The whereabouts of the gully had become all important. It filled my mind, to the exclusion of other things.

'Let me lead out another pitch, towards that next bay,' I said. 'Then we'll know for sure what we're up against.'

Chris did not hesitate. 'Okay, but take off your sack, you'll be quicker. You can haul it up after you, if we decide to continue.'

Without my sack I moved quickly and easily. After a few minutes, I had covered about thirty metres, still in the uppermost bay. I stopped, looked up and felt my heart sink. Tucked into the side of the bay was a broad shining ribbon, plunging steeply onto the ice. It looked to be vertical. Above, it seemed to twist leftward and pass through an overhanging balcony of granite.

'It's desperate! This is the gully and it's desperate!' I anguished.

David had joined Chris and they were talking again, about whether we should go on or not. I felt so confused. All this talk and debate had tripped up my momentum. I was suddenly negative. Finally I heard David speak.

'If this is our highpoint, I'd better film it,' he said.

I tiptoed down to the others. David looked determined, Chris a little dazed. Steve stayed on the previous stance. We abseiled diagonally back to the last campsite. What doubts I had were quickly dissolved once we started to descend. Gravity was now on our side, there could be no turning back. David was masterminding the whole descent. From the ledge we traversed north in the crevasse across the face, for about a hundred metres, from where we abseiled directly down the face. David and Steve refused to abseil on a single screw, so Chris and I brought up the rear taking out the back-up as we came. In four full-length abseils we reached the camp above the séracs, where we spent the night.

Chris told me that he was sorry that he shouted at me. I lied to him that it hadn't bothered me.

In the morning, the 11th May, we briefly questioned whether to leave our tents and sleeping bags here for a second attempt. Not wishing to commit ourselves either way, we decided against it and left soon after light with David ahead again, abseiling for three more ropelengths until we were beyond the ice groove. Rather than leave an ice screw here, David impressively reverse climbed the pitch. We virtually ran down Central Highway, facing outwards for most of the way. The snow felt so secure after the two days of green ice that we had endured. We quickly traversed to the Promontory, reaching our cache of gear there at about midday. It was fantastically hot and we stripped down to our thermal underwear in anticipation for the abseils down the upper gully of the lower ridge. We descended from a stake and swung into the gully, and from there we kept close to the rocks on the right, in order to save ice screws. We had used about fifteen already. At last we reached the rock step and one by one we jumared up it, before finally tumbling like rag dolls down the fixed ropes to our camp above the scree slope. A reception party of Charlie, Jess, Iain and Krishna was there. I had never enjoyed a mug of tea more and Krishna had made some delicious momos, small samosas packed with melted cheese and spinach, especially for our arrival.

'Now then, my darlings,' said a warm and amiable Charlie. 'Didn't expect to see you so soon.'

'Bad luck, team,' said Iain. I could see that he had a barrage of questions to ask us. 'Difficult, was it?'

Iain insisted on carrying my sack, and I insisted that he didn't. We quarrelled. As a compromise I carried my sack but he took most of its contents and I was thus able to dance effortlessly down the scree, put my head down and push for camp which I reached alone two hours later, just as it was beginning to darken. The first thing that struck me was how much greener it was. There were alpine flowers, too, bright dots of yellow and blue. Nima came out of the cook tent to greet me. Francis bounded from his tent looking incredibly excited.

'Francis! What's the matter? Have you found the yeti?'

'Naw!' he said coyly. 'Found yeti. Oh yes, thelly funny!' He started giggling. 'We have been watching *you*!' he squealed and started to jump up and down. 'Another try?'

'Yes, of course.'

'Oh thelly good!'

That evening we had a party, in celebration of Jess's birthday and our safe return. Charlie and Iain produced the last of the scotch and announced that the beer was ready for consumption. In addition Charlie had ordered some local brew from Chang bu Jiang. Krishna and Nima cooked a lasagne, courtesy of Safeways, and we brought the ghetto-blaster into the mess tent. As if that wasn't enough, Hinkes arrived with letters and his dry sense of humour. The scene became more and more debauched, as if a spirit that had been bottled in everyone was finally released. It was one of the finest evenings I can remember.

13

A further look

Over the next three days we rested. These were unhurried days and the most mellow of the expedition. I felt no disappointment in our climb, for I knew that we would have another try. And on the next attempt, I told myself, we would be fitter and stronger. At night the simple act of lying inside my tent enclosed in the warmth of my sleeping bag, reading or listening to my Walkman took on an exaggerated level of pleasure. Each morning, after Krishna had brought me 'bed tea', I dozed until the sun forced me up. During the day I enjoyed wandering far from camp, through the pasture and its flowers to find a warm boulder which I could lean against and sleep, or read or gaze knowingly up at the face. The gully in the headwall looked so easy from below. I smiled. I held no grudge. From my warm sheltered perch I could follow every pitch of the climb. That face and I, we knew each other now. And our relationship was far from over.

Charlie and Jess had left camp the day after we had come down. They had walked up the Upper Menlung Glacier to try to get better views of the East Ridge and brought back Polaroid photographs which told us very little about the ridge that we did not already know. But Charlie and Jess were buoyant about their adventure and rekindled our own hopes about the ridge. It should be possible, they assured us, to walk above the glacier, on its true right bank, far beyond the East Ridge, from where we could better assess the climbing possibilities. Like me, Jess had been taken with the elegant peak, simply marked as 6301m on the map, and he had easily persuaded Alan, with Iain's blessing, to attempt it. They planned to leave from camp on the 16th. Chris, David, Steve and I decided to return to the East Ridge and camp beneath it on the 15th. On the 16th we would traverse around the base of the ridge and look at the other side and, all being well, make our attempt on the mountain the next day.

Krishna volunteered to come with us to our camp to cook for us. Charlie and Nima also helped with our loads. We walked for about four kilometres, keeping as close to the mountain as we could, until we reached the terrace that Jess and Charlie had mentioned. Below on the right, the glacier was a jumbled wasteland of scree ridges, black ice cliffs and pools of water skimmed with ice, like frosted glass. We continued on the terrace for another hour until it tapered away to nothing. A kilometre of rubble lay between us and its continuation. Above on the left, rose the concave South-East Face of Menlungtse; guarded by a hanging glacier which extended down the face and across our line of travel. This face, entirely snow and ice, would provide the easiest route up Menlungtse, but it was constantly swept by avalanche and was unjustifiably dangerous. Our glacial obstacle made unattractive viewing and Charlie decided that he had come far enough and we agreed to split his load among us. Before we could implement our plan, Nima, to my amazement threw the entire load onto his back to supplement what he was already carrying and set off unerringly.

We descended down the rubble, hopping from boulder to boulder, walking with a jarred rhythm. My heavy sack pushed me down and I felt a stabbing pain in my knees. We each chose our own route across the rocks, and for an hour I picked my way towards the far side where I caught Chris up at the base of the final slope. He seemed to be toiling.

'I don't know,' he sighed laboriously. 'I'm *really* tired.'

'Horrible stuff to walk on,' I offered.

'Andy . . .' He drew a deep breath. 'I'm not as fit as I was. I'm only going to hold you back, aren't I? You go on the ridge as a three.'

I had half-expected him to say something along those lines. He had been much slower than the rest of us to recover from our climb on the West Face. I felt suddenly very fond of him.

'No! I mean . . . so what? We can climb at whatever pace we like! There's no problem!'

'That's good of you . . .'

'Rubbish!'

'Well, if you don't mind . . . I'll give it a go.'

Above the scree we rejoined the terrace and came across a tiny round lake in a depression. Its water was absolutely still and it reflected the fluted white peaks on the frontier ridge with Nepal. We pitched three dome tents on its grassy banks, one for Krishna and the other two between Chris, David, Steve and me. A blunt rib led up from the lake and onto a shoulder from where the East Ridge began. We decided to spend the rest of the afternoon here, and in the morning continue along

143

the terrace for another few kilometres around the other side of the ridge. We unpacked the rucsacs. David and Steve produced one pile of gear and Chris and I another. There was a serious omission.

'Have you got the rope?' Chris said to me.

'No, I thought you packed it.'

'Oh, dear me!' he whispered. 'It's a balls up.'

We gave Nima a message for Charlie that we needed the rope sending up from camp. 'Urgent!' he wrote and Nima scurried off. Krishna buried himself in his task, two paraffin burners roaring in front of his tent. After dark it was colder here than at Base Camp and we dressed ourselves in our duvets and changed into mountain boots just to sit around.

In the morning we set out quite early, Steve and David first and, an hour later, Chris and I. After a kilometre the terrace petered out and we found ourselves traversing a scree slope above the glacier that feeds the Upper Menlung from the north. The north side of the ridge was now right above us, but we were too close in to assess it properly. We could see tracks leading out into the middle of the glacier, although we could not see David or Steve.

'Let's go down there . . .'

'You go,' Chris said quickly. 'I'll not bother.' He handed me his binoculars.

I shrugged, 'Okay,' and set off alone.

'You all right on your own?' he called after me. 'I mean the slots. Sorry, I'll come if you like.'

'No, don't worry. I'll keep on their tracks. I won't kill myself. See you.'

As I heeled down the scree and snow onto the glacier, I realised that Chris had already given up on the mountain. He seemed more relaxed than the previous day, and to have come to terms with his decision. Despite that, he was bound to be disappointed.

The snow was wet and slippery, and it reflected the sun's glare. But there were no slots. After about twenty minutes of brisk walking I reached the end of David and Steve's tracks. They had gone back to camp, I concluded. I sat down on my rucsac and looked up at the East Ridge. It looked difficult. 'Waste of time,' I grunted out loud.

The crest was hideously broken and corniced, as we knew already. The north side of the ridge, which we had not yet seen, was almost as steep and unaccommodating as the south side, a jungle of séracs, avalanche runnels and snow flutings which would have been laborious and dangerous to traverse. I sat for a few minutes, then picked myself up and slouched back towards Chris.

144

'Desperate,' I told him.

We reached our camp at around midday. David and Steve were there. Krishna handed us each a brew and some rice. David raised his eyebrows. 'Did you get a look?'

'Yes. We're wasting our time,' I said.

We sat down on the grass. Each of us knew that we needed now to make a decision, and an important one, of what to do. The options were few; to go back onto the West Face, try another route altogether or give up on Menlungtse. Our setting, away from the distractions of camp, was a good one in which to talk.

'I think we should go back to the West Face,' I opened.

'I've got to admit,' Chris contributed, 'I'm simply too tired to go back on the hill. I'm pulling out.'

David and Steve looked at each other. They did not look as surprised as I had expected them to.

'So am I,' said David.

'What?' Chris stared at him briefly in disbelief. 'What's wrong with you?'

'I'm fine, physically. Just don't feel like going back on the hill, that's all,' he said easily.

Chris was astonished, and did not disguise the fact. 'Well, I'm bloody surprised at you,' he said righteously, adding, 'In fact, I'm disappointed.'

I looked at the ground, embarrassed. How could he say that? We sat in an awkward silence. This wasn't Chris speaking, but the personification of his own frustration. It was unlike him. I knew it. David knew it too, and I was impressed by the coolness of his response.

'I came on this trip for all sorts of reasons. The climbing, sure, but also for the travel across Tibet, meeting the villagers, for the scenery. It happens that I don't feel too good about the West Face.'

David continued, talking mostly at Chris. He had climbed Everest in 1984, when two Nepalese climbers, one of them a Sherpa, had also tried for the summit but had slipped and fallen. When he had been on Everest the following year the bodies of these two climbers were found in a hideous condition. David had collected the bits in a large bag and disposed of them in a crevasse.

'Yes, I admire you for that,' interjected Chris who had been there at the same time.

Even by raising this subject, it was clear that David had been deeply affected. The reason for dropping out was valid but he offered another, as if he feared that it would go misunderstood. 'There's a monsoon expected. I don't want to be on that face when a dump of snow comes.'

145

David and Steve had brought a long term forecast of the weather patterns for the Everest region. Its author, a friend of theirs, had based his computer model on previous observations of the monsoon's advance across the Indian subcontinent. Looking back through our diaries and comparing their comments of the weather in April and early May with the computer's predictions, we noted that the forecast had an uncanny accuracy. A period of stormy weather, at least over Everest, was predicted in about five or six days.

Steve had not shown his cards and was placed in a difficult position. If he genuinely did not want to go back onto the West Face, he could not say so without Chris being 'disappointed' in him, and he would be preventing me from climbing on. If he *did* want to go back to the West Face, then he could be seen as condoning Chris's criticism of David. He pulled out.

That left me. I stood up and walked over to the edge of the lake. Its water was calm, and I tried to think clearly. David was by far the best and fittest climber of our group. I felt no disappointment, only shock. I looked up at the South-East Face. I wondered, could I solo that – if I was fast? Madly, I convinced myself I could, but all the way down as well? Abseil ropes, twenty ice screws, bivouac gear, stove . . . and the avalanche risk? Forget it. I looked across the Upper Menlung Glacier to Point 6301m. Could I climb that? Maybe I could. I remembered that Jess and Alan had planned to try it. *Hinkes! Of course!* It dawned on me. I walked briskly over to the others. I felt the tension in the air long before I reached them.

'I've been thinking,' I said, 'I reckon Hinkes might be keen on the West Face. What do you reckon?'

Chris nodded his head. 'I've already thought the same thing.'

At that moment Charlie arrived. He had brought the other rope.

'Charlie!' Chris called out. 'What a star!' His arrival had been timely.

'Where's Hinkes?' I asked.

'He's at camp. He and Jess are going up that.' He pointed across the glacier. 'They're leaving this afternoon.'

'I'd better run! I'll have to cut them off.'

'What?'

Within five minutes I had packed my rucsac and started out to Base Camp.

'You can tell Jess that I'll substitute for Alan,' Chris said as I was leaving. I crossed the moraine to the terrace and half ran, half walked through the grass and boulders, fearful of missing them. I also had time to think about what Chris had said. His feelings had been too strong to

146

curb, and what had been said was not a reflection of what he really meant. Chris had proved to me during the last two months that he was a climber first, all else second. He relished the romantic struggle, man versus mountain. He had developed a close relationship with Menlungtse, and saw David as the strength in our team. With David gone, he realised that the mountain might not be climbed and it was this that bothered him most. It had seemed such a waste. I wonder now, had Hinkes not agreed to climb with me, would Chris have reversed his decision?

From the glacier snout, looking down to the grassy meadows and to Base Camp, I spotted three figures heading towards the glacier. They were in the middle of the valley and I was on the true right bank, so I ran as quickly as I could across the top of the snout. When I was above them I relaxed, sitting among the rocks to catch my breath. Then I descended directly. The leading figure was Nima. Behind him was Jess.

'Andy, hi!'

Oh no, I thought. Why has he got to be so cheerful. Doesn't he know that I've come to ruin his plans? I bet he has been looking forward to this climb with Hinkes. How shall I do this? Oh dear, climbing is so selfish.

'Hello, Jess.'

'No joy on the ridge?'

'No joy,' I confirmed. 'Listen, Jess. Umm, where's Alan?'

'Right behind.'

'I'd like to invite him to try the West Face with me. The others have, well, dropped out.'

'I'm sure he'll agree,' he said blankly.

'Yes, so am I. But what about you?'

He shrugged. 'It's better that you and Alan try the face.'

I was grateful to Jess, particularly as I suspected that he was more upset than he would admit. He had not tried to deter me with emotion. Quite the reverse; he was immediately supportive of the idea and helped assuage my guilt.

'I think you'll find that Chris will be keen to try Point 6301 with you,' I said, more to ease my own conscience than gladden Jess.

Alan arrived and I explained the new game plan. He was very excited. I knew this because he was more quiet than usual, like someone who had been offered a job at an interview. He wanted the job, but he didn't want to show that it really mattered that much. All four of us returned to camp. Alan and I walked together discussing when to leave, how much

147

food, what gear. We studied the headwall, and decided against the gully line.

'Let's just go to the bottom, and blast a route straight through the middle!' You might have said that we were confident.

'We had better clear this with Iain,' Alan said, pouring cold water on my excitement.

'Yes, of course.'

Iain was delighted. 'That's a much better idea. We'll watch from camp! Great!'

When Alan had returned from Kathmandu he had handed Iain a message from his editor, offering no support for the plight of the girl with the hole in her heart. Iain had been momentarily melancholy, but resigned. The note had also said that he was needed at his desk. But he had no intention of going back home, and the prospect of another spectacle above camp only added to his determination.

That evening bad weather moved in and threatened to prohibit our climb. In the morning there was a dusting of snow at Base Camp. The sun quickly disposed of it to reveal dry warm grass once again. But the mountain had also been dumped upon and avalanches were so frequent that at times we did not bother to look up at the face when the roar and cracking sounds reached us. Most of the big avalanches on the West Face came from the séracs below the level of the Promontory, and their behaviour was unpredictable. The real danger came from small avalanches above the level of the sérac band, sometimes no more than sloughs of fresh snow sliding off the face.

David and Steve offered to take our sacks up to the top of the fixed rope, to give us a head start. It was a spontaneous and warm gesture which strengthened my high regard for them both. Chris and Jess teamed up for their attempt on Point 6301m. That night, beside the resplendent glow of the five-metre dome, in which the others sat around the paraffin lamp, Hinkes and I sorted our equipment for the climb. We laid out ice screws, pitons, ropes, jumars, sleeping bags, mats, clothing, headtorches, bivouac food, gas, stove, cameras, films and tent. For Alan, especially, weight was of paramount importance, for he was not fully acclimatised. He was fit, no doubt, but he had not been above 5400 metres during the expedition. By midnight we were finally satisfied and left the sacks in the dome tent for David and Steve to collect in the morning. We would carry only crampons, harness and jumars.

David and Steve had already left when we rose in the morning. The weather was poor and I half-expected to see them return from the mountain at any moment, having abandoned their task. But they did not return until long after dark. Throughout the day I had felt myself growing more and more nervous. When David, brushed in snow, poked his head through the door of the mess tent where everyone had assembled and said, 'Your sacks are there, all ready and waiting,' my stomach seemed to fall to the floor.

We planned to depart at two o'clock and it was now already ten. I ran through the night to my tent and fought against the cold nylon of my sleeping bag for warmth. When it came, I relaxed my body and coaxed myself into sleep. Four hours passed without my knowing it. I groped in the dark and killed the electronic intrusion of my alarm clock. The cold gripped my arm tightly and I withdrew it into my cocoon, lying very still and concentrating on my eyelids. They were heavy and I let them close. As I drifted slowly back to sleep I sprung them open again and shook my head furiously. I sat upright, breathing quickly and deeply. I found my torch and started to dress, thermal leggings and top, small woollen jumper, salopettes, thin socks, freezer bags, thick socks, cotton windshirt, balaclava, thin gloves and double boots. I did not lace the boots but walked to the mess tent and kicked them off and went inside. There was a flask of tea Krishna had left us in the middle of the floor. I poured a drink and waited for Hinkes to arrive. Then we sat quietly together for a few minutes gathering our energy. At two in the morning, we left.

Chris was awake. He poked his head out from his tent, as we walked past it. 'Best of luck, lads. I hope you do it.' He was whispering, conscious of the time.

'Thanks a lot. See you in a few days.'

'Cheers. And take care.'

14

Avalanche on the face

The rest of the camp did not stir. We stumbled through the grass and rubble slopes towards the mountain. I had appreciated Chris's gesture. My own thoughts were not towards the summit, nor even the headwall, but simply to find our way to the bottom of the route as quickly and as efficiently as possible. Route-finding was my responsibility now. For morale, as much as for safety reasons, a step-at-a-time approach was the best one to adopt. And yet I accepted from the beginning that a time would come, sooner or later, when I would grow impatient. I knew that I had to watch for that moment very carefully and not let it consume me, as it had on Chogolisa, with near disastrous results.

We carried day sacks with only harnesses and climbing ropes, two lengths of sixty metres, and ski sticks to make the scree slope a little more bearable. Yet we made slow progress and stopped frequently. Alan and I, suddenly lethargic, had simultaneously developed dysentery. I almost ground to a complete halt at one point, and fell into my pool of headtorch light. I briefly considered turning back, but decided that we had nothing to lose. I had built myself up for this climb, I could not give up without an effort. By the time we had reached the first of the fixed ropes dawn had passed, and I was able to look around me. The sky was broken, dappled with turquoise and white. Gauri Sankar's North-East Face held a cold glow. Alan found his sack at the first rope and was suddenly twenty kilograms heavier. I started upward as he squatted for what was to be his last attack of diarrhoea that day. I too had felt my innards settling.

Thankfully the anchors were exposed. The ropes themselves were buried deep into the snow. As I bulldozed my way up the first rope I tugged it outwards furiously. Each time it cut through the snow, like a wire through cheese, I found myself falling backward for a metre down the slope. At the top of the cone I donned my sack and dropped into the

150

upper gully. The snow was deeper than before. I uncoiled our climbing ropes and started out up the gully, kicking a line of steps towards the narrows. We were making very fast time, exchanging leads right up to the final ice wall. Where Steve had led a difficult pitch on hard ice, I was able to kick buckets in the snow for my feet. Alan led the final pitch onto the Promontory. It was not yet midday and I felt fitter than at any other time on the expedition. But Alan was tired.

'Let's rest here tomorrow,' he said.

'Really?' I was disappointed.

Alan then came out with an argument that it was sometimes better to creep up a mountain and then creep back down. 'It's a question of strategy,' he concluded.

'Sort of take the mountain by surprise, you mean?'

'Yes, I suppose.'

'Bollocks.'

'Well, I'm whacked anyway.'

I told myself not to forget that I had been at 6600 metres just two weeks previously, and he had not even been within 1200 metres of that height. 'Acclimatise as we go, then,' I offered.

'Yes, sort of. Tomorrow is brew-me-crazy day.' He had drifted into Geordiespeak. 'Why eye man, I luv a canny cuppa.'

We sat out, basking in the sun, recharging, breathing the thin air. There was no wind, no other noise than the constant purring of the stove and the occasional cracking of séracs, now beneath us. As night descended and the snow all around us started to flush with a chilled lustre, temperatures began to fall rapidly. We retreated into our tiny tent and drank hot soup and another brew. As we had already decided to rest the next day, I took a sleeping pill for the first time in my life.

'You can get addicted to them,' Alan informed me. Blissfully I listened to his conversation wafting further away, like I was on the shore and he was on a boat bound for Newcastle.

In the morning, our perch above the North-West ridge remained shaded. Alan got out to take some photographs while I relaxed into a long lie in, the sort that comes on Saturdays at home when outside the moors and crags are slashed with rain. Snatches of Alan's voice came through the walls of the tent. He approved of the day. He loved the mountains more than anyone else I knew. No question, they were more important than anything else in his life. Even his daughter, Fiona. He had shown me a photograph of her holding up four fingers to signify her age. He wanted to leave the picture on the summit, so he had it wrapped in polythene inside his rucsac. I remembered a time eight weeks previously when he and I were on the flightdeck of our Boeing 747 from London to Karachi. The captain, Johnny Sadiq, had allowed us to use the radio phone. I had rung my father who thought I had been kidnapped and Alan spoke to Fiona.

'Hello, Horris!' he had said. 'It's Daddy! I'm at 37,000 feet! I love you, Fiona.'

Fiona lived with her mother in Birmingham. He had never married and I wondered if he ever would. His climbing totally dominated his life. Despite this, he was a rational climber, careful and, in the present situation, quite content to rest beneath the face. Just before midday, an hour after I had emerged from the tent to find Alan sitting over a stove with a broad grin, the sun's direct rays reached us, and the temperature in our little suntrap suddenly kicked upward.

'Might as well get in some serious sunbathing.' He faked a resigned tone, as he leaned into the tent and produced his Karrimat. Then he stripped to his underpants and smeared himself in sun cream. 'This is *hell*!'

'Terrible, isn't it.'

'Why don't we stay here a few days, and then go down and tell them that we did it. They'll believe *you*.'

'They can see the face.'

'Only joking.'

'How many other climbs have you not done, Hinkes?'

By five o'clock, the view across the frontier ridge into Nepal, with its characteristic afternoon clouds, had become a familiar sight. I was growing a little impatient. 'Early rise, tomorrow,' I said. There was no response. Alan was asleep.

We left the next morning at six o'clock, two hours before dawn. Tibet uses a Beijing-based clock, which differs by about two and a half hours from sun time. As clocks in Tibet are as rare as trees, most of the team preferred to adopt the Nepalese clock, more consistent with the sun. However, Alan and I decided to use Beijing time on our climb, which psychologically lengthened the evenings. Light flooded in when we were halfway across the hanging terrace above the séracs, heading for the Central Highway.

'Let's get a dawn shot,' Alan suggested, producing his camera. I had been warned of his fondness for photography. I had nevertheless found it strange, when we had packed, that he wanted to take ten films on the mountain. For the next hour he asked me to stop every twenty paces to take a picture. 'No, face me. Great. Now look at Gauri Sankar, turn

around, let me get your rucsac, this way a bit, I want to see your label . . .'
Then I couldn't cope any more.

I turned to him. '*Hinkes!* Do you think we can just climb this
mountain?'

'Sorry. I thought you didn't mind.'

'I don't,' I lied.

'Good . . .'

'But less of the posed stuff. Can't you just take pictures of me
climbing.'

'Okay, just a few posed ones then?'

In Central Highway we moved together, quickly. Alan did not appear
to be tired at all. By mid-morning, we reached the ice groove pitch which
I led, hardly noticing its difficulty. Above, we traversed to the right, the
way that David and Steve had gone. There was an obvious runnel
twisting up through the séracs, which we followed for three pitches up
to the huge crevasse. All signs of previous inhabitants had been obliterated. It was barely midday, but the sun had climbed high, and it cast its
light across the icefield above. Alan squinted upwards.

'Wild!' he gasped.

Nothing had changed. The hideous uniformity of green ice looked as
formidable as before with its smooth rippled surface as if a lake had
frozen under a soft summer breeze. I felt suddenly weak. We had a brew,
and took off our harnesses to walk about freely. Across the frontier
clouds were building up, as normal. They no longer concerned me.
Above, the sky was clear. Rather than follow our previous line of ascent,
we decided to go direct up the face, the way we had abseiled. We hoped
to find the abandoned ice screws and use them as belays. By going direct
we would reduce the amount of climbing on the green ice, but equally
we would put the second in the firing line.

Hinkes led the first pitch, traversing a few metres out and then picking
rhythmically, but slowly upward. He cast a long spider-shadow behind
him. His image diminished each time I framed him in the viewfinder of
my camera. I tilted it for effect, at first making him crawl along the slope,
and then lean out impetuously from a vertical wall. After half an hour
he was almost out of rope and I called to him.

'Ten feet!'

'Only ten? There's a screw about twenty above me.'

'Sorry, mate. Ten feet.'

I had overlooked that when we had abseiled a fortnight before we
had reached the crevasse on the stretch in the rope. It would have been
impossible for Alan to exert the necessary force to stretch the ropes

enough, while climbing, to reach the belay. He placed two screws and shouted down the ice. 'Safe.'

'Okay,' I responded, undoing the rope from my belay plate.

Each pitch took an hour, legs burning, eyes scanning ahead for the fissures that occasionally darted across the ice. Some were no more than hair lines, others wide enough to accommodate the picks of our axes. Some of the horizontal cracks were over a centimetre across; wide enough to take the side of our boots, allowing us to transfer our weight onto our heels, thus resting the muscles in our legs. After five hours we came to the traverse right along the crevasse, which led to the site of our next camp.

It looked different. There was more snow, which had filled the floor to greater depths with large powder cones where stuff had slid from the frictionless bare slope above, and spindrift had drifted. I had not noticed, until now, that we were in the grasp of approaching clouds that had filled the Menlung valley and obscured Gauri Sankar from sight. Silently we dumped our sacks towards the back of the crevasse, beneath the protecting wall of ice above, removed our harnesses and crampons and started to trample a trench for the tent. There was a sudden urgency between us, as the air darkened. Snow was suddenly in the air, some coming from the clouds, some picked up by the wind gusting in all directions. I removed my shades, their glass clogged with snow, and sealed my clothing against the wind. I gathered the ropes together and ran them through my fingers, feeding them into a loose pile in the snow ready for moving off in the morning. Above, behind the ripping wind and fast flying mist, was the headwall of Menlungtse's West Face, suddenly remote. We slunk into the tent and quickly zipped the entrance shut behind us.

In the night it continued to snow large soft flakes that stuck to every surface. When we shook the tent we could hear the snow sliding off the walls outside. Alan had collected fragments of sérac ice which he had stored in a polythene bag brought for the purpose. We spent three hours melting them for soup and brews of tea. We ate oatcakes, on which we smeared Primula cheese or rubbed a clove of garlic. We also had some chocolate. Our rest day on the Promontory had been costly on food and gas and our supplies were almost finished; one more night of food, perhaps two of gas.

It was like a scene from an Edgar Allan Poe story, as Alan put it. The walls slowly caved in under the ever increasing weight of snow, as if two Sumo wrestlers, one on each side, were slowly rolling together sandwiching the tent between them. Although we were protected by the icy wall above us, tiny sloughs of snow poured into the crevasse and eddied in towards the tent. Sooner or later, we knew we would have to repitch it. Neither of us quite had the enthusiasm. Alan was lying down with his feet pressed into the snowhole tube that extended out of the back of the tent. It had compressed around his legs like a mould. I sat upright, with backache, yet half asleep tending the stove. Suddenly there was a loud rumble from above.

'Alan, listen!'

'Avalanche!'

His eyes sprang open. There could be no mistaking that noise. I listened to the approaching slide, frantically trying to picture our tent in relation to the lip of our protecting wall. Then it came, thundering like an express train, drowning every other sound. Predictions were academic now. I shone the torch in Alan's face.

'It's going over our heads!' he shouted from point blank range.

At that moment the tent was crushed against our bodies, the two walls touched and the flame of the stove was extinguished. The roar continued, unabated.

'Over our heads!' he bellowed again, from somewhere around me.

It could not have lasted more than ten seconds, but it felt as if a minute had passed before the air was peaceful again. Thankfully, the crumpled tent fabric had not torn, but the internal poles had ripped from their guiding ties. One of them was bent through ninety degrees. Alan had been right. The avalanche had missed us, but for a brief moment, at the point of impact on the ledge around us, there had been a blast of snow, filling every nook and cranny of space in the crevasse. This is what had caused our tent to collapse. I fought with my boots and salopettes and a minute later evacuated the tent to dig it out with my mittened hands. Only the top projected above the level of snow. Alan stayed inside for a little while longer struggling with his boots. He forced the poles back into position before clambering out. We excavated the squashed tent. For the second time we trampled a space big enough for it. Through the beams of our torches I could see snowflakes falling. It took more than two hours to rehouse ourselves.

Our alarm was especially unwelcome that morning, 22nd May. I poked my head out of the tent. We had been partially reburied in the night. But the air was extraordinarily still and cold, and the sky studded with stars. I reclined back and dozed. Alan had not stirred. I drifted in and out of consciousness for an hour. Finally, I sat up and scooped some snow from outside the entrance of the tent with our pan and stacked it above the stove, between the three lengths of chain suspended from the ceiling. I lit it, and the familiar purring returned. A small blue flame, perfectly calm, burned in the faint yellow glow of daylight that had diffused through the walls.

'What time is it?' Alan grunted.

'Eight.'

'Shit.'

After we had drunk tea, I pulled on my boots, first emptying them of snow. I exited, and leaned back into the tent for my duvet jacket. I had worn all my other clothing in the night in anticipation of another burial.

'Hinkes, it's a beautiful day.' Then, I was struck with a horrid realisation. 'The ropes!'

'What about them?'

'Where are they?'

'They're by the tent door.'

'But we've *moved* the tent!'

It was farcical. I did not recognise a single feature in the snow, and all of our tracks from the night had been obliterated. The ledge seemed to be at least a metre higher than the day before. I started to dig furiously and Alan came out to help. After an hour of random bulldozing, we stopped.

'This is useless. We'll have to do this logically,' I said. We moved the tent away from the area and drew out a grid. We agreed to dig each section to a metre depth and then after prodding below that with an ice axe, we would abandon it and go onto another section, until we found the ropes.

'Looks like this is another rest and brew-me-crazy day.' Alan looked resignedly at the perfect blue skies.

'You call this a rest!' I interjected, angry that we should have been so stupid, and missed a perfect opportunity to climb the headwall. Nepal was smothered in clouds, but all the peaks of the Rolwaling had punched their summits clear, like village steeples in English morning mist. Northwest, along the length of the crevasse, Xixabangma stood, a hundred kilometres distant, above the clouds. It had been a year since Alan had climbed it. 'Perfect summitting weather over there as well,' he said.

After two more hours of searching, in which time I twice sat down and held my head in despair, Alan spotted a tiny patch of blue colour at the bottom of a long thin column where he had thrust his ice axe shaft.

'Thank Christ!' he said.

I leaped up. 'What?'

'The rope . . . I think?'

We scrabbled down through the snow with our hands, throwing it

156

behind us like crazed dogs unearthing a bone, until there before us beyond any doubt was a tiny loop of rope protruding from the snow. Alan hooked his axe behind it and pulled it out like a huge worm. Although we could now relax, it was midday before we had uncovered the remaining 119 metres of rope.

'Let's think of the options,' Alan said. 'And going down isn't one of them.'

'I quite agree. And neither is waiting here. What does that leave us?'

'I reckon we should go up . . .'

'Fine.' Hinkes was baffling me, as usual.

'. . . tomorrow. But leave the tent here, and all its contents. Take just a camera, a headtorch each and maybe the stove in case we get benighted.'

We repitched the tent for the last time and spent the rest of the day lying out, enjoying the wide open spaces and putting detailed final touches to our plan. We agreed that to climb directly to the headwall would be our best option. I didn't trust the gully, and to reach it by a diagonal rising traverse would be both strenuous and expensive on time. We would need to move fast, we realised, if we were to make the farthest summit and back. Early the next morning, on 23rd May, we emerged from the tent into a cloudy and blustery day. The conditions were, as Alan put it, 'typically Scottish'. We hesitated, waiting for the weather to show its cards, but at about nine o'clock with no real change we started out towards the headwall. It was our last chance for the summit.

15

The headwall and the summit

I carried a rucsac that contained all our gear for the day. We had intended to alternate the sack so that the leader of a pitch never wore it, but it was so light that I kept it on for most of the day and barely noticed it apart from at one crucial section. We had decided to do our route-finding as we went. On the third pitch of sixty metres, Alan reached the top of the green ice shield, beneath the pale pink wall of granite. The clouds were beginning to free themselves and seemed to be evaporating from all around us. Across the face, the icy rim of the right skyline shone like a golden thread. It was already twelve o'clock.

I changed into a pair of ski gloves, stuffing my gauntlets down my front, and took over the lead up the final few metres of ice that washed up against the rock. A ramp, about half a metre wide and seamed to its vertical host by a brush stroke of snow, extended up and left. Behind the line of snow I found a crack which took the picks of my axes. The points of my crampons found other indentations. As each metre passed, so my comfort in this new environment grew. I could no longer simply crawl upwards in a mechanical fashion as we had done on the ice, employing energy but little thought. Now I really had to work, to study the architecture and look ahead, visualising the moves as a chess player would do. Rashness had no place here. Although I was the first person to enter into this enormous pink and white amphitheatre, it did not feel unfamiliar, almost as if I had rehearsed the moves. After most of the rope had been spent and I could follow its trace through three or four nut runners back to Alan, the ramp petered out and a small bulging wall took its place. Above, I could see a snowy slab clinging dubiously to the rock beneath. It led to an icy smear, a streak that clung like candle wax, thinning upward. I found a thread runner and bridged up as high as I could above it. At the end of an outstretched arm, my axe found névé snow and with a burst of energy I pulled myself up. Above I found ice

158

thick enough to take ice screws. I placed two, then kicked a small ledge for my feet and leaned out.

'Safe!' I cried.

I was perched above a vertical step that fell in about thirty metres onto the green ice below. I saw the slack rope that Alan was controlling sag in a loop below me on the ice.

'Taking in!' I responded.

I hauled up the rope and a moment later Alan retrieved his ice screws and started to climb. He was stiff from belaying, and he stopped frequently to blow on his hands. 'Good four, that,' he said when he arrived on my stance. He set out again, onto the daub of ice, reclined at about seventy degrees against the granite, just about shallow enough an angle not to feel vertical. When I had fed about half of the rope through my belay plate, Alan stopped. He had reached a tiny overlap which deterred further ice. A crack three metres to the right cut through the overlap, then opened into an elegant groove, choked white in its deepest recesses. The slab of rock between him and the crack was no more than dusted with snow. He lunged right. I heard the grating of steel on rock and his accentuated breathing. But I could not see what was holding him on. I glanced nervously across the ropes, sagging slightly on a runner. He made no attempt to move; perhaps he couldn't; but simply froze and surveyed the possibilities. He looked especially vulnerable like that.

'This crack line looks hard to start. Gets better after that,' he said, a few moments later as if preparing me for something. He placed a Friend in the crack and tugged on it. 'Uumm,' he mused. Then he shuffled up a little, paused and lowered himself back into the security of his Friend. 'You try,' he concluded.

I followed the smear and lunge pitch a little too quickly, almost falling in my haste on the slabby traverse and arrived at the stance, panting hard.

'You okay?' Alan enquired. I nodded silently.

The crack was vertical at first, widening into a flake and then a stunning little dièdre, curving gently right towards the crest of an arête. Although the back of the groove was white with snow, the walls were bare, their granite as flawless as we had come to expect.

'I'll see,' I offered, 'can't promise much.'

'If we can't climb this headwall, we can always go down. No big deal. But let's keep at it, eh?'

It was true, we could retreat, and in safety. Subconsciously we were both a little doubtful about our prospects. The sun had already swung

159

its afternoon rays onto the face, and Nepal's lowland clouds were beginning to spill over the frontier. Without tents and bivouac equipment, the lack of time was our greatest threat. I shuffled past Alan, first pulling on him and then his belay and stretched up, finding a small ledge for the pick of my right-hand axe.

'Alan, watch me.' I cranked up and kicked my left boot as hard as I could into the crack. It held. I stood on it.

'Great for a pic!' Alan cheered. I ignored him.

Groping with my other gloved hand in the crack, I found a solid fist-jam, my axe hanging from its strap around my wrist. Pulling into the rock and releasing my other axe, I lifted it high above my head and hooked it over a chockstone in the crack. I straightened my arm, and relaxed their muscles, so that I could feel the strain tugging from within my shoulders. I placed the front points of my right boot on the original flat ledge, which caused my left hand to rip from the crack. I palmed it against the rock on the left. I was totally absorbed. I stood up on the right foot, first transferring my weight from the left and shivering it from the crack. With my left axe I reached as high as I could into the back of the groove where it opened out like the base of a peapod. I hit only rock beneath powdery snow. 'Shit!' My right calf muscles began to complain. Rather desperately I kicked my left foot back into the crack and pushed up again, leaning into the base of the groove, scratching both my axes across the snow. I found a patch of névé and sank my teeth into it. I exhaled and pulled up into a resting position.

'Look this way,' Alan requested.

I did as he said. 'Thanks,' he said, putting away his camera.

'You *were* belaying me then?'

'Yes, yes of course,' he replied flatly, but I doubted it very much.

I gazed up the groove towards the sun and the deep blue sky. It promised much easier climbing. 'Brilliant, Hinkes!' I said jubilantly. 'This climbing is brilliant!' The drag of fatigue was forgotten. Here, above and below, was the principal reason why I had come to Tibet. I do not ever remember being so inwardly happy. I stemmed up the groove for thirty metres, revelling in the sunshine, letting its warm rays soak into me. I curved upward and onto the spur that powered up to the top of the face. There were more cracks, flakes, bottomless grooves, chimneys, each of them virgin, just waiting to be found. 'This way!' they called to me. 'No, this way!'

The face was made up of a succession of arêtes and gullies. The latter were fault lines and, as such, contained breccia, loose and shattered rock. They also contained snow and ice, and were generally easier to

160

climb. But the spurs were safer and even, in the sun, warm to the touch. As if by fate, we had followed a line of weakness right onto the crest of one of these spurs in the middle of a sea of rock, fantastically exposed over two kilometres above the valley floor. The rope tugged gently as soon as I reached my intended belay and Alan's call drifted up the groove.

'Rope's out.'

'Safe!'

'Okay.'

I felt the rope slacken, and I leaned back into my sentry box belay. Gauri Sankar's facing flank was shaded, though majestic, above the shining white cloth of cloud. All of the peaks of the Rolwaling winked at me above the blanket, exaggerating their height. Alan followed the pitch with impressive ease and occupied a small ledge below me. I could see that he was happy, too, though a little tired, and unusually quiet. We looked up the face, gauging our progress. We were almost halfway. We agreed to follow the spur but realised at its top that we would be unable to exit directly onto the summit ridge. The very top of the face looked to be overhanging and above the spur we could see only jutting roofs lent by smooth parallel-sided cracks. Randy Leavitt, whom I had met at Urdokas in 1986, had perfected a technique for climbing such 'off width' cracks which involved hanging upside down from his feet in the crack. I doubted it was the sort of thing that we could easily emulate at 7000 metres in a pair of crampons. However, on the left, where the fault line penetrated the upper barrier of overhangs, a deep cleft chimney had been cut. Although the chimney was vertical or beyond, it provided the key to the summit ridge.

'You carry on,' Alan said. 'You'll be quicker.'

Alan was obviously suffering the effects of altitude more acutely than I, but I was happy to lead. I followed the crest of the arête, consistent at about Severe standard, finding plenty of runner placements. I kept my axes hooked onto the sides of my rucsac belt and removed my gloves. I was climbing in paradise. After forty metres, I reached a series of flakes that offered a traverse line back left towards the gully, and ultimately the chimney, now only seventy metres above. I took it, and found myself swinging on a series of enormous holds across a vertical wall shouting my delight. The exposure was outrageous, the climbing the best I had ever done.

'How much rope?' I called as loudly as I could.

'Twenty feet,' was the faint reply.

I decided to run it all out, thinking that with sixty-metre ropes we might just be able to top out on the next pitch. 'It's unreal!' I whispered to myself. The chimney was about fifteen metres high, and coming across from its base was a traverse that looked like a ledge. Directly below the right-hand end of the ledge was a shattered series of cracks and protruding flakes. I was faced with a short steep groove in crackless granite to reach them. I placed a two-metre sling behind the last of the flakes that I had traversed and set off up, using a technique I had, scratching and torqueing, pulling and pushing, and sometimes just willing. I reached the base of the shattered cracks, and nestled myself among small detached blocks. The headwall was vertical. I placed a small nut in a crack behind an ominous flake and also a blade piton, which I only managed to hammer half way in. The angle of the rock forced me to rely on the belay to support some of my weight. I leant back gently on my sling, feeling suddenly vulnerable and apprehensive. I put Alan's ropes through my belay plate.

'Alan, when you're ready!'

A minute later, he called back. 'Okay.'

'And don't fall off.' I was ready with the sentence. Cryptically, I had informed him that my belay was little more than psychological.

'Okay,' Alan replied, apparently unperturbed.

As before, he climbed slowly and smoothly. My eyes followed him up the crest of the arête and then out across the vertical wall. He stopped below the groove, reluctant to remove the sling runner.

'What's your belay *really* like, Fanshawe?'

'A tied-off peg and a nut behind an expanding flake.'

'Well this is a bomber. I'll stop here. I reckon you'll make it through the chimney on these ropes. That can be your first runner.' He nodded at my belay. 'It's five o'clock already, China time.'

It did make sense. My belay was dubious as it was. As our main anchor, for the crux section of our climb, it was madness. 'You're on,' I said, failing to suppress my excitement, more keen than ever to commit myself to the crux of the climb. Was this summit fever? I did not ponder the question but glanced at the chimney and felt the adrenalin pumping within me, a feeling that stayed with me for three hours.

'What gear do you want?' Alan asked.

I glanced at my harness and the straps of my rucsac, then at the gash up above. 'Just a couple of slings. Doesn't look like I can lace it anyway. Looks like a pile of choss, in fact.'

Alan tied the slings and one or two Friends onto the rope, and I pulled them up. Then I dropped the loop of rope and Alan took it in. 'When you're ready then, matey.'

162

Nervously, I turned to face the climb. The rock was shattered. A large flake protruded perpendicularly from the crack. Another flake clung to the wall on the right. Both were loose, but one of them was compulsory. I chose the first flake. It offered a thrutchy layback of sorts and ultimately a good handhold on its top. But each time I pulled, it moved. Eventually I summoned the courage and, signalling to Alan, I pulled as high as I could, keeping my body close in, and slapped my hand in swift dynamic movements up the inside of the flake. It wobbled and grated. At last I had moved my feet high enough for my hand to reach the top edge of the flake, where I found a good hold. Still no alternative seemed possible. There was just me and this big flake, about as heavy as each other and apparently as detached.

'Keep the rope free of this flake if you can, Alan.'

'You've put both ropes in the runner. There's nothing I can do about it.'

I looked down, noting reluctantly that my ropes indeed ran straight across the offending flake which would have jerked or cut my lifeline had it come away. The only solace was that Alan was tucked neatly under an overhang for whatever was about to happen. I placed my feet into the crack and teetered up, caressing the flake. It held firm, and allowed me to pass up to where we were beyond each other's influence. I gave myself a moment's rest and continued up to the start of the traverse line. A ledge, ten centimetres wide, offered good footholds and a thin horizontal crack at eye level provided security for my ice axe and ice hammer picks. The blocks of granite and their bordering fractures had a fresh feel about them as if the whole wall had recently been quarried. I recognised splinters and dust of granite, that I had seen in mines after blasting. Seemingly I was standing in the middle of a vertical wall of detached blocks, held together by their own weight and size; a delicate equilibrium that was now being subjected to another element. I tried to make myself weightless, standing on tiptoes, pulling gently with my axes, futile all of it.

By the end of the traverse I had dislodged many large rocks and sent Alan scurrying into his cubbyhole for shelter several times. But the climbing had been easy and the rope looped freely across the wall to the original belay. The chimney leaned over me. To reach it I had a choice; climb the shattered wall that I had traversed or directly up the gully. The gully, to its advantage, was off-vertical but it contained no recognisable rock, just pulverised granite rubble. Powder snow offered even less support. I glanced back at Alan.

'Desperate!'

163

He nodded his head in sympathy. 'There's no other way.'

I was standing on a large detached block, at least twice my weight. I placed a two-metre sling around it, then thought for a while and removed it again. I could not take the risk that, had I fallen, it would have held. Had it been ripped from the face, attached to the rope it would have bounced with me down the mountainside. I doubted that Alan could stop us both. So I set off up the gully, comforting myself that with or without the block runner, a fall would be fatal. I threw myself at the gully, just wide enough to bridge across, and made initially fast progress up the ten or so metres to the final chasm. But I had been too hasty, and made moves that I doubted I could reverse. I had kicked footholds in the gravel, which had decomposed and run down the face when I had stepped above them. Occasionally larger rocks protruded, but once again I had dislodged them and they had fallen, rattling off the side walls. Now as the angle steepened, I had ground to a standstill. This was the most committing climbing I had ever done. Where the gully reared up into the chimney, it shed its snow and gravel bed, exposing better holds. But now vertical, I was beginning to feel the physical strain. Time had become a factor, for how long could I hold on against the numbness and cramp in my stretched out legs and the pumped weakness in my arms? I shuffled upward, heading for a ledge on the right wall with a huge spike above it. I was becoming more and more clumsy. Alan was quiet on his ledge, out of sight down below. A rope between climbers is an effective way of transmitting messages and Alan had deduced, just by the unevenness with which he was being asked to pay out the rope that I was not at all happy. I imagined that I was standing on a time bomb, and at any moment my footholds would crumble and throw me down the face. Convinced that I had to move quickly, I stepped up right onto a patch of snow where the shallow angle could accommodate it. I felt my boot bite on something, I did not question what. Pushing hard on my foot, I stretched up and hooked my axe onto the ledge. A few seconds later I stood up with my arms wrapped behind the spike. I had spent all my energy, and terrified myself. I looked down at Alan and shook my head. He did not respond. I banged the spike with my hammer; it felt solid, and I threw a sling over it. All about me the ground fell away vertically.

'Runner on!' I shouted to Alan, 'thank God!'

It was nearly seven o'clock, an hour before sunset. Alan knew that if I was to belay and bring him up, it would be almost dark, and ten degrees colder before he was able to try the final fifteen metres of climbing. Whether we succeeded or failed depended on whether I could climb the

164

chimney. In a two-month expedition, the balance lay in the next hour. The best that Alan could do was to encourage me. He had an uphill struggle, because I was virtually sure that I wanted to abseil off. And yet at the same time, I doubt that I could have done that, after coming so far. I could actually see the crest of the summit ridge above.

'What does it look like?'

'Horrible! Impossible!' My response was automatic, conditioned even.

It was not really a chimney at all, but a crack less than half a metre wide splitting a slightly overhanging wall. The rock on either side looked more solid than I had expected but the angle scared me.

'How hard do you really reckon? What grade would you give it?' he continued.

'Maybe VS,' I answered, 'maybe even Severe. But it's loose and I'm wasted!'

'Take off your rucsac,' Alan encouraged, 'and your crampons. And your gloves. Just pretend you're on Stanage. You wouldn't hesitate there, would you? You'd piss up it.'

I did as he said. If nothing else, having a task took my mind momentarily off the climbing. I hung all these items on the sling. I kept my axes ready in case I needed them for extra reach, or for whatever other purpose I could think of.

'Now, just *go* for it!' I heard Alan say from somewhere very distant.

I turned and climbed up for two metres, into a position where I was straddling the crack. I found small uncut holds on the walls for my feet. Inside the crack I was offered side-pulls. So far so good. I searched the side walls for cracks that would take a runner, but could not find any. I climbed as boldly as I dared, leaning out of the crack to watch my feet carefully, placing them as accurately as I could. I was flowing upward. After another metre, the crack widened and the side-pulls diminished, but good holds appeared on the walls. I pulled steeply up, contorting my body, twisting it to keep my centre of gravity close to the wall. Then I became suddenly frightened. I had seen a crack for a nut, high out of reach on the right wall. It brought the seriousness of my position screaming into my ear. I was five metres vertically above my last piece, almost fifty metres above Alan, silent again. I unclipped a bunch of wires from my harness and stretched with one of them for the crack. They wouldn't reach.

'*Shit!*' I released a little adrenalin but it came flooding back in, more powerfully than ever before, a tidal wave of fear. I blew hard. 'Keep calm, you bastard,' I whispered. 'But move! Fucking move!' I gripped the wires in my teeth and lurched up again, locking my knee in the crack

165

to relieve my forearms, whose muscles were screaming. My brain tried to control them, but they were dead meat. I snatched at the wires with my one free hand, almost dropping the lot, and threw the most likely size at the fissure. 'Yes! It fits!' I left all the other wires hanging there and hurriedly clipped a small extension sling into their karabiner. Finally I attached the rope. I was safe, but the problem was not over. I launched out again finding a good incut hold immediately, then another and another. I pulled up steeply for one more metre to where the crack widened even more. The rest was easy. I slipped my body inside the crack and chimneyed up into oblivion.

I could hardly see as I arrived at the top, for my eyes had filled with tears. All that remained of the West Face of Menlungtse was a five-metre snow slope. I found a block at the very top of the wall and cut into the snow behind, eventually fixing a sling and a belay. Then I sat and let myself weep. I had overdosed on adrenalin. The summit did not occupy my mind, just the exhilaration of climbing the face, in particular the final pitch. It had taken three hours to cover just fifty metres, the same amount of time it would take someone fitter than me to run a marathon; over twenty-six miles. Soon, I would begin to think of the next section of the climb, but for now I was blissfully happy.

I called to Hinkes to follow. He climbed up the groove to my belay and then pulled steeply over the crumbling wall and across the shattered wall.

'Well done, matey!' he said. 'Not easy that.' He was directly below me. 'No point in climbing this bit,' he declared. 'We're short on time as it is. Looks pretty hard though, for twenty-three thousand.'

I pulled on the rope and kept it tight. He donned the rucsac and made the moves up the final crack.

'Pull! Yes, quite good climbing this . . . Pull!' He arrived at my belay. We had climbed the face.

I re-fitted my crampons and we collected and coiled the ropes in the last few minutes of sunshine that we were given before the sun dipped slowly behind the western cloud banks. We climbed up onto the crest and looked out for the first time to the north and east. The first thing that struck me was that Cho Oyu looked surprisingly near, barely twenty kilometres across the dark swirling clouds. Its front face was lit, towering above the softly filtered dusk. Behind and on the right, stood Gyachung Kang, similar in profile but far, far away. Looking down the face, I watched the snow slopes falling away, tumbling over crevasse and sérac edge. My eyes were drawn right inevitably, to the eastern summit of Menlungtse. I had not expected to see it, and its sight shocked me. The

166

summit rose to a pinpoint, like an elegant steeple, glowing in a warm pastel hue. Further right I looked steeply up towards the western summit. The way was clear for our climb to the top. I could see a broad dome and a long gently waving crest of snow coming down to meet us. The eastern summit could wait, or at least *we* could. With no food or bivouac equipment, there was no possibility of spending the night at 7000 metres. Many climbers would not have thought twice about enduring an uncomfortable bivouac. But we were too tired and did not even discuss it as an option. Instead, we stashed one of the ropes and the rucsac, first retrieving the headtorches and set off for the West summit. It was eight o'clock.

The way looked easy, but it was not. The first pitch of fifty metres traversed over steep granite slabs. The snow cover was superficial, and the protection nil, but after the verticality to which we had become accustomed it felt delicate, but harmless. Beyond, we climbed back up to the crest and continued, moving together at last, slowly upwards. The Menlung valley was filled with cloud and Gauri Sankar was already under wraps. Higher, the ridge thinned to a razor edge, and the slopes on either side fell more steeply away. The wind picked up and it began to snow. We dropped down a few paces to the north-east side and traversed on our front points across hard névé snow. Now we were *really* at risk, from ourselves, tired and growing impatient. After thirty metres we rejoined the crest. On the western side I looked down a broad gully of steep snow. The gully! I tried not to look too hard, fearing that the more I knew about it the more depressed I would become. Could it really have been as easy as it looked? The snow continued to fall, and as the darkness gripped more and more tightly, so the wind intensified. There was no pleasure left in the physical act of climbing, but we knew that if we did not go on now, we would regret it.

We plodded, each in his own pool of light dancing at our feet. At ten o'clock we reached the top of the dome of snow that I had seen from below. It was not the summit, for further along the ridge we could make out a sharper and higher turret. Reluctantly we pushed on. The ridge was broad and the visibility had improved. We dropped the coils of rope and continued with a full sixty metres dragging in the snow between us. I resumed the lead, breaking an ugly scar in the naturally sculptured snow. Exhausted, I started to count breaths and steps, as I had done on Chogolisa. At 10.30 p.m. I reached a point where I could look down in all directions. I stood on the West summit.

I leaned forward and clasped my knees and stood very still while I caught my breath. I looked back down to Alan's torch bobbing slowly

167

up and down. The night had settled and the moon risen. It was a very strange and lovely feeling to be perched on that summit. The darkness exaggerated my feeling of isolation and the space between the other mountains. The clouds that smothered all below reflected the moonlight and I was aware of their uniformity. The sky was constant, too, a sweeping black infinity that seemed a little more accessible than usual. And then there were the other peaks, Gauri Sankar, Xixabangma, Cho Oyu, Gyachung Kang, hovering as unearthly worlds across the void.

The East summit formed a pale moonlit outline across a snowy saddle, and would have been a straightforward climb. I felt no disappointment in not reaching its top. We had pioneered a route up the West Face of the mountain, and we had reached the West summit. It was a suitable prize. I felt sure that we had opened up a route that would be repeated, maybe even become a classic climb.

I shouted to Alan. 'I'm there!'

'Oh, thank God!' he replied.

He came up to me and we embraced. 'We've done it, matey!' he said. Then we resumed our own private thoughts and stared wonderously about. At last Alan produced his photograph of Fiona and looked at it for a few seconds. 'Hello, Horris,' he said. But he couldn't bring himself to leave it on the summit, as he had intended, and put it back into his pocket. 'I'll keep you next to me for a safe descent,' he whispered to her image.

I removed the beads that JP had given me and dug a hole in the snow and placed them there. Finally Alan produced a scarf David had given him that had been blessed by a senior lama and threw it as high in the air as he could. It was so light that the wind took it immediately and we followed it for as long as the semi-darkness would allow. As it fluttered across Tibet, its prayers were being sung.

We stayed for only a few minutes on the summit before following our prints back down. We moved together the whole way to the stash at the top of the headwall, which we reached at about midnight, Beijing time. We rigged up an abseil anchor from two pitons hammered in the rock, where we were absolutely certain that the rope would not jam, threaded one of the ropes through the sling and tied it to the other, then threw them down the face. Hinkes went first sliding down the double rope, swinging freely on the initially vertical wall. After he had left, I became suddenly touched by a feeling of isolation. I also felt very tired. We had been on the go constantly for fifteen hours and not drunk any liquid in all that time. As I deteriorated, Alan seemed to pick up, and he took control of the task in hand. His headtorch bulb blew as he descended, which he replaced as he hung on the rope, so that it was ten minutes before he reached his previous final belay and called for me to come.

'Test the ropes,' I shouted down, hoarsely.

He pulled on one of the ropes, and the other, beyond the knot, slid easily through the sling.

'Okay,' he said.

I reached Alan and clipped myself into his anchor and he set off down again, this time aiming into the gully. A few minutes later I heard the banging of a peg. 'Okay, when you're ready.'

I slid down to him, and clipped in again. Thus we continued down the face. On the fourth abseil, Alan found himself near the bottom of the headwall on smooth granite slabs, swinging like a pendulum, with only a metre of spare rope below him. He couldn't find a belay. At last, on full rope stretch he found a patch of green ice, feeding up from the ice shield and placed a screw at arm's length. He clipped in via a short sling and slunk onto it. When he unclipped from the rope it sprang upwards like an unleashed spring. He had descended sixty-five metres on sixty-metre ropes, and was left isolated, hanging helplessly on a solitary ice screw in the darkness.

As I came down the rope he called up to me, 'It's a long ab. I've got a sling and a karabiner ready for you here. *Don't* let go of the rope, whatever you do!' I reached him on rope stretch and he clipped me in and threaded one of the ropes through the anchor. 'Okay, then.' I let the ropes rip through my friction device and one of them shot skyward. He pulled the other through the belay. Three more abseils took us directly to the tent on level ground at last.

I opened the tent and found a rock on my sleeping bag and a dusting of snow. I shone my torch on the outside of the tent and saw a hole in the fabric which the rock had punctured. I put the rock in my pocket. A geologist and friend, Mike Searle, who had a research post at Leicester, had asked me to bring back some granite from the summit. This I had failed to do, but the sight of the rock on my sleeping bag jogged my memory. The specimen had probably come from at least near the summit. We immediately put on a brew, filling the pan with snow, then putting our heads back to wait for it to melt. We awoke with the tent full of steam. On our second attempt we did no better and again fell asleep, steaming the tent out as before. On the third try, we managed to melt enough snow for half a mug each of lukewarm black tea. I drank it in a single gulp and went back to sleep.

We awoke late in the morning, had a mug of soup each and packed up the tent to set off, hoping to reach the Promontory before the sun melted the snow. The liquid triggered my bladder, or so it seemed, but my urine was bright yellow and viscous, like syrup. I went to the lip of the ledge and looked down into the valley, as I had done many times before. But something was not quite right.

'Alan, look! Camp has gone!'

'Don't be ridiculous!' he said without looking.

'No, I swear . . . at least the yellow dome has.' I could not be sure but I thought I saw a tiny swarm of black dots on the valley floor around where camp was. 'Look! Yaks! The buggers are leaving!'

'They must have seen us coming down.'

'What, in the middle of the night?'

'Sure, why not?'

We made very fast progress, traversing the crevasse and finding the previously abandoned screws. We abseiled right down to Central Highway in less than two hours, where we heeled and down-climbed to the terrace and along to the Promontory, waiting there for a couple of hours, before swinging down into the ovenlike heat of the upper gully, where again we found the abandoned abseil anchors of the previous descent. To jumar up the rock step in my exhaustion took me close to an hour. I waited at the top for Alan to come up. When he appeared I started my final few abseils down the fixed ropes to the base of the mountain. Alan was a few minutes behind me.

'Charming this,' I said to myself, when I reached the bottom of the ropes. 'They move camp, and then don't even come up to tell us!' I punched deep holes in the soft snow down towards where we had left our ski poles. Around the final corner, and faced with only fifty metres of snow, to my delight I saw Iain and Chris.

'Hey!' I cried out.

They jumped up and waved. 'Where's Alan?' Chris shouted back.

'He's coming.'

There was a short pause, as if they were waiting for me to tell them something. 'Well? How did you get on?'

'You don't know?'

There was another pause as I stumbled up to my waist in the soft infuriating snow. So they *can't* have seen us coming down the headwall, I thought. 'Only the West summit I'm afraid,' I said. I can't imagine what had got into me. What was I 'afraid' of. What did I mean 'only the West summit'. I was overjoyed by our climb.

'*Really* well done!' said Chris spontaneously, suddenly back in his Sandhurst voice. They had brought a flask of tea and some sardines and some of Krishna's momoes, and I sat and munched some, while we waited for Alan. Chris clipped a small microphone to my salopettes.

'Hey, what are you doing?'

'It's nothing. Just pretend it's not there,' he said like a guilty schoolboy. 'Here, have another sardine.'

'Where's camp?' I continued my interrogation. It felt like a stupid question, once I had said it, but it wasn't.

'Halfway to Chang bu Jiang,' Chris said. 'We're going there now.'

Alan arrived and we ate and drank everything that we were offered and after half an hour rose to leave.

'Where are the ski poles?' Alan asked.

'What do you mean?'

'They were just here, under this pile of rocks.'

'They're gone?' said Iain suddenly taking a keen interest. 'Let's get a picture!'

'Iain, it's hardly the work of the yeti!'

'Why not? Could they have blown away?'

'No . . .'

'Well there you are then, QED – quite easily done.'

We continued to search but had to conclude that they had been taken. We could even see where the rocks had been unearthed.

'They were definitely here?' Iain asked.

'Yes. Just here,' Alan said. 'I even left some bog roll, here under this stone. They've taken that as well!'

It did seem very intriguing, particularly as no one knew that we had come this way. Certainly a Tibetan would have no normal reason to come up this scree ridge to 5300 metres. They would need ESP, we concluded, to know that we had left our sticks here.

'ESP! The yeti!' said Chris jubilantly. 'I knew that my theory was right.'

Nobody was as delighted as Iain. 'A double scoop,' he murmured as we started off down the ridge towards Chang bu Jiang.

16

Home

'Thelly good!' Francis ran out to greet us as we crossed the grass and boulders towards our temporary camp. 'I think you have *done* it!'

'Yes, sort of . . .'

'You get a picture?' Francis could not contain his excitement.

'It was dark.'

He gave me one of his cheeky smiles. 'No picture?'

'No, Francis,' I laughed. It was certainly a fantastic welcome.

'But you cannot get certificate from CMA without *picture*!'

Jess and Charlie had also come out to greet us. They looked genuinely elated. Jess had had a long day with Chris on Point 6301m, reaching only a hundred metres from the top. I could tell that both were pleased with their excursion. As we got nearer camp, David and Steve came out as well. They had seen us approaching and made a flask of tea which they offered with a couple of plastic mugs.

'You did good,' David said. 'You guys were tenacious.'

I said, 'Thanks.'

'Pity about the main top.'

'Sure.'

We lodged ourselves inside the kitchen tent, where Krishna and Nima had a meal prepared and Charlie produced the last of the wine. We talked about the climb but also I learnt that Charlie and Iain had found the skins of two bharal on the glacier below the East Ridge. The skins were fresh and there were no bones scattered nearby. A Tibetan, we were reminded by those who believed in the yeti, would have kept the skins to make clothes or to sleep on. A snow leopard would have left bones in the vicinity. Charlie had been very careful to collect all the turds in the area to take home with the bharal skins. Two weeks later, he declared them in the Red Channel at Heathrow Airport and was waved hastily through. But minutes before his appearing on Wogan the

Department of Agriculture and Fisheries impounded the skins and left Charlie with only a freezer bag full of shit to brandish at Wogan.

I soon began to feel drunk and very tired. The others had already erected my tent and I went to it and slept solidly, revelling in the space. In the morning of 25th May we started for home. I was carrying just a small rucsac, bounding effortlessly along the mud path, bordered with fresh green grasses and brightly coloured alpine flowers. For the people of Chang bu Jiang, the summer was just beginning. The monsoon was rolling in and soon the yaks would return to the alpine pastures beneath Menlungtse.

After an hour, I felt an urge to turn around. The pyramidal North Face of Menlungtse formed an enormous dark tooth, framed in a backlit sky. From the side of the face two kilometres behind, the East summit seemed to be winking at me and I wondered when it would be finally climbed, and whether I would return. I was a little sad to be leaving. I questioned why we had not been more tenacious and climbed through the night from the West summit to reach the top by dawn. So easy to say! Regrets were futile. We could not change what had happened. Simply, we had listened to our instincts; just as Chris, Steve and David had done, a week before. To have betrayed those inner feelings would have been to discard the very fabric of decision-making.

The rhododendron forest was in mid-flower and bursting with other life. And it was hot. As we tilted down the Menlung Chu, the temperatures climbed. I stripped to my waist and tossed my two-month shock of hair away from my face. The sweat on my brow stung my eyes. In the early afternoon I caught sight of the Chue gompa, and an hour later I reached it and hesitated briefly before kicking up the valley to Chang bu Jiang and the start of a long climb home.

David and Steve were in the Army compound drinking chang. As the afternoon passed, more of our group assembled there with an endless supply of drink. David insisted that Menlungtse was unclimbed. And we agreed with him. But he laboured his point. I found him very tiresome at first, but later as our arguments became personalised, and the quantity of consumed chang increased, I could see that our conference had degenerated into a harmless slanging match that continued unabated until we were slurring our words so much that we had to stop. But I recognised that David had exorcised a great deal of frustration from his system.

In the morning the herders were slow in collecting our loads and setting off and David spent the time with the local people, particularly the children of the village. He had a very gentle, open manner with them,

173

and I admired him for that. Clearly he was enduring something of a psychological struggle, coming to terms with his decision to give up on the mountain. I did not doubt that he was regretting that decision, and that this had been his motivation for playing down our own climb to the West summit. The blow-out the night before appeared to have settled him.

That day we reached Darzang, at about 4200 metres, where we ate and slept in the village headman's home. I noticed that one of the houses had no windows or doors, but it wasn't until I saw a man squatting on its roof that I discovered what it was. I wondered what they intended to do when it was full. It was certainly an improvement on Chang bu Jiang, where I had found turds at the bottom of most of the best boulder problems.

Chris had sent a message for there to be a truck on the other side of the Fusi La on the 28th but, as there was some doubt that it had got through, David, Steve and I decided to cover the distance to the roadhead in a single day, against the others' two, and then, if a truck did not arrive, we could set off to Tingri and organise one. We carried sleeping bags in case the Cho Oyu camp was deserted. I welcomed an opportunity to open up and move quickly across the terrain. I also enjoyed walking with David and Steve, particularly as I knew that at Tingri we would split up. Chris, Jess and Francis planned to go home via Lhasa and Beijing to see the CMA. Chris had invited me to go with them across China. Thus the expedition was, in many ways, about to end.

But I quickly pulled ahead of the other two. I felt fitter than I had ever been, a result of good eating and strenuous living. I climbed quickly out of the Rongshar Gorge and onto the rolling terrain of the Fusi La, stripped of snow. On the other side I dropped steeply down towards the formidable bulk of Cho Oyu and the Tibetan plateau, still lifeless and grey after all those weeks.

I followed the road down from the pass, which meandered through a series of switchbacks. David and Steve cut directly across them and pulled ahead of me again. I came upon a small group of cloth tents shared between two or three nomadic families. I marched over to them and sat on the ground between their tents while everyone stood around, looking down on me. The smell of yaks on their bodies was remarkable.

'Chang bu Jiang,' I said, pointing over the pass. 'Jobo Garu, Jobo Tseringma,' making a steeple with my hands. They shook their heads gently. Some of the children whispered to each other and then started to giggle. Their elders ignored them, and continued to fix me with their blank expressions. 'Chomolungma,' I said, more quietly.

174

'Chomolungma!' said a man, in a high pitch. It was the first time I had heard him speak, but I felt sure from his tone that he had understood the word. Chomolungma is the local name for Everest, literally Mother Goddess of the Earth. But I had misled him. I was a fraud.

'No,' I shook my head. 'No Chomolungma.' And then with emphasis, 'Jobo Garu.'

The man resumed his blankness. 'Jobo Garu,' he repeated.

I produced my camera and everybody took a step back. 'Here, take a look.' I held the camera out to the man who had spoken. He took it and everybody gathered round him again. He studied the object carefully, turning it over in his hands. He looked at me, smiled and handed it to the others, who passed it around the group. Finally it came back to the man and he offered it to me.

'Thank you,' I said to him. Everybody laughed, not just the children now.

'Fan Que,' they imitated.

The children had gained confidence and their curiosity in me was a force too strong for them to resist. They gathered around me very closely and I gave one of them my Walkman, after first switching it on. I demonstrated what to do with the speakers. In the same way as before they passed the machine among their group and returned it to me. Their faces were filled with wonder.

I stood up and offered my hand to the man. He hesitated then took it with both of his and gripped it tightly. I shouldered my rucsac and walked away. None of the children ran after me, but I could feel their gazes on my back. I turned and waved at the motionless group, all of their faces turned towards me, smiling broadly.

At the Cho Oyu camp I met up with David and Steve and an Austrian expedition who had already climbed Xixabangma and who now wanted to make a fast ascent of Cho Oyu. We spent an enjoyable evening with them, eating some of their luxurious food and sleeping in their mess tent. In the morning the truck arrived, right on cue, and we rode with it higher up the road back towards the Fusi La where we stopped and waited. In the middle of the morning the team arrived with the yaks and Chris and Jess paid their herders off. By the evening we had made it to Tingri.

Galen Rowell, the American wilderness photographer, was there, doing a shoot for the *National Geographic Magazine*. Even as he shook hands with Chris, who he had not seen for several years, he viewed him through his lens and unleashed his autowind. 'Just stock,' he apologised. Some apology. He told us that an Anglo-American team had climbed a

175

new route on the Kangchung Face of Everest and that they were due to be in Lhasa any day. Most of our team knew the only British member, Stephen Venables, and I wondered whether we would be able to meet up. Early the next morning a jeep rolled into the compound and its driver and Francis conversed.

'Okay, let's go,' Francis said.

It happened so quickly. We said our goodbyes to the others. I knew that I would see most of them again in London for a press conference, but not the Americans, nor our Nepalese lads.

'Cheers, Steve, Dave. Enjoy your ride to Kathmandu.'

'Yeh, cheers. Good one. See you again!' I really hoped that I would. I embraced Krishna and Nima and clambered into the Mitsubishi.

Our journey to Lhasa took us two days, on the first bouncing over unmetalled roads for 300 kilometres to Xigaze, the second city of Tibet, near the mighty Tsangpo river. Lhasa lived up to none of my expectations. Through its size it had lost charm, but gained no grandeur. I wandered about its streets trying to soak up some of its atmosphere. Apart from its religious buildings, it appeared to be a perfectly average and impoverished sprawling town. The Potala was certainly impressive in its size and dominance, though not as beautiful from street level as I had expected. The concrete and corrugated iron buildings of Lhasa were so encroaching that I was given only glimpses of the Potala's white walls, and tiny windows. A dead dog was floating in the stagnant river. I visited the Jokhang Temple, but was not allowed inside the Potala and I wonder whether it was this disappointment that tainted my impression of the city.

We stayed in the Holiday Inn in Lhasa where we met Reinhold Messner who refused to let us know why he was in Tibet. Reinhold claimed to have seen the yeti.

'So are you looking for the yeti on this trip?' asked Chris.

'No, I am not,' he said. He convinced nobody.

The Everest team were also staying at the Holiday Inn, though not Stephen Venables, who had travelled home via Kathmandu. Steve had reached the summit but contracted quite serious frostbite, as did two of the Americans, Ed Webster and Rob Anderson. Ed in particular was suffering terribly and had every finger on both his hands bandaged. He and Rob had reached the South summit of Everest, behind Stephen, but they had been exhausted and close to collapse, so had decided to retreat to the South Col. Earlier, Ed had taken off his gloves and taken photographs of dawn on Lhotse, which is how, he told us, he had first developed frostbite. Dehydration, oxygen starvation and a treacherous

176

descent in a delirious condition to Base Camp, where the others had given up hope of ever seeing them again, made it worse. Ed and Mimi Zieman, the expedition doctor who had worked around the clock for three weeks, allowed me to sit in while she redressed his wounds. I did so shamelessly, because I was curious. Messner, whose two feet share just three toes, had confirmed to Ed that he would lose his fingers, but declined a private viewing.

We went to Mimi's room. 'It's not nice,' she said to me. 'I'd like to warn you.'

'Thanks. I bet you didn't think you would be so busy – I mean with three casualties,' I added.

'No. I've never seen frostbite before. More used to stab wounds.'

'I beg your pardon?'

'I work in Casualty,' she said, 'in the Bronx.'

She carefully cut away the existing bandage, to the clenched cries of pain from Ed. I was horrified at what I saw. From the second joint each of his fingers had been reduced to a shrivelled black stick, barely the width of a pencil. After an hour, when they had patiently applied all the fresh dressings, Ed disappeared back to the group. I walked back with Mimi.

'That's dreadful. And he's so cheerful.'

'Believe me, Andy,' she said softly, 'he's suffering inside.'

My admiration for Ed Webster was total. For a man who had come within an hour of the highest point on earth and been forced to retreat and who was now facing the loss of eight fingers, Ed had a brave face. He joked, not about his wounds, but about life and its peculiarities, anything that would raise a smile and help with the pain. He talked in positive terms about everything and everybody.

At the airport, waiting for our flight to Chengdu, the next stage of the journey to Beijing, we were able to study a sort of tourist's charter and code of ethics. Clauses 3 and 4 read:

Foreigners are no allowed to crowd around watching and photographing disturbances manipulated by a few splittists and they should not do any distorted propaganda cocerning disturbances, which is not in agreement with the facts.

In accordance with our laws we shall mete out punishment to the trouble makers who stir up support and participate in the disturbance manipulated by a few splittists.

An adjacent notice informed us that we could not carry TNT onto the plane.

Our flight over Eastern Tibet offered impressive views of some of the world's most uncharted mountains. We flew close to Namche Barwa, at 7756 metres the highest unclimbed peak in the world. Even more impressive was the Tsangpo river, where it cut a fiercely deep gorge around the mountain to flow south as the Brahmaputra to the Indian Ocean.

We spent two nights in Chengdu, which is below sea level, arranging connecting flights to Beijing and sleeping. Here Francis had come into his own, while the Americans' interpreter was useless. 'Don't scream like a dog, or you'll never get out of here!' was what he had told an anxious Mimi who was pressuring him to arrange an earlier flight for Ed. Francis went back to the agency and stormed straight to the front of the queue. He thrust Ed's bandaged hands across the counter.

'We need a ticket, *immediately*!' Francis bawled at them in a way that really gave them no option. Ed, and all of his team, were on the next flight to Beijing.

Our own foursome arrived in Beijing a day after the Americans and spent the remaining few days of the expedition socialising with them and liaising with the CMA. In a lengthy and tedious financial meeting, Jess turned an overdraft on our account into a credit. The Association also laid on a banquet of the most expensive Chinese food, and invited all of China's most eminent mountaineers and bureaucrats. I was impressed by their hospitality.

'So was I on *my* first banquet,' Chris informed me, 'until I got the bill for it. Did you know we're paying for our share?' I didn't.

At last on 7th June, after three days in the city and a celebratory meal with the Everest team, we went to the airport for our long flight home. On the outward journey PIA had uprated our tickets to first class. I explained this fact to Francis. 'See what you can do,' I said to him.

'Oh yes, no problem,' said our ever confident fixer, marching straight to the front of the queue as usual.

'No, stop!' I said to him, suddenly embarrassed.

'Quickly! Give-me your tic-kets,' he said with urgency. 'Smoke or no?'

'Um . . . not,' I said.

Francis entered into rapid dialogue with the clerk. After a minute he turned to me again. He looked stunned. 'She says first class seats not available.'

'That's okay, Francis, really. No problem,' I said.

'No! I mean *yes* – pro-blem! Must be some mistake.'

The others in the queue started to look a little perturbed. I looked

178

away, while Francis raised his voice switching back into Mandarin. I put my head in my hand.

'Francis! Please!' I said.

'But she says we can only have *one* first class,' he said disbelievingly.

'One?'

'Yes, only one!'

'We'll take it!'

He fell silent and looked quizzically at me. 'One okay?'

'Yes, Francis,' Chris intervened, then turning to me, 'you take it.'

We said goodbye to Francis. He ran between us, giving us each a hug. 'I shall miss you!' he said, smiling broadly.

'See you,' I said to him, though doubting that I ever would. Francis had been the perfect official. He had suffered the brunt of our humour, smiled happily through it all, and ultimately gained our greatest respect.

In the early morning the Boeing jet flew across the huge expanse of Tibet and Xinjiang. 'Ladies and gentlemen,' came the announcement after several more hours of dozing, 'K2, Pakistan's highest mountain is visible on the left side.' My eyes were drawn instinctively to the highest mountains of the Karakoram far away on the horizon: K2, Broad Peak and the mighty Gasherbrums. It took a trained eye to know where to look and I imagine that I was the only person on the plane to be looking beyond K2, to an elegant trapezium that Conway had called the Great White Roof. I was filled with pleasure – Chogolisa.

In Beijing we had lived in style. By comparison my newly acquired semi in Manchester now seemed bare and unwelcoming. But I had arrived at the beginning of the British summer, in time for a full season of rock-climbing. There were good things to look forward to.

I revelled once again in my work, recharged by an absence from the hurly burly life of a mountaineering bureaucrat. Dennis looked a little more drained, constantly defending himself from the interminable political flak of his enemies, but his wit and wisdom and capacity for story-telling had not faltered. I listened each day to a new story and wondered when he would tell me one that I had already heard. He never did. Not even Lesley, his secretary and most trusted confidante, had heard two the same. I remembered at K2 Base Camp, John Barry, who had recently retired from his post of Director at Plas y Brenin and a long-time supporter of Dennis, saying to me, 'You've got a good job, you. No matter what cock-ups you make, it's Dennis who gets the blame. People will always see to that!' But Dennis was rarely suppressed for long; springing back with a quip of his much imitated Yorkshire inflection. In the spring of 1989 he left the Council, set on doing other things, and I resigned also, to visit Makalu and to write this book. Dennis had been the perfect leader and one of the greatest assets to the sport.

Over New Year prior to Menlungtse, I had visited the limestone region around Alicante and Valencia and it was here that I met Caroline. She was climbing above the beautiful hillside village of Chulilla, and had come for a few days from Madrid where she was living. She was vibrant like Spain. We talked in a bar in the square, surrounded by brightly clad *chicos*. I admired their ease.

'*¡Hola! Soy Juan Carlos. ¿Eres de Madrid, no?*' said one of the youths.

'*Me llamo, Carolina. Estoy trabajando allí.*'

She had a natural, fluent way with these people. I understood little of what they were saying, only that it had freshness and spontaneity, unbound by stiff British etiquette.

'*¿Quieres beber algo?*'

'*Gracias. Una cerveza por favor . . .*'

'*¿Y tu amigo?*'

'*Andy Si. ¡Ya lo creo! Una cana tambien.*'

'What did he say?'

'He's buying you a beer.'

I wrote to her as soon as I returned to Manchester. The mild wet Scottish winter seemed to be prompting me as if I was seeking compensation for the poor conditions. And I wrote three times from Menlungtse. Her own letters were frequent, long and impulsive, about the crags and life of Madrid and the children she taught and loved.

We met again briefly in Britain in July before she travelled to America for six weeks. In September she returned to Madrid and we made plans to meet again at Christmas. But the lure was too great and I spent several weekends of the autumn in Spain. We travelled widely in Caroline's rusty Renault 4 van, walking and climbing in Andalucia, the Gredos, Guadalajara and Toledo. At first Spain was a buoyant blur. We rushed through the landscape, with barely an idle minute, climbing in the warm sun and descending from the hilltops in the gathering dusk. Later, the days cooled and we drew closer together. Inevitably in the evenings we retreated to the *pueblo blanco* and its tight cobbled streets, littered with autumnal colour. Here we would find a bar, and a collection of old men over a game of dominoes and a bottle of wine. Sometimes we slept in the Renault perched on the steep twisting roads above the lights of the white village, sometimes in the olive groves, sometimes in a classic Spanish *pension*.

180

Over New Year in Fez in Morocco, we decided to get married and set a date for the spring of 1990. It had seemed the most natural thing to do.

17

Calm

Makalu, for which I had had permission since 1987, loomed nearer. In the final weeks before departure I had suffered pressures like I had never endured, shuffling priorities between my BMC work, sponsors, film crews and the other members of the team. In July 1989 I was sent a Fax at the BMC. It laid down conditions then ended, '. . . or I resign. Saunders.' I laughed, then felt my insides hollow out in anguish.

Tony Saunders was an architect in London and I had met him through the BMC, an organisation that he called a 'loose collection of sub-committees'. He was competitive to the extreme, but self-effacing of his own achievements and extremely knowledgeable, having enormous respect for some climbers, whom I had never heard of, and paltry regard for most of the others. Rather involuntarily, I suspect, Tony had dropped his first name and his friends had adopted Victor, his middle one. Presumably they did so because it had a better ring to it when prefixed by 'Slippery'; for he was simply impossible to tie down. The more direct the question, the more indirect his answer. Once he rang from a railway station and asked me to pick him up.

'Are you at Stockport?' I asked.

'I might be,' he said. It had been his automatic response.

'Well are you?'

'I think so . . . Yes.'

He was always very guarded about his own plans, but infuriated by secrecy in others. He reminded me of Gollum in *The Lord of the Rings*; a slight frame with dark intense features and an affinity for greasy, wet rock climbs, as if their lack of friction were advantageous.

'What was the crux like, Vic?'

'Wet.'

'Oh, well, that was lucky then.'

And he was similarly at home in the cold. His early climbs, such as winter ascents of the North Face of the Eiger and the Shield Direct on Ben Nevis, both in 1979, were succeeded by impressive firsts in Bhutan, the Caucasus and Pakistan including the desperate Golden Pillar of Spantik in 1987.

We were having our problems. Three weeks before projected departure, we had found a sponsor, Blackspur Group Plc. Kees and Annette, Victor's friends were coming to shoot news footage which could be sent back to Britain by mail runner, but they also wanted to make a small film of their own. Peter and Harriet Getzels who, under the ambiguous but intriguing banner Passion Pictures, were filming for Channel Four, now insisted that they could not work in those conditions. Didn't we know that another lens would ruin everything, they probed.

'But you want a Sherpa film. Kees is doing a climber film,' Victor persuaded.

'Yes, but we need climber action.'

'You knew about Kees.' This was not an enquiry.

'No, we didn't!'

Victor was dumbstruck for a full minute. Did he hear them correctly, he wanted to know. Were these guys real? Their terse riposte sent him reeling, cursing, mistrusting. He had my every sympathy. Our sponsors suggested a meeting, and we tried, we really did. But it broke at three a.m. unresolved. We were leaving in a week. The freight had already gone. This is when Victor sent me his Fax. At the eleventh hour it all slotted loosely into place, but I do not remember being so tired in my whole life.

On 30th July I met the others at the airport. Caroline came to see me off. I hated to leave her for three months and I began to question whether I really wanted to go to the Himalaya at all. Certainly I was in no condition to climb a mountain.

Four weeks passed. Above our grassy terrace where we had formed a small village of dome tents, the South Face of Makalu rose, undeterred, for almost three and a half kilometres. I had never seen such a daunting mountain, so plastered in fresh snow. The South-East Ridge that we had come to climb snaked steeply down from the summit to a col from where it traversed a knife-edge peak, finally petering out on a grassy saddle just above our camp. Steve Sustad smiled to himself.

'It's desperate, right?' he said.

'Sure.'

'The hanging valley will be waist-deep in snow, I know it.'

And who could argue with him? In 1984, with Doug Scott and Frenchman Jean Afanassieff he had come within 200 metres of the summit and turned back when Jean, with the words 'I go,' had turned downslope and set off back to camp. Doug and Steve had looked at each other, shrugged and followed suit. The descent was made even more harsh by deep snow in the Eastern Basin, what Steve had called the hanging valley. Rather than stick to the South-East Ridge all the way up, it was easier, Steve argued, to drop into the basin behind the ridge and climb the headwall at the back to regain the ridge near the summit. Thus, even descending, one is faced with a 300-metre climb.

'Once you're in that valley,' he reminded us, 'there's no way out but up. Like climbing an 8000-metre peak just to get down.'

'You can't bail out into Tibet, then?' I asked, as the Devil's advocate. Stephen laughed. I had a great respect for Steve, our quietly spoken and unflappable American. In a small wiry frame, he had packed a lot of strength, yet he had a passive and tolerant nature.

We had reached Base Camp on 27th August, one whole month after we had first arrived in Kathmandu. Import hassles had cost us a fortnight, and the walk-in had taken us another, when we suffered a porter strike and then a riot. 160 porters had smashed their sticks on the ground in a frenzy. 'What a pain in the ass,' had come Steve's resigned and hoarse whisper beside me.

Base Camp was perched amid clean granite boulders on a grassy shelf at 4900 metres, just below the snout of the Upper Barun Glacier. We christened the area Haute Fontainebleau, after the forested sandstone bouldering area in France where Parisian rock-climbers do their training. We scattered our dome tents and they clung to the earth like limpets to sea-swept rocks, our home for the coming weeks. Camp, and the outwash plain of the glacier, were strewn with litter when we arrived; tin cans and foil food wrappers that previous expeditions had apparently thrown on a fire miraculously expecting them to burn. It was a disgusting sight and one that brought Rob Collister, one of the team, close to tears of rage. We collected some of the rubbish and employed our porters to carry it out and bury it permanently near Tashigon. There were ten climbers in our group, a mix of friends, including Ulric and Hamish.

I knew what it felt like to want to climb a mountain, to have an apprehensive yet determined gut feeling. That sensation did not appear. Our Sherpas built a shrine and strung out prayer flags. Then they performed a small ceremony. I poked my head out of my tent when I heard their cheers, but it was too late. I had missed the puja.

Early in the expedition a few of us traversed around the west side of Makalu to the Advance Base Camp, the site at 5400 metres that the

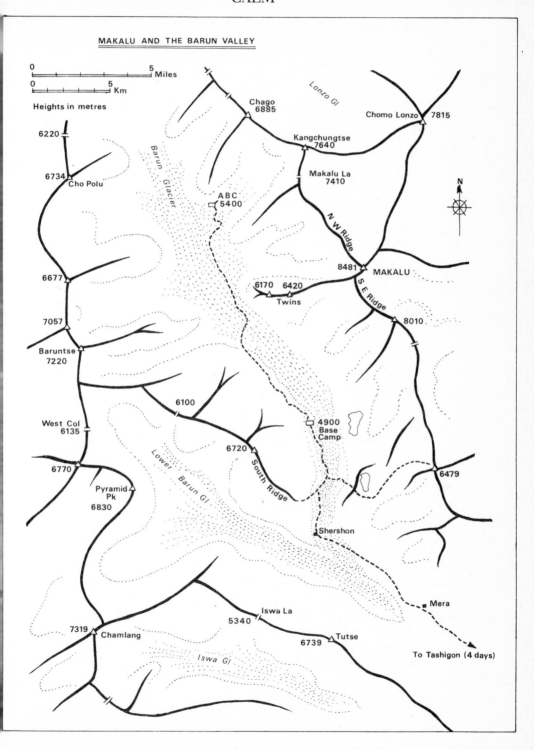

MAKALU AND THE BARUN VALLEY

0 — 5 Miles
0 — 5 Km

Heights in metres

6220
6734 Cho Polu
6677
7057
Baruntse 7220
West Col 6135
6770
Pyramid Pk 6830

Barun Glacier
ABC 5400
Chago 6885
Lonzo Gl
Kangchungtse 7640
Chomo Lonzo 7815
Makalu La 7410
N W Ridge
8481 MAKALU
6170 6420 Twins
S E Ridge
8010

6100
4900 Base Camp
6720
South Ridge
6479
Lower Barun Gl
Shershon

N

Iswa La 5340
7319 Chamlang
6739 Tutse
Mera
Iswa Gl
To Tashigon (4 days)

French expedition of 1955 had used on the first ascent via the Makalu La on the northside. It was perched in a small depression on a terrace high on the spur of splintered rocks and scree between the Upper Barun and Chago Glaciers. A small stagnant lake provided water. We spent two days there, acclimatising above camp up to 6000 metres, and socialising with a Catalan expedition attempting the original 1955 route. I was touched by the naked beauty of the area, the huge mountains all about, Everest and Lhotse in the west, Baruntse the south, Kangchungtse the north and Makalu itself, rising more steeply than ever before. The West Face was frightening, capped immediately beneath the summit by a vertical headwall of smooth granite. Towards Kangchungtse, I could trace the route that the Catalans would follow up the Chago Glacier to the Makalu La and then up near the North-West Ridge to the summit. The ridge was backlit each morning, highlighted by a single thread of light where the wind had thrown spindrift snow into the air. I enjoyed the crisp dawn light most of all, when the fluttering prayer flags were still frosted and the mist was heavy in the hollow of our camp. I sat and waited, wrapped warmly inside my duvet jacket, breathing the thin air. The East Face of Everest was the first to be flooded with light. It held a soft yellow glow but just as quickly it was drained, white again. Slowly the lower mountains, above the far bank of the Barun, caught the glow of the sun, and held my gaze, each in turn. Baruntse was a huge snowy hulk, its lower neighbours above the Sherpani Col were sharp and pointed like single brush strokes of brilliant white paint. I could feel my heart opening out.

Our Sirdar, Nati Sherpa, and I wanted to accompany Steve and Vic on another acclimatising foray, but Mingma, Nati's brother, refused to let him leave camp. Mingma was one of our kitchen hands and he had been down at the Barun meltwater river washing his clothes, when he had suddenly felt very cold and ripped his hand from the water. He looked up and saw Sherpas walking down the river. He turned away and looked again, but they had vanished. He ran all the way back to camp. The figures, Mingma believed, were the ghosts of those who had died on Makalu and he was convinced that he would be the next. He lay in his tent shivering violently. Gill, our doctor, could find nothing physically wrong with him. The other Sherpas summoned a local Lama from lower in the valley who chanted, burned leaves and threw rice around the tent. Mingma did recover, but not right away and he still looked forlorn.

The monsoon weather was kind with the morning more settled than after midday. Although it was common for there to be less than an hour of sunshine each day, it was rarely windy and normally warm. We knew

186

that above the clouds Makalu would be enjoying fine weather. Our 6500-metre mountain offered a fruitful outing. We walked in two days to its base, below the West Face, and camped there, at about 5900 metres. The next day, carrying just a camera and a water bottle we climbed unroped up the steep face and along the summit ridge to the top.

From the base of the face, the next morning, I looked covetously at an elegant pillar of rock. It led to a small shoulder at 6010 metres, from where an icy arête cut upward to a gleaming white summit marked as 6720m on our map between Chamlang and Base Camp. I easily persuaded Ulric to climb it with me. He went further and suggested we traverse the peak.

'We can follow this skyline here after the summit,' he said, pointing to the jagged white crest two kilometres above camp, 'and come out at the Sherpani Col. We could do three or four summits!'

He was as ambitious as ever. In the years since Chogolisa he had barely changed. In 1987 in Ecuador he had made the first true ascent of the West Ridge Direct of El Obispo, a route that I climbed, avoiding the obvious crux section in 1984. Ulric and Hamish still climbed together frequently and planned to be the first pair to try the traverse of Makalu, the way that Steve had tried in 1984.

We threaded through the mist to the bottom of our spur. My rucsac carried four days' food and gas, bivouac equipment and an assortment of gear for our technical climb. I was exhausted by the effort. I led the first pitch. As soon as I started to climb my fatigue waned. We wandered happily up the blunt crested pillar, pitch after pitch of impeccable climbing. I reflected that apart from one hot day at Stanage Edge in the Peak District, I hadn't climbed with Ulric in over three years. It did not seem to have mattered, for we were climbing quickly and confidently together. After 200 metres the angle eased and we moved together for speed. The rock deteriorated and we slunk upwards on the shattered crest. A rather temporary looking ramp led onto open snow slopes. We camped in the mist on a toadstool of rock high above the void, listening to the roar of avalanches satisfyingly far below.

Another day of mixed climbing to negotiate gendarmes on the ridge brought us a small col at about 6000 metres. Above lay a short icefall guarding the upper slopes.

On the first pitch of the next day I inched my way up a hideously rotten ice arête, a cold black abyss on each side. Every step was hollow, plunging me through into a void that I did not dare investigate. My headtorch chose this moment to blow its bulb, and I continued the pitch in the light of Ulric's faint glow twenty metres below, gratefully uncertain of the risks I was facing. After forty metres the snow became firm again and I climbed up a little further to belay on my ice axe. Ulric followed as it grew light. The mist had dropped and it swirled up at the shoulder like an ocean wave. Above, the sky was clear and a beautiful view was opening out south to the smothered lowlands of Nepal and east to Kangchenjunga and Jannu in Sikkim. I could see the peak that I had climbed and I followed the line that we had taken to the summit. I admired its elegance with satisfaction and wished momentarily that Vic and Steve could see the view. Behind lay Tibet. I looked as far as I could but nowhere was the ceiling of cloud broken.

We unroped and an interminable snow slope led in nine hours to a corniced ridge, and finally a snow mushroom that was the top. It was three o'clock, and the afternoon clouds had wrapped around us. We peered down the other side but could not see where to go, so we camped on the top of the mountain, anticipating our dawn vista. We were at 6720 metres, higher than my top camp on Menlungtse and I would not have expected to sleep. I writhed and tossed fitfully all night sliding deeper into my pit when I felt cold and fighting to escape it when the claustrophobia came. Not for the first time I wondered why I voluntarily put myself to such extremes of tiredness and discomfort. As before we slept head to foot. In the morning, when it was light enough to see, but when the sun was still below the eastern horizon, Ulric poked his head out of the tent.

'What a beauty!' he said, calmly. 'The best day of the trip!'

'What can you see?' I said without thinking.

'Everything!'

He crawled slowly out onto our summit perch and stood up by the entrance of the tent. As he moved away he revealed Everest framed in the doorway, just beginning to glow. I scampered up, pulled on my inner boots and joined him.

It was the finest view I can remember. Of the six highest summits in the world we could see five of them. Only K2 was absent. Soon all the East Faces were brightly lit and we were bathed in sunlight. The ground fell away steeply in all directions. Our massif, scattered at our feet, towered above the confluence of the Upper and Lower Barun Glaciers. The Lower Barun and Base Camp two kilometres vertically below were obscured by a huge grey arm of cloud extending out into Nepal's muffled lowland, isolating our cluster of peaks on an island of snow. There were rivers down there, thick forests, villages, hills, a whole expanse of Asia hidden beneath a perfectly smooth bank of cloud. And not a single thermal had yet pierced its flawless silver surface. The sacred Tutse and the long line of Chamlang summits across the southern ocean formed other detached worlds. Tutse's eastern flank shifted colour through a spectrum of pastel hues as the day broke. At one moment it glowed purple. To the north-east, against the glare of a Tibetan sun, my other summit dominated another quarter. Four years before, and with fresh eyes, I had observed the chaotic confusion of the Karakoram. But now I viewed an ordered range of peaks. Each mountain group gathered at the foot of Makalu had identity. And a charm. In the west, fifty kilometres distant above the Khumbu, I recognised a small, sharp needle, Men-lungtse. I was older, satisfied and calm.

Makalu, except the highest ramparts of its Eastern Cwm, was shaded dark, inert and brooding. Symbolically so, for I viewed it with no more enthusiasm now than when I had arrived at camp two weeks before. It suddenly became very clear to me that I should give it up. I felt released, as if the present climb had flushed the confusion from my mind. I briefly considered telling Ulric but decided to wait until camp.

Ulric suggested tentatively that we abandon the traverse and I noted his reluctance with some surprise. It had been the first time that I had seen him hesitate. Three years before I doubt that we would have chosen to retreat. Ulric was no less enthusiastic but he had matured. In his mind he was measuring his energy and gauging it against what he would need for his main objective. His gaze lingered much longer than mine on the South-East Ridge.

We packed up the tent and set off unroped, heeling back down. I threw myself down the slope, half-sliding my crampons through the inch of crust, half-braking against the speed. I was joyful to be moving so fast. In a single hour we reached the site of our previous morning and in another two were at the first night's bivouac. Now for the rock. Ulric started to climb down solo. I followed reluctantly at first but slowly loosening up as we descended into the thick mist. Sensations of exposure and risk were lost in the cloud and we swung confidently on the holds, edging on the smallest intermediary footholds to save the long groping stretches. Could we descend the whole mountain without tying on? I asked myself. Ulric seemed to know the answer already, as he raced on down. He stopped at the top of the first four pitches of the climb, a section of Very Severe that he had led three days earlier. He looked down. Surely not!

'Ulric, my leg's a bit dicky . . . I'd like to abseil this bit, please.'

'Naturally,' he replied.

Forty minutes later we were running the scree and grass slopes back

189

to Base Camp. It was snowing when we arrived at two o'clock on 14th September. I crashed into the mess tent and the Sherpas rushed around to fetch a brew. After I had rested I took Mike Woolridge, with whom I shared the Makalu permit, to one side and told him that I was giving up. He expressed surprise.

'You look happier now, than when we arrived,' he said.

Ulric looked twice as confused, fell silent and said simply, 'Why?'

'I'm exhausted, mate,' I said. 'I just can't get my mind around the mountain.'

He looked at me curiously, in the same way perhaps that I had contemplated David Breashears a year before. He raised his eyebrows, then blanked his expression.

I was in no mood to justify myself. I had resigned myself to the fact that I was unfit to climb Makalu. Physically, I was in good shape and well acclimatised. But mentally I was left unguarded. It was a new feeling and not one that I had immediately approved. But I was now ready to go with it. I missed Caroline and at first I accepted that this was the major reason for my unrest. Yet equally I recognised that, had I been content with the mountain, I would not be thinking so much of home.

'Missing her might be an effect,' said Mike thoughtfully. 'The cause could be much deeper.'

Whatever, I was not prepared to go against my own grain. The mountain will always be there. I can return.

I left camp with Mingma, on 17th September. When I reached the last point where we could see Base Camp, I stopped and turned round. This is the acid test I thought. Will I want to go back? The answer was a resounding 'No'.

With a quick glance up to the South Face of Makalu, I turned my back on the mountain and my friends and tilted for home.

18

Afterwards

It was the twelfth day of the new year 1990, and another cloudless day was about to close in a week of perfect settled, cold, dry weather. We watched the face grow dark as dusk fell. A tiny section above and left of the Exit Cracks was sunlit for a few brief minutes. This was the extent of any sunshine that any part of the face had seen at any time of that day. We had never been here before, nor even considered climbing this mountain. Route-finding, we had been told, was crucial, so we studied the face for as long as the light would allow.

Our view was a familiar one, from the countless photographs and diagrams that we had studied or seen in passing. A light sensation rose in my stomach, a mixture of excitement and apprehension. We traced the history of the face. The Hinterstoisser Traverse, the stone-pitted Second Icefield, Death Bivouac, and the perfect logic of the upper wall – the Ramp, the Traverse of the Gods, the Spider and the Exit Cracks.

Ulric and I had met up as soon as he had returned from Makalu. A heavy dump of snow had prohibited his traverse attempt. Victor and Steve had made an audacious first ascent of the West Face of Kangchungtse and reached the summit just as the snow storm came. They survived an epic retreat but Steve returned at once to Britain with frostbite. The others stayed and attempted the *voie normal*, but continued heavy snow brought high avalanche risks and hampered their progress.

In November Ulric and I had discussed coming to the Alps but we left arrangements open so that we could remain flexible on the weather. On the Wednesday I rang Mark Diggins, a British Guide in Chamonix.

'The conditions are fantastic!' he said. 'And the forecast is clear . . .' And then glumly, 'It's rubbish for skiing.'

I rang Ulric. The next evening I met him in London off a train from Edinburgh and we caught a night ferry to Calais. We drove through the night in my Nova to Grindelwald and caught the next train to Kleine Scheidegg. Dusk was gathering on the North Face of the Eiger.

Early the next morning we started and climbed unroped as far as the Difficult Crack. Perfect conditions prevailed. The air was cold and still. We reached the Hinterstoisser late in the afternoon and scratched across it and up a short crack at its end to the Swallows' Nest, banked out with winter snow as we had expected. We continued and, at the top of the First Icefield, cut two generous scoops in the ice, temporary residence for the night. We watched the western horizon nervously but it did not threaten. We slept deeply, thankfully tired. The dawn was deathly cold. Ulric's thermometer indicated minus twenty degrees. There were no clouds, not a breath of wind.

We struggled, but succeeded in climbing the vertical wall between us and the Second Icefield, the Ice Hose pitch. Cratered black ice beneath a veneer of snow then extended for 200 metres left to the Flat Iron and Death Bivouac. We moved together. The loop of rope between us snagged on rocks embedded in the ice; rocks that had once rested in the upper part of the face. Death Bivouac was also banked out, we could not bivouac there, but we were climbing quickly and did not doubt that we would reach the Traverse of the Gods that day. The Ramp was difficult to climb and its steepness threw us back. Herringbone clouds appeared and swept quickly overhead.

'We've got eight hours before it hits us,' I commented to Ulric, who did not need to be told that a depression had arrived and with it, no doubt, fresh snow.

On the fourth pitch of the Ramp Ulric led out a desperate ropelength, stemming impetuously out across an overhanging crack. He removed his gloves to climb and the holds felt sticky as the moisture on his skin instantly froze to the rock. Next, I led a reluctant bulge glossed with verglas ice, really frightening myself for the first time on the route. Ulric's pitch onto the Brittle Ledge above, the key to the upper face, was masterful. The climbing had suddenly turned from strenuous to delicate and he made that transition naturally. He tiptoed up a crumbling wall, careful not to dislodge rocks that would have funnelled onto me, but equally careful not to fall, for there was no protection and, if he had, he might have killed us both. Another difficult pitch was climbed in the dark and then a scramble up to reach the Traverse of the Gods and a perfect site for the night, big enough for us both to lie out. Thicker clouds rolled in and I prepared myself for the approaching moment when the snow would arrive. I slept fitfully, aware that I had perhaps never been as committed to reaching a summit in my life. Miraculously, the snow never came and, although on the northern horizon the sky had blacked out and it was snowing, the sky overhead remained clear. I could barely believe our luck.

At five o'clock we prepared to leave. I was shaking. An outrageous moment had just passed when I had woken with my head overhanging the wall below. I had looked vertically down the face and drawn a sharp gasping breath before realising where I was. The Traverse of the Gods is aptly named.

I found rocks and gravel in the bottom of my sleeping bag, two or three handfuls which I tossed down the mountain, but no gloves and no hat. What had I done?

'Osmosis,' explained Ulric. 'Outside there were rocks and inside there was essential equipment. The rocks moved in and the equipment was thrown down the face.'

The remainder of the route provided the best climbing that I had ever done. Ulric and I were better together now than at any other time and we were able to enjoy the phenomenal exposure. And what a place to be! My front points scratched the slaty rocks, the rest of my boot overhung the vertical face. Eiger, don't turn on me now! I thought glancing at the icy clear sky and cloud blanket over Interlaken. No chance. The Spider lay silent and did not even flinch as we passed. The Exit Cracks. Which way? Icy grooves, squeeze chimneys and limestone slabs led us upwards to the foot of the final long dièdre. The mountain had a sting in its tail; the stacked Hymnbook pitch.

I set to work bridging up the dry walls. Downward-facing slates greeted my crampons and refused to accept even the most useless of runners. A twenty-kilo rucsac dragged me down. Twenty metres above Ulric I was still desperately looking for a runner. Then I saw a peg winking at me out of reach about two metres above. I went for it too soon. I got in a mess and tried to shuffle myself upwards but I could not make the moves. My arms were pumped through the effort, my legs cramped and my fingers, numbed white from the cold, were slowly uncurling. In the final throes of desperation, facing a fall that would have killed me, I committed myself and stretched my ice axe out above me, putting the pick through the eye of the piton and cranking up as much as I could. My mind was distorted through fear. Next I fumbled with a karabiner and displaced the pick of my axe through the peg. I wobbled on for another twenty metres to a belay. I breathed very deeply and slowly.

Ulric led one more hard pitch and we emerged onto easy ground with every difficulty behind us. We untied, each trailing a rope behind us up

193

the Summit Icefield. More black ice led to a final razor edge, the summit ridge. I concentrated on my feet and swung them in wide arcs to keep the points of my crampons off my gaiters. It was an unnaturally clumsy and frightening way to finish our climb. Only when we came to the place where the slope fell in all directions did I accept that we had climbed the face. A perfect vista greeted our efforts with all of Switzerland laid out before us. The dying winter sunshine warmed my face.

Across the miles of shattered hills Mont Blanc stood proud. I briefly reflected on my climbs there with John and other friends. My epic above Chamonix brought a little smile. And thinking of John had the same effect. At last it seemed I could see the good times. What had happened, had happened. At least we were friends at the end.

'Where shall we go now?' asked Ulric.

'Let's go to Italy, to Finale. I can show you what it's like to climb in the sun, clipping bolts!'

'Okay, you're on. Then we'll go to Nice . . . Monaco! Swim in the sea!'

Ulric put his stride towards *terra firma*, and I watched him losing height. Then he stopped and looked back at me.

'You coming?' He grinned widely.

'Yes. I'm right behind you.'

We heeled down the western slopes of the mountain, pausing at a suitable perch to gaze down the dark sweep of North Wall. Beneath, the lights of Kleine Scheidegg were beginning to ignite and filter up through the lingering evening clouds.

APPENDIX I

CHOGOLISA EXPEDITION
SUMMARY AND CHRONOLOGY

Title	BRITISH CHOGOLISA EXPEDITION 1986
Area	Upper Baltoro Glacier, Karakoram, Pakistan.
Dates	27th June–12th September 1986
Achieved	First traverse and fifth ascent of Chogolisa and Bride Peak (7665m, 7654m) by SW Ridge and NE Ridge, 10th–15th August.
Personnel	Climbers: Andy Fanshawe (Leader), Liam Elliot, Hamish Irvine, Ulric Jessop and Simon Lamb
	Liaison Officer: Captain Gulzar Jamal
	Cook: Mohammed Ali
	Sirdar: Hamsa Ali (Satpara)

Diary

27 June	Andy, Liam, Hamish and Ulric fly to Karachi.
28 June	Board train to Rawalpindi.
29 June	Arrive Rawalpindi/Islamabad. Begin preparations and freight gear by Karakoram Highway to Skardu.
3 July	Simon arrives. Meet with Liaison Officer, Gulzar.
6 July	Briefing with Ministry of Tourism.
8 July	All team fly to Skardu. Meet Hamsa and Mohammed Ali.
11 July	Jeep to Dasso, roadhead.
12 July	Start walk-in with 32 porters.
16 July	Reach Paiju at snout of Baltoro Glacier.
18 July	Rest day at Urdokas.
22 July	Reach Base Camp at junction of Vigne and Upper Baltoro Glaciers.
24 July	Visit K2 Base Camp.
30 July	Liam, Hamish, Ulric and Simon leave for recce of north-east side of Bride Peak.

195

31 July	Andy follows after others.
1 August	Liam, Hamish, Ulric and Simon reach c.7000 metres on Ice Dome of Bride Peak. Andy reaches c.6500 metres.
2 August	All return to Base Camp.
3–4 Aug	Rest, prepare for traverse.
5–9 Aug	Grounded at Base Camp by bad weather.
10 August	Depart on traverse. Camp below Vigne Face.
11 August	Climb to c.6200 metres on Vigne Face.
12 August	Reach top of Face. Camp at site of Austrian Camp IV, c.6800 metres.
13 August	Long day to c.7400 metres.
14 August	Liam, Hamish, Ulric reach summit 7.30 a.m. Andy and Simon reach summit 8.02 a.m. Traverse to Bride Peak in late morning. Andy and Ulric climb summit tower. All descend to col at 7000 metres. Arrive 7 p.m. Ulric, lost, arrives at 10 p.m.
15 August	Andy reaches Base Camp at 6 p.m. Others camp at 6400 metres.
16 August	Others arrive at Base Camp 4 p.m.
19 August	Leave Base Camp. Andy and Simon reach Goro, others Broad Peak Base Camp.
23 August	Liam, Hamish and Ulric set off on West Face of Broad Peak, reaching c.6800 metres. Simon and Andy reach Jolla.
24 August	Liam, Hamish, Ulric reach c.7700 metres. Andy and Simon reach Askole.
25 August	Liam killed at c.7900 metres. Hamish and Ulric start descent. Andy and Simon enter Braldu Gorge.
26 August	Andy and Simon reach Skardu. Hamish and Ulric reach Base Camp.
31 August	Andy and Simon learn of death. Fly to Islamabad.
2 Sept	Andy and Simon fly to Gilgit, then take bus to Skardu.
6 Sept	Hamish, Ulric, Gulzar and Mohammed Ali reach Skardu.
7 Sept	Jeep to Islamabad.
9 Sept	De-briefing at Ministry.
11 Sept	Fly home.

MENLUNGTSE EXPEDITION
SUMMARY AND CHRONOLOGY

Title	MENLUNGTSE AND THE SEARCH FOR THE YETI
Area	Menlung Valley, Rolwaling, Autonomous Region of Tibet in the People's Republic of China.
Dates	23rd March–8th June 1988
Achieved	First ascent Menlungtse West (7023m) by West Face, 19th–23rd May.
Personnel	Climbers: Chris Bonington (Leader), David Breashears (USA), Andy Fanshawe and Steve Shea (USA)
	Support: Dr Charles Clarke and Jess Stock
	BBC Unit: John-Paul Davidson (director), Nigel Meakin (cameraman) and Arthur Chesterman (sound recordist)
	Mail on Sunday: Iain Walker (journalist), David O'Neil (photographer) and Alan Hinkes (courier)
	Interpreter: Fan Xiachan ('Francis')
	Cooks: Krishna Bahardur Rai and Nima Chotor Sherpa
Diary	
23 March	David B, Steve and Jess fly to Kathmandu, start arrangements. Meet Krishna and Nima.
30 March	Chris, Andy, Charlie, Iain, David O'N, Alan, Nigel, Arthur fly to Kathmandu.
3 April	John-Paul arrives from Bhutan. Receive telex from CMA.
9 April	Clearance to proceed.
10 April	Puja ceremony.
12 April	Reach Friendship Bridge and meet Francis.
13 April	Cross border into Tibet. Load truck and reach

Nyalam.

14 April	Via Lalung La, c.5200 metres, to Tingri.
15 April	Chris and Francis round up yaks from villages.
16 April	Truck to roadhead at Cho Oyu Base Camp.
18 April	Meet yaks and start walk-in.
19 April	Over Fusi La, c.5200 metres.
21 April	Reach Chang bu Jiang, c.3500 metres.
23 April	Visit Chue Gompa.
24 April	Start final stage of walk-in up Menlung Chu.
27 April	Reach Base Camp, c.4600 metres.
28 April	Alan leaves on mail run to Kathmandu.
29 April	Chris, David B, Andy and Steve make recce to East Ridge.
1 May	Chris, David B, Andy and Steve climb Point 5733m. Views to Menlungtse West Face. John-Paul, Nigel and Arthur leave for home.
7 May	David O'N leaves for home. Chris, David B, Andy and Steve start on first attempt on West Face. Reach Promontory at 5800 metres.
8 May	Reach 6250 metres on West Face.
9 May	Reach 6600 metres on West Face.
10 May	Reach base of headwall, c.6700 metres. Return to camp at 6250m.
11 May	Retreat to base of mountain. Alan arrives from Kathmandu with mail.
15 May	Chris, David B, Andy, Steve and Krishna return and camp beneath East Ridge.
16 May	Further inspection. Abandon attempt plans. Chris, David B and Steve drop out of another attempt on West Face.
19 May	Andy and Alan leave on attempt on West Face. Reach Promontory.
20 May	Rest day on Promontory. Chris and Jess attempt Point 6301m and reach 100 metres from summit.
21 May	Andy and Alan reach 6600 metres on West Face. Heavy snow in night. Tents and ropes buried.
22 May	Four hours looking for ropes! Rest day.
23 May	Andy and Alan climb through headwall of West Face. Reach summit of Menlungtse West at 10.30 p.m. Return to camp at 6600 metres at 2 a.m.
24 May	Chris, David B, Steve, Charlie, Jess, Iain, Francis,

198

	Krishna and Nima dismantle Base Camp. Andy and Alan descend face to base of mountain.
25 May	All reach Chang bu Jiang.
28 May	All reach Tingri.
29 May	Chris, Andy, Jess and Francis take jeep to Xigaze. Others leave for Kathmandu.
30 May	Chris *et al.* reach Lhasa. Others reach Kathmandu.
1 June	Reach Chengdu.
3 June	Reach Beijing.
7–8 June	Fly home.

THE HISTORY OF ATTEMPTS AND ASCENTS OF CHOGOLISA AND MENLUNGTSE

CHOGOLISA

According to G. O. Dyhrenfurth's list of the highest mountains in the world over 7300 metres, Chogolisa ranks as number 46. This ranking would be three places higher if Dyhrenfurth had adopted the current assessment of its height. Alan Rouse, in *Mountain Magazine* (No 104, 1985), compiled a different list which acknowledges secondary and even tertiary summits within the same massif. Some peaks, such as Kangchenjunga, have four entries and by this reckoning there are twenty-two peaks, one of them unclimbed, over 8000 metres high. Chogolisa has two entries: the higher South-West summit at 7665 metres (ranked 68th) and the North-East summit, that I have referred to as Bride Peak, at 7654 metres (ranked 71st). Currently the most exhaustive list of the 7000-metre peaks is in Jill Neate's *High Asia*.

However one juggles the statistics, Chogolisa is a high mountain, in an important arena. Considering it is situated in such a popular range of mountains, access to which is controlled by one of the more enlightened Himalayan countries, it is perhaps surprising that it has received so little attention from mountaineers. Quite possibly, it is its proximity to higher, more famous mountains that has protected it from the sort of traffic that K2, Broad Peak and the Gasherbrums have grown used to. In 1986 there were fourteen expeditions on K2 and two on Chogolisa, though it was an unusually busy season for both peaks.

The first Westerner to survey the Upper Baltoro region was the Briton Godwin Austen in 1861, as part of the British Survey of India. But it was William Martin Conway in 1892, whilst on his remarkable traverse of the Karakoram via the Hispar, Biafo and Baltoro Glaciers, who first drew specific attention to Chogolisa, referring to it as the Great White Roof, a term which is aptly descriptive of its classic trapezium shape when viewed from Concordia. He reached the summit of Pioneer Peak, a satellite peak to Baltoro Kangri, on this expedition and accompanied by 'coolies' who carried his easel and canvas he produced a remarkably accurate crayon drawing of the North-East summit, or Bride Peak as he called it; good enough to be used to plan a route, except the glaciers will have changed considerably in a century! But he made no attempt to climb the mountain.

The first attempt to climb Chogolisa came in 1909 by an Italian expedition led by the Duke of Abruzzi, after first trying K2. They fixed a number of camps on the North-East Ridge of Bride Peak. On the expedition's third determined attempt they reached a rock step at 7400 metres. After two hours they had negotiated it, but bad weather had moved in and after a further two hours the Duke made the decision to retreat within 200 metres of the summit of Bride Peak. They had thus set a new altitude record which was to stand for thirteen years, until 1922 when the British reached c.8500 metres on the north side of Everest. Abruzzi put his name to the South-East Ridge of K2 and the glacier beneath the North-East flank of Bride Peak.

The next serious attempt on Bride Peak came in 1957. Austrians Kurt Diemberger and Hermann Buhl, having successfully climbed Broad Peak a few days earlier, attempted an alpine-style ascent of the East Ridge. Having negotiated the ice dome, a huge icy fin that rises on the East Ridge to over 7150 metres, they reached the col at about 7000 metres below the heavily corniced snowy ridge that rises to the summit. Here they camped and after a period of stormy weather continued, but turned back soon after from 7400 metres in deteriorating weather. Buhl, according to Diemberger, was unusually tired, and he quickly fell behind. Missing his companion, Diemberger retraced his steps to discover the trace of Buhl's boot prints disappearing through a cornice. He had plunged hundreds of metres to his death.

A year later, in 1958, a Japanese party from the University of Kyoto, following the intended line of Buhl and Diemberger, succeeded, using supplementary oxygen, in reaching the small rocky perch of Bride Peak's summit. M. Fujihara and K. Hirai, the summiteers, made their ascent on 4th August in deep snow often up to their waists. They could see along the ridge to the South-West summit, which later surveys would reveal to be some eleven metres higher.

In 1975 came the first ascent of Chogolisa. An Austrian team led by Eduard Koblmuller approached from the south. Their eleven-day walk brought them to their Base Camp site on the confluence of the Kaberi and Kondus Glaciers where their low-altitude porters could go no further. The expedition adopted a siege approach. Between Camps II and III lay a long, difficult icefall and between III and IV a 1000-metre fifty-degree iceface. They disposed of 1200 metres of rope in these sections. Above camp IV, on a col at about 6800 metres, they negotiated the remaining two kilometres of the South-West Ridge to the top in lightweight fashion. G. Ammerer and F. Pressl reached the summit on 3rd August, followed two days later by the second summit pair of A. Furtner and H. Sturm.

In 1980 there were two expeditions to the south side of Chogolisa. An accident on the Austrian route above the Kaberi Glacier caused both teams to abandon their attempt. The three members of a Canadian/ USA party led by Howard Weaver (US) were descending from their highpoint of 6850 metres (the site of the 1975 Camp IV) on the south side of the South-West Ridge when John Wittmayer (Can) and Weaver, roped together, fell almost 1000 metres, miraculously sliding over the bergschrund and coming to rest on the Kaberi Glacier. But they were still extremely remote from their Base Camp. Douglas Cannalte (US), the other climber descended alone and found them delirious, badly injured and with severe frostbite. Cannalte gave them shelter in his tent and descended for help. An avalanche then struck, flattening the tent and burying their gear. They crawled to another tent on the glacier, only to be blasted in the air currents of another much larger avalanche. Meanwhile, Cannalte had reached a deserted tent belonging to a Japanese expedition led by Shunsuke Tamura. From here he was able to make radio contact with some of the Japanese climbers who were fixing ropes above 7000 metres on the South-West Ridge. All descended at once to help, reaching the Kaberi Glacier on 21st July, three days after the fall. Weaver could walk, with help but Wittmayer had to be carried by stretcher. A joint rescue by both expeditions resulted in the pair reaching the jeep roadhead on 29th July. The Japanese had, by this stage, run out of supplies and could not continue on the mountain.

In June 1983 a West German team led by Georg Brosig made an elegant second ascent of Chogolisa. Their Base Camp was situated at the confluence of the Vigne and Upper Baltoro Glaciers and their Advance Base below the North-West Face of the mountain. They climbed rapidly with only one bivouac on ascent at 6800 metres. Brosig, Adi (Heinz) Fischer and Hubert Wendlinger were the summiteers.

In 1984, Joel Coqueugniot (French) made a solo ascent of one of the northern satellite peaks in the massif at about 6350 metres, and a mixed European team were successful on the South-West summit, on a line similar to the West Germans'. On 10th June, Hans and Alice Zebrowski (German), Louis Deuber (Swiss), Richard Franzl (Austrian) and Harald Navé (Austrian) reached the summit. Alice Zebrowski had become the first woman to climb Chogolisa. Both teams were operating from the Baltoro. A third party of eight French climbers, led by Christian Blot, climbing from the Kaberi Glacier reached the South-West summit by a new route on the South Face and South-West Ridge. As in 1975, this team had fixed the entire route on the South Face between 5750 and 7000 metres. The two pairs of Brigitte Aucher and Philippe Dubois and Jean-Marie Galmiche and Eric Monier reached the summit on 26th July. However, on descent, Aucher and Dubois were killed in an avalanche on the summit snowfields.

In 1986 a Spanish team of eight climbers, led by Sebastian Alvaro, made the second ascent of Bride Peak by a new route on the North Face, direct from the Upper Baltoro Glacier. The lower portion of their climb threaded on sixty-degree ice through séracs to a hollow on the ridge at 6300 metres. Félix de Pablo and José-Carlos Tamayo reached the top on 22nd June, followed a day later by Ramón Portilla and Gregorio Ariz. The team found a Japanese doll on the summit, left in 1958 – interestingly on the exact day that Portilla was born! Also that year the mountain received its first complete traverse by a British team led by Andy Fanshawe and comprising Liam Elliot, Hamish Irvine, Ulric Jessop and Simon Lamb. From the head of the Vigne they climbed the North-West Face to the col at 6800 metres where the Austrian team had made their camp IV. They reached the summit on the 14th of August from where they traversed the summit ridge to Bride Peak the same day, descending in the evening to the col where Buhl had died. All five members completed the traverse.

In 1987, a Lyonnaise expedition led by Jean-Etienne Hénault succeeded in climbing the North-West Face route. Two of the six members, Henault and Pascal Poizat, reached the South-West summit on 13th August. They had fixed 500 metres on the lower part of the route.

There are no other recorded ascents of Chogolisa since 1987.

MENLUNGTSE

According to Rouse's above-mentioned list, Menlungtse (7181 metres) and Menlungtse West (7023 metres) are the 245th and 347th highest peaks in the world. Menlungtse lies in the Rolwaling Himalaya, wholly in Tibet and relatively inaccessible from Nepal which is why Menlungtse has only recently had legitimate and serious attempts on its summits.

The Rongshar Gorge into which the Menlung Chu flows was first visited by Westerners in the 1920s as part of the British Everest expeditions of 1921 and 1924. It was not until 1951 that the Menlung valley itself was reached when Eric Shipton and Michael Ward, having successfully reconnoitred the future South Col route to the summit of Everest, poached across the border from Nepal via the Dingjung La. They passed beneath the south and west faces of a steep granite peak that they named Menlungtse, unaware of its local name, Jobo Garu. It was here that they produced the now famous photographs of prints that they ascribed to the yeti. They descended the Rongshar Gorge across the border back into Nepal.

In the post-monsoon season of 1954 a Swiss expedition, led by Raymond Lambert, made an unofficial attempt on Menlungtse. Initially intending to attempt Gauri Sankar, they crossed the border into Tibet by the Menlung La to explore possibilities on Menlungtse. Having abandoned this attempt, they then crossed the Dingjung La to try Cho Oyu, still without success.

In the spring of 1987 Chris Bonington led an Anglo-Norwegian expedition with Jim Fotheringham, Odd Eliassen and Bjorn Myrer-Lund. They approached by what is now the standard route, from Tingri on the Tibetan Plain, across the Fusi La, down the Rongshar Chu to the village of Chang bu Jiang and up the Menlung Chu to Base Camp. This expedition chose a very difficult route on the far right side of the West Face, and this, coupled with unusually stormy weather, stopped them at about 6400 metres.

In the spring of 1988 Bonington returned with a different team of David Breashears, Andy Fanshawe and Steve Shea. Alan Hinkes accompanied the team as a courier for the newspaper that sponsored the expedition. The team abandoned their original plan of climbing the heavily corniced East Ridge and instead tried a line on the West Face. Fanshawe and Hinkes climbed the face, including a steep granite headwall at its top, to reach the summit of Menlungtse West on 23rd May. They were too tired to attempt the obvious traverse to the main peak.

In the spring of 1989 Americans Jim Wickwire and John Roskelley failed to reach Menlungtse as unrest and a student-led rebellion in China was crushed by the People's Army. Twelve months later in 1990 they returned and Roskelley, with Greg Child, reached a highpoint of 6400 metres on the East Ridge on 13th May. Bad cornices hampered further progress. They tried no other routes.

At the time of writing, Menlungtse's main eastern summit (7181 metres) remains one of the world's most beautiful and difficult unclimbed peaks.

EXPEDITION SUPPORTERS AND SPONSORS

The expeditions to Chogolisa, Menlungtse and Makalu were possible only because they were supported generously by a number of individuals, trusts and companies. In listing them here I acknowledge their contribution and extend my warmest thanks.

Main Supporters/Grants

BRITISH MOUNTAINEERING COUNCIL   Grant aid
The National Body for Mountaineering fosters the interests of mountaineering and walking in the UK, and of British mountaineers and walkers overseas. Among its many duties the BMC campaigns for the free access to moorland and crags, plays an important role in the setting of technical standards for equipment and administers Sports Council grants for British overseas expeditions.

EDINBURGH UNIVERSITY MOUNTAINEERING CLUB   Grant aid

MOUNT EVEREST FOUNDATION   Grant aid
The MEF was set up with the proceeds of a lecture tour after the 1953 Everest Expedition and currently gives over £20,000 in grants annually to British or New Zealand expeditions which are attempting first ascents or engaged in exploration or scientific research in the mountain environment.

NICK ESTCOURT MEMORIAL TRUST   Annual award (1986)
The Nick Estcourt Trust was set up after Nick Estcourt's death on K2 in 1979 and gives one grant (currently of £1000) each year to a young and innovative British expedition.

SANG AWARD   Grant aid
The Sang Award is administered by the Scottish Mountaineering Club.

The main sponsors for the Menlungtse expedition were:
    Berghaus, manufacturers and distributors of specialist outdoor clothing, footwear and rucsacs; BBC Natural History Unit; Dodd and Co,

Accountants; William Hill, Bookmakers; the *Mail on Sunday*; Safeway Foodstores Ltd.

The main sponsor for the Makalu expedition was the Blackspur Group Plc, who lease finance for large industrial scale printers.

Suppliers

Allcord: Camp icescrews, axes, Cousin ropes, Witco snow shovels; Arova Mammut AG: ropes, harnesses, karabiners; Batchelors: Base Camp food; Berghaus: shell clothing, rucsacs, boots; British Airways Cargo: air freight ('86); British Mountaineering Council: insurance; Camping Gaz: gas and burners; Cascade Designs Ltd: Thermarest mats; Duracell: batteries; Epigas: gas and burners; Europa Sports: Lowe rucsacs; Javlin: salopettes; Jessops (photographers): Fuji films; Kodak: film; Leki: ski poles; Mountain Sports: Hirsch burners; Mountain Technology (Glencoe): ice axes; Nomad: boxes; North Cape: thermal underwear; Pakistan International Airways: air freight ('88); Phoenix Mountaineering: windsuits, helmets; Pindisports: miscellaneous; RAB Down Equipment: sleeping bags; Sanctuary Mountain Sports: Markill pans; S.O.S. Air Cargo: air freight ('89); Sony (UK): radios, tape recorders; Swiss Cutlery (London) Ltd: Swiss Army knives; Graham Tiso: porter stockings; Troll Safety Equipment: harnesses; Ultimate Equipment Ltd: Base Camp tents, helmets; Uvex: sunglasses and goggles; W. L. Gore: tent fabric; White Horse: whisky; Wild Country: mountain tents, climbing hardware; Yale: padlocks.

Individuals

Jeremy Adams; Mr Alfredi (Govt Co-ordinator, Skardu); Chris Bonington; Col Bill Clements (Military Attaché, Beijing); Geoff Cohen; Ralph Fanshawe; Angela Geal; Dennis Gray (BMC General Secretary); Tim Greening (Karakoram Experience); John Haig (Vice-Consul, Islamabad); William Hanbury-Tenison; Mr Kelleher (Barclays Bank, South Kensington); Tony Lack; Marian Lawrence (PIA); Keith Rugg; Wendy McCall; Ray Scott; Lesley Smithson; Paul Stretford (Blackspur); Dick Turnbull; Roger Withers.

If I have inadvertently omitted any suppliers and individuals from the above may I apologise and thank them here.

206

211